Moments in Time:

A Memoir

Moments in Time:

A Memoir

∞

Donald F. Megnin

Copyright © 2010 by Donald F. Megnin.

Library of Congress Control Number: 2009913296
ISBN: Hardcover   978-1-4500-1204-1
               Softcover   978-1-4500-1203-4
               Ebook   978-1-4500-1205-8

All rights reserved. No part of this book may be reproduced or transmitted in any form or by any means, electronic or mechanical, including photocopying, recording, or by any information storage and retrieval system, without permission in writing from the copyright owner.

This book was printed in the United States of America.

To order additional copies of this book, contact:
Xlibris Corporation
1-888-795-4274
www.Xlibris.com
Orders@Xlibris.com
71374

Contents

Preface 6
Foreword 7
Dedication 8

I.   A New Career 9
II.   Settling into the First Ward Methodist Church 25
III.   Full-Time Graduate Study 38
IV.   Dissertation Research 47
V.   Candidating, Buying Farm, and Writing My Dissertation 67
VI.   Settling in on the Farm 94
VII.   Moving to Butler—Sabbatical Leave 109
VIII. Ventures into Politics 124
IX.   Life's Changes 128
X.   Our Involvement with Rotary International 133
XI.   Highlights of the Eighties 138
XII.   Highlights of the Early Nineties 153
XIII. Beginning Retirement 170
XIV.   Purchase of Sugar Mill Home 184
XV.   Moving to Erie Village 186
XVI.   Overseas Travel 192
XVII. Life's Changing Moments 207

Preface

As a sequel to my autobiography (A Farm Boy Sees The World), this volume is a continuation, but highlights the attendance in seminary, meeting the person who was and is literally the turning point of my life (Julie), the subsequent new direction which our lives took from that point onward, is portrayed in a detail similar to that of a living diary. Ironically, the argument between my father and mother over whether I should attend seminary or not proved to be the wisdom of my mother in contrast to the dogmatism of my father. Had I not gone to seminary, which my mother strongly supported in contrast to my father, who couldn't understand why I would even consider such a choice, my life has become a reflection of the hope, the values and the intrinsic beliefs of my mother in the universal goodness of all peoples, I like to believe has been exemplified in the lives of Julie and myself.

Moments in Time is a remarkable journey of one who believes in the goodness of people to do their best even in the most extraordinary of circumstances in which they may find themselves from time to time. There is often no other course of action to undertake than carrying on what our previous efforts have produced for the moment in which we are encapsulated. Each one must choose which direction he/she shall or shall not go. This story is an attempt to portray what our lives have reflected and produced over these many years of our existence.

Foreword

For a young man who planned on becoming a minister and met the woman in seminary who has become his wife, his life was forever changed. We not only started off serving a church, but began to undertake graduate courses in international politics on a part time basis. I became acquainted with a Syracuse university professor who has most influenced my life and changed the direction in which we were going in the ministry to the field of teaching. My wife had already been an elementary school teacher and understood the requirements for teaching. She encouraged me to continue on in this new path. My years of constant political discussions with my father on international topics no doubt also had an enormous influence on helping me to decide to study in the field of international politics. As one who grew up in an immigrant family which kept its ties alive with our German relatives, I grew in appreciation of using my first language in order to communicate with them in our many visits to Germany over the course of several decades. Both my wife's and my German fluency has also been highly instrumental in taking groups of American students to Germany and Austria for purposes of travel and study.

What follows is the year by year resume of more than fifty years of our lives on a remarkable journey of "moments in time". In the scope of a person's life, his/her activities are what results in accomplishing achievements which, in the scale of historical time, is miniscule to the world at large, but represents the results of the efforts, difficulties and overcoming of obstacles which every generation confronts. After a lifetime of love, work and meeting daily challenges, the outcomes should speak for themselves.

Dedication

    This Memoir is dedicated to my wife, our family, friends, professors, students and institutions which have influenced our entire lives to culminate in a rare and privileged experience of learning the importance of truth, trust, justice and the need to try to improve life wherever we find it. If it were not for the kindness and generosity of Walter A. Bolton to make it financially possible to attend Syracuse University, this opportunity might never have been reached.

    The linkage of persons and institutions is a profound recognition of how the minds of individuals can be developed to transcend the limitations of poverty, discrimination, and injustice which is often the experience of many persons unable to overcome the deprivations into which they are born. It is, therefore, also necessary to promote educational opportunities as widely as possible so that the development of the mind is never treated lightly or indifferently by the society into which the child is born and raised. Syracuse and Boston Universities are the premier institutions of higher learning which have most profoundly influenced my life and that of my wife. I trust our years at Slippery Rock University have also been of value to the students with whom we interacted and found such pleasure in getting to know and working with them through the years.

I.

A New Career

Moving to Boston to attend seminary (the Boston University School of Theology) in September of 1957 proved to be the singular most significant action which I have ever undertaken. Not only the intellectual stimulation of the educational environment was enhancing, but also it was where I met Julia Mae King.

Upon returning home from my summer's work at Volkmar's cooperage mill in Whitesburg, Pennsylvania, I loaded my 1955 Chevrolet and drove to Boston. I had never been to Boston before. The nearest I had come was to the Berkshire Mountains to attend the Boston Pops music festival a few years earlier with members of the DeWitt Community Church's College Club while still in college. I had been given directions from Bob Bolton about how to reach Boston University. He and Nancy were working at the Milton Methodist Church at the time. They had gone to Boston earlier in the summer. I had no problem finding the university. The twin towers (one on the end of the seminary and the other on the end of the College of Liberal Arts) reminded me of two phallic symbols similar to what I had seen at various Hindu temples in India. The towers were on either side of the square in front of the Boston University Chapel. I couldn't help but be impressed. Whoever designed the structures had promoted the idea of unity between theology on one side of the square and the intellectual pursuit of knowledge on the other.

I parked behind the seminary and walked into the dean's office.

"Hi. I'm Donald Megnin. I'm going to be one of your students this fall."

"Hello. I'm Dorothy Lord, the dean's secretary. We've been expecting you."

She held out her hand and we shook hands.

"You can take the elevator on the end of the hall to the third floor. You'll be rooming with George Carter. He's already here. If you have any other questions, we're always available here in Dean Muelder's office."

"Thank you Ms. Lord. That's all I have to do?"

"There will be an orientation on Monday morning in the chapel for all of you new seminarians. We'll expect to see you there. Classes will start on Tuesday."

I left and found the elevator just down the hall from her office. Upon reaching the third floor, I found room 302. It was on the left, the second room down the hall from the elevator. Upon entering the room, I saw my roommate.

"Well, you must be George Carter," I said as I came into the room.

"Yeah. I'm George Carter. What's your name?"

"I'm Don Megnin."

George had gotten up from his chair and we shook hands.

"I'm from California. Where are you from?"

"I'm from Central New York near Syracuse."

He pointed at the second bed. "This is yours, Don. Since I got here first, I picked out the nicest one!" he laughed.

"That's the way it is, George. The early bird gets the worm!"

George proved to be a very congenial roommate. He told me he grew up in Georgia and his family had moved to California when he was in high school. He still had a very heavy Southern accent. The men in the room next to us were black seminarians. George liked to joke with Gastrel Riley (a tall and very distinguished-looking student). "Wait until I get my sheets and hood, Gastrel. Then we'll see how brave you are!" he laughed.

Since I had been working at the community church that previous year, I read a notice on the seminary bulletin board that the Waltham Methodist Church needed a youth minister. The job entails about twenty hours per week. If you are interested, please contact the Reverend Ernest Bell.

I drove out to Waltham and talked with the minister.

"Where are you from, Don?"

"I'm from Upstate New York. I've worked for a few years as an intern in a large community church near Syracuse. This past year, I was an associate pastor at this same church working with the Youth Fellowship and the College Club besides hospital and new member calling. Your job sounds as though it would be a continuation of what I've been doing."

"The job takes about twenty hours a week, Don. We can't pay you very much, but we can pay you twenty dollars a week. If you're ready to accept the job, I'm ready to say you can start this coming Sunday evening."

"Okay. I'll be here this next Sunday evening at six o'clock. Is that when you start the Youth Fellowship?"

"Yes. If you would like, you could also teach an adult Sunday school class between our two services. You can choose whatever you would like. Once you've made a selection of the materials, I'll alert the congregation and have the secretary order the books."

"Fine, Ernie. I'll be here this coming Sunday evening for the Youth Fellowship."

Classes started the day after Labor Day. The first semester was an interesting mix of Old Testament taught by Dr. Harrell Beck, the philosophy of religion taught by Dr. Peter Bertocci, church history taught by Dr. Theodore Booth, the psychology of religion taught be Dr. William Douglas, New Testament theology taught by Dr. Harold DeWolfe, and religious literature taught be Professor Harold Ehrensberger.

The courses taught by Beck and Bertocci elicited the most discussion. The questions asked of Dr. Beck were mostly for clarification of what he presented. The questions for Dr. Bertocci, on the other hand, were questioning his premises. Unfortunately, in retrospect, I realize now I wasn't asking the right questions. It was taken for granted that all of the seminarians held the same basic premises: (1) a belief in a supreme being, (2) a father figure who is in charge of the unfolding scheme and growth of life, (3) that human beings live in a calculating universe based on immutable laws whose future depends upon how they interacted with each other and with their environment, and (4) all of life was to be viewed as the result of a continuing evolution in the growth and development of knowledge by the human species seeking to improve life wherever we were to be employed. The Christian religious tradition was viewed as the continuing backdrop underlying the beginning and the end of life's circumstances. The ancient leaders, kings, prophets, and forerunners of the Old and New Testament were to be read as the preparers of "the way." All people should ultimately become Christian. While world religions was taught as part of the curriculum, it was taken for granted that no one would ever really convert or follow the path of some other religious leader. Jesus of Nazareth was the one true leader of all religions, and any other expression of religion was simply to be studied because it was also part of the whole human mosaic of history. We attended chapel each morning at 10:00 a.m. as part of the daily routine to make sure we had the opportunity to pray and become enlightened about the various aspects of the Christian religion, including Methodism.

Another important aspect of our theological education was that all of students would become involved in some aspect of religion either as ministers, workers for religious foundations, or social service agencies that were sponsored by the church. The connection between religious studies and active involvement in some aspect of a related field was a given. Since our tuition was paid by the various conferences of the Methodist Church, our futures were to be directly related to involvement in the life of this church.

Besides the work in the local churches and our theological studies, as seminarians, we were encouraged to participate in a monthly social get-together within the seminary community. Professor Edward Nadel, from the university's Physical Education Department, came once a month to teach us folk dancing in our cafeteria. It was expected we would need to have this experience in order to assist us in working with our youth groups in the churches to which we would be assigned. The cafeteria was called the "refectory" and was the room in the basement of the seminary building in which we had our breakfasts and lunches each of the weekdays. It was only closed on weekends. We also had visiting speakers once a month in the refectory on some social, international, or religious issue that the faculty thought would be helpful for us to envision our role in the wider society as we would be posted in our own churches.

One of the interesting aspects of having our refectory closed on the weekends meant we had to rely upon our own resources. We soon discovered one of the best places to go was on Beacon Street: Ma Rieser's Diner. It was only three blocks to the east of the seminary (745 Commonwealth Avenue) and the meal would include a glass of milk, a bowl of soup, a main course, and dessert, all for one dollar! It was not only the best buy anyone could find in the Boston area, but was about the best meal for the price any of us had ever had! George and I visited Ma Rieser's regularly on weekends when we were at the seminary. We could have gone to the university mensa where the cost would have been about the same, but could never quite equal what we got for a dollar at the diner! Down the avenue, within a few blocks of the seminary, was another restaurant that had excellent hamburgers and fries which we often visited late at night during finals.

Since our dormitory was exclusively for men, the women seminarians had to find their own accommodations. There were apartments available near the university and within walking distance of the seminary. Most of the women chose to share the cost of renting an apartment. There were usually two or three bedrooms so that often the apartments had sufficient space for five or six women. Two of the students with whom George and I became acquainted were Darlene Evans and Carolyn Cox from Tucson, Arizona. Their apartment was just across the street from the Boston Red Sox Fenway Park entrance. In thanks for their generosity and hospitality dinner, we took them to a movie or a lecture on occasion.

With the beginning of the spring semester in 1958, I received a letter of invitation from Fred Stoerker, director of the Ecumenical Voluntary Service Organization in New York City. He asked if I might be interested in participating in the first cultural group exchange with the Soviet Union during the summer of 1958. He went on to explain that four groups were participating in this exchange by recruiting ten graduate students each for a total of forty students. Not only his organization (the Ecumenical Voluntary Service Organization), but the Lilly Foundation, the American Friends Service Committee, and the Lyle Foundation were joining in the recruitment effort. Since I had participated in the Ecumenical Voluntary Service Organization's program in Berlin during the summer of 1956, he thought I might be interested. I wrote back to him to find out what it would cost and what the closing date for applying would be. His return letter indicated it would cost approximately $1,200 per participant and the deadline for application was March 1. Since I did not have the $1,200, I talked it over with my roommate.

"Well, I've been invited to participate in the first US-USSR Cultural Exchange Program this summer, George, but I don't see how I can pay for it."

"What's the cost for the trip, Don?"

"It's twelve hundred dollars. I receive twenty dollars a week from the Waltham Methodist Church as youth minister, but I haven't saved enough for the trip."

"You know, Don, I'm not coming back to seminary this next year. I'm going to work at a church in the Northern California District. How would it be if I bought your car for $1,200? I'm going to need a car, and I could drive it home this summer after school is out."

"Are you sure you want to do that, George?"

"I wouldn't have offered, if I weren't serious."

"Okay, George, you've got yourself a deal!"

George paid me the twelve hundred dollars in a check, which I took to the bank and deposited in my account. We agreed he would have the car at the end of the semester. I returned to the farm via the courtesy of Bob and Nancy Bolton at the end of May. Bob and Nancy made several trips from Boston to Central New York to visit their families after the semester was finished. I sent Ecumenical Voluntary Services a check for the trip and participated in learning some rudimentary Russian during the spring semester conducted by one of the graduate participants in the program from Harvard.

Towards the end of June, I took the train to New York City for the two-day-orientation sessions for all of the participants. We then traveled on a Greyhound bus to Quebec, Canada, where we boarded the *Arosa Star* ocean liner for the trip to Hamburg, Germany. The shipboard language and history sessions continued for the week we were on board. Upon arriving in Hamburg, we took a train to Moscow going through West Germany, East Germany, Poland, the three Baltic states, stopping briefly in Leningrad, before proceeding to Moscow. Since the entire forty-person complement of the exchange was divided into four groups, it gave us an opportunity to become acquainted with the members of the group to which we were assigned in New York. Our group was headed by Dr. Robert Bowers, a history professor from Hanover College in Indiana. Each of the groups was already clustered around their leaders during the orientation sessions before our departure from New York. The entire exchange program for the United States was headed by Dr. Ralph Fisher, a history professor from Yale University.

Upon our arrival in Moscow, we were grouped together and sent to different regions of the Soviet Union. Our group of ten, plus our leader, were sent to the southern part of the European Soviet Union. We traveled by rail and then by boat down the Volga River to Stalingrad, followed by Rostov and ending in Lazarevskya on the Black Sea. Our guides were Vladmir and Elena, who introduced us to various Russian engineers, teachers, students, and party members at each of our stops along the way. The shipboard facilities included not only sleeping quarters (two persons per room) but also all of our meals. The purpose of the trip was to establish as many contacts as we could with different groups of people at each of these stops. One of the most impressive historical stops was at Stalingrad on the Volga River. We were given a tour of the battlegrounds between the German invaders and the Soviet defenders of the city during October 1942 and to early 1943. From the six hundred thousand German soldiers comprising the Sixth Army Group, only ninety thousand survived and were taken prisoners by the Soviet defenders at the end of January.

"It was the most crucial battle of World War II on the Soviet front," our guide told us. "Our forces were victorious over the Nazi hordes, who thought they could defeat our brave Soviet defenders of the motherland!"

Having talked with German members of these invading forces, I was told by them also that from Stalingrad onward, the momentum of the war changed from one of German initiative to one of German resistance and retreat before the Soviet forces until the defeat of the German forces in Germany in 1945!

Upon reaching the Black Sea at Lazarevskya, we stayed at the tourist spa for a week and went swimming, participated in calisthenics, and visited local tea and wine plantations in the nearby Caucasus Mountains. The meetings with the local hosts were always very friendly and cordial with the parting words "We hope to meet you again."

I must have gone swimming too often when the temperature was cool. I started coughing before we left the seacoast, and by the time we had arrived in Kiev on our way north through the Ukraine, I couldn't stop coughing.

"We'd better go to the hospital, Don, and see what's causing your coughing," Bob Bowers said. "You can't go on like this without some medication."

He took me to the city hospital. The doctor who looked at me confirmed what he advised: I'd have to stay under her care at least during the time the group was touring in the Ukraine. Fortunately for me, the doctor spoke German so that I could talk with her each time she came to see how I was progressing under her care.

"Herr Megnin, Ich muss Ihnen einen heitzung systeme geben, Wir muessen diesen Hussten besetzen." (Mr. Megnin, I'm going to have to use my heat control system to lessen your cough.)

She proceeded to heat up what looked like glass vials and placed six of them on my back. They were like vacuum cups which seemed to draw out the heat from my chest. She also gave me medications which seemed to help ease the constant coughing. By the time the group was ready to leave Kiev, Bob stopped to see if I could rejoin them for our trip to Leningrad. She thought if I continued taking the medication which she prescribed, I should be able to rejoin the group. The coughing had eased considerably. I was no longer viewed as a danger to the health of my colleagues.

We took the train to Leningrad and were lodged in a hotel near the Hermitage Museum. The tour was an excellent introduction to the arts and history not only of the Soviet Union but of Russia. It is probably one of the best-organized and maintained museums in the world. It also housed the best works of art from the Berlin Museum which the Soviet forces had taken following the downfall of the

Nazi regime. While most of these items have now been returned to Berlin, there were still some works which remained in the Hermitage. Following our tour and visits to various schools and historical sites on the Baltic Sea, we boarded another train from Leningrad proceeding through Estonia, Latvia, Poland, and Czechoslovakia before continuing on to Hamburg for the trip home. While the group continued on to Hamburg, I got off in Prague and took a plane to Stuttgart to visit our relatives in Germany for a few days. The relatives were surprised to see me. It must have been a bitter pill for Tante Lise and cousins Marianne, Hermann, and Lisele to hear of my trip to and from Leningrad where her husband and their father had been killed during the German withdrawal from this front in January of 1945.

After a two-day visit, I caught a flight from Stuttgart to Hamburg in order to rejoin the group returning to the States on the *Arosa Star*. It had been an excellent experience overall, and we also had had an opportunity to engage in a question-and-answer session with the chairman of the Soviet Youth division on Soviet television.

As a consequence of having taken so many slides, I was invited by my classmates to come to their churches and give programs on this trip. Practically every Sunday evening for the next year, I presented my slides to a different church throughout the Boston area.

With George Carter no longer in seminary that next year, I had to look for another roommate. Lamar Jacks, from Memphis, Tennessee, also had to find another roommate since he's decided to move into an off-campus apartment. Lamar wasn't interested in moving out of the seminary dormitory. In talking it over, Lamar suggested we should move to the top floor and share a suite together. It was much larger than the single rooms we had had previously. We chose a corner room overlooking the Charles River with a view of MIT and Cambridge in one direction and Commonwealth Avenue in the other. For our last two years in seminary, we shared this suite.

In retrospect, September 1958 was also to be the most memorable encounter which I had in the School of Theology. I met Julia Mae King, from Goshen, Indiana. She had graduated from Manchester College, North Manchester, Indiana, in 1953. After spending two years teaching fifth grade in the Mt. Morris School District in Mt. Morris, Illinois, she then moved to Lawrence, Kansas, to be near her boy friend, Leonard Wiebe, a grad student at the University of Kansas. With this romance going nowhere, she met a student of medicine, Charles Tschopp, who was studying at Kansas University in Lawrence, Kansas. When Charles became an intern in Kansas City, Julie moved there to be closer to him and joined the Shawnee Mission School District. She then taught unified studies to junior high pupils. With this romance also going nowhere, she left Kansas City after two years. During the summer of 1956, she worked as a student helping to rebuild a school as pat of a work camp in Germany. These experiences left a mark upon her in stimulating her interest in pursuing religious education. Upon her return to the States, she enrolled at Peabody College for religious education in Nashville, Tennessee. Not finding this program challenging enough, she decided to apply to the Boston University School of Theology. She was accepted in the Religion in Higher Education program as a student and began her seminary studies in September 1958. It was then that I met Julie for the first time.

Julie moved into an apartment with three other women called "the penthouse" on Montfort Street approximately three blocks from the seminary. It was called the penthouse because of its unique position vis-à-vis the other apartments on the street. The penthouse was the only apartment on the fifth floor of a four-floor apartment building. Her roommates were Donna Lingel, Liz Wolfskill, and Emily Jackson, who were fellow students of theology, and Debbie Norris, who worked in Dean Muelder's office as a secretary. Following Jackie's graduation from seminary, Sally Hayden replaced her. She was a third-grade teacher in Ipswitch, a suburb of Boston. Sally and Julie had been elementary teachers together in Mt. Morris, Illinois. Of all of the women students in the seminary, Julie was one of the only ones who had her own car. Most of the students (male and female) used the MTA rail system, which went down Commonwealth Avenue directly in front of the School of Theology. Over the next two years, our relationship grew from one of casual interest in each other to what proved to be an inseparable one!

Since I no longer had a car in September 1958, I had to depend upon others for a means of transportation to and from the weekly Sunday evening programs on the Soviet Union trip which I was giving. I also could no longer continue working at the Waltham Methodist Church without a car. I had called Ernie Bell and told him I no longer had a car to drive back and forth.

"Then I guess you won't be able to work here anymore, will you, Don? You need a car to commute back and forth."

"That's why I thought I better call you, Ernie. I won't be able to be your youth coordinator any longer."

"Well, I wish you good luck, Don. Maybe something will open up near you in one of the churches where you won't need a car."

"Actually, there is an opening here at the BU Chapel for which I've applied. It's to develop a program for the children of persons who attend the services each Sunday morning."

"That would be great for you. Thanks for calling and I hope you get the job."

"Thanks, Ernie. I've enjoyed my time at your church this past year."

I applied for the job at Marsh Chapel. Dr. Howard Thurman was very gracious in the interview.

"Don, what we need here in the chapel is some kind of a program for the children of people who come here each Sunday morning to our service. We've never had such a children's religious education program before. I'd like to have you develop one."

"What type of materials should I use, Dr. Thurman? Should it be Methodist?"

"Whatever you think would be most appropriate, Don. Since we have a really mixed congregation of people from a variety of backgrounds, you probably should look for a curriculum which would be ecumenical, yet helpful to the children to understand the historical development of religion in the Christian context."

"That sounds like a good idea, Dr. Thurman. I'll see what I can find as I look over the materials in the various publishing houses here in Boston."

"Whatever you think is appropriate is okay by me, Don. You're in charge. Just give the bill to my secretary after you've made your selection and I'll see that it's paid."

This was a propitious start over the next two years in developing the Children's Religious Education Program in Marsh Chapel. Dr. Thurman gave me the leeway to choose whatever type of material I thought would be most appropriate for his mixed congregation. The materials which I chose were from the Unitarian Publishing House. I was impressed with the rationality of the books. There was not a given belief system which is usually required by other denominations as the core of their faith system. I appreciated the right for persons (including children) to make up their own minds concerning what they chose to believe or not believe. The relationship of early religious concepts were also integrated so that children could understand the historical context in which belief systems (all religions) have developed.

Dean Thurman was a good man for whom to work. He was very generous in his work ethic and expected no less of his employees than he did of himself. The only disappointment for me was that he never invited me to participate in the chapel's Sunday-morning services. He had another assistant, Bill Whipple, a graduate student in the School of Theology, who was Dr. Thurman's worship leader. He conducted and presided over the weekly Sunday-morning service. I had done the same for Alex Carmichael on occasion and would very much have been pleased to be asked to do the same in Marsh Chapel. But I was never asked. It seemed rather odd to me that on one occasion, Dr. Thurman called me at ten thirty at night and asked, "Don, I'm sorry to bother you, but could you go over to the dean of the Law School's house and see what you can do to prevent the dean's son from assaulting him? Dean Long is very upset and thinks his life is in danger. I don't know if this is true or not, but see what you can do."

"Okay, Dean. I guess I'd better take my pajamas along, just in case I have to spend the night."

"Yes, that's a good idea. You may have to spend the night with them so that nothing happens to the dean."

On my way over to Dean Long's house I couldn't help but reflect upon the fact that Bill Whipple was much bigger and a rather imposing man with a very rugged build. He was a professional fisherman before enrolling in the School of Theology. In contrast to Bill, I was only five feet eight inches tall; Bill was probably six feet three inches tall and much bigger than I. Maybe Bill wasn't available, I thought, giving the dean the benefit of the doubt. Interestingly enough, there had been a fight going on outside of the apartment of Darlene Evans and Caroyln Cox one evening as I was going back to my room. I tried to break up. I thought I was helping the one man who seemed to be getting the worse of the beating when, to my shock, they both turned on me! Fortunately, a couple of fellow seminarians came along and pulled them off me and waited until one of the men left in his car.

"I guess you won't try and be the peacemaker again, Don, without some help in the future!" George reminded me.

"I've never had that happen to me before, George. Whenever I've helped break up a fight in the past, I was able to separate the men without getting myself involved at the same time!"

I continued on my way to the address Dr. Thurman had given me. I rang the doorbell and a very agitated older man opened the door. The front window had been smashed. I asked the dean what had happened.

"My son threw a book at me and it went through the window!"

I entered the hallway and noticed the dean stood behind me. He wanted to make sure I was between him and his son! His son moved to grab his father.

"Keep your hands off your father!" I told him.

"And if I don't?"

"You won't want to find out. Your dad is to be left alone!"

The son muttered to himself and went into the living room to play the piano.

"What's the problem, Dean Long? Why is your son so angry with you?"

"He wants to borrow money from me, and I told him he's already had more than enough! I won't give him any more! Did Howard Thurman send you over?"

Yes. He just called me. He said he was engaged in something else and couldn't come himself. I work for him at the chapel."

"I'm afraid my son is going to kill me! You're the only one who stands between us. You'll stay the night, won't you?"

"I told Dr. Thurman I'd see what I could do. If I have to stay the night, then that's what I'll do."

"I'd like to go to bed," Dean Long told me. "I'll sleep in this bed next to the window. Maybe you ought to sleep in the bed nearest the door just in case my son tries to come in."

"Okay."

I told his son, "We're going to bed. You are to stay out of the bedroom. I'm sleeping next to the door, and if you try to come in, you won't be able. I'll throw you out again!"

"Ha! That'll be the day!"

I spent the night half-asleep and half-awake, making sure the son didn't try to come into our bedroom. The next morning, Dean long arose and asked, "Where's my son?"

"He's not here, Dr. Long. I think he went out last night and hasn't come back."

"Thanks for coming last night. I'll keep the doors locked and he won't be able to come in if he comes back. He has his own apartment over in Cambridge. He probably went over there."

"Are you sure you'll be all right?"

"Yes, and tell Dr. Thurman thanks from me for sending you over last night. I might not have survived if you hadn't come."

I reported to Dr. Thurman and told him what had happened.

"Thanks, Don. I didn't know I was sending you into a family quarrel last night. It's probably a good thing you were there from what you've told me."

The seminary had not only a student government organization for the student body but also a social action organization called Christian Social Witness (CSW). It was my privilege to have been voted president of this organization prior to my departure after the spring semester. We held monthly meetings to discuss various domestic and foreign issues with members of our faculty whom we had recruited as resource persons to enable us to understand what the Christian position should be on war, poverty, crime, newly independent nations, conspicuous consumption, and management-labor issues in our capitalist system. My cabinet was composed of four other students. We met weekly to plan for the topics we wished to have presented to the seminary community. Each of the four members were also seminarians, and one of the most active members of my cabinet was headed by Julie King. Her responsibility was international relations. The programs were stimulating, and, as I noted earlier, some actions which we undertook were difficult for nonseminarians to understand. In particular, when the ROTC candidates wished to hold a parade down Commonwealth Avenue, we blocked their access to the street by arraying ourselves in front of them as they stood in formation and were ready to march. Needless to say, our passive resistance was not appreciated by the officers or the students in charge of this event!

During the summer of 1959, I worked at the DeWitt Community Church in charge of obtaining weekly preachers for the summer services, calling on the sick and hospitalized, and visiting potential new members of the church. On those Sundays in which I was unable to obtain a guest preacher, I ended up leading the services and giving the sermons myself. For these services, I received three hundred dollars a month. These funds helped pay for my final year in seminary.

I returned to Boston in September courtesy of Bob and Nancy Bolton. I hitched a ride with them. I continued as the director of the Children's Chapel program each Sunday. Fortunately, I was able to recruit teachers from the seminary to teach the eight classes in the Children's Chapel program. One of my most faithful volunteers, again, was Julie King. She helped recruit other teachers from the School of Theology to teach each week. Without her help and the students whom she recruited, there would not have been a Children's Chapel program!

On October 4, 1959, I started dating Julie King. It had taken a long time for me to recognize her as the person most genuine, loving, and considerate of the needs of other persons. Since I had to depend so often upon others to obtain rides to the churches each week to present my Soviet Union program, she suggested, "Why don't you use my car, Don? I don't need it on Sunday evenings. It would save someone going back and forth to get you and return you to the seminary. You might want to fill up on gas occasionally, but I don't need my car that often."

"Thank you very much, Julie. I really appreciate your generosity. I'll fill it up each time I use it."

We attended a movie on our first date. Each weekend, thereafter, we went out together for a bite to eat, to visit one of her friends, or to simply to get together to attend a lecture or play games with our friends. I shall never forget how guilty I felt in early September when I was escorting Martha Davis out of the School of Theology on a date and Julie held the door open for us to exit. She smiled at me as if to say, "You poor boy. You don't know what you're getting into!"

I couldn't help but ask myself the same question. Why are you dating this person and not Julie? It was Reg Smart, an architect from Australia and a fellow student in seminary, who said to me, "Don, of all the girls you've taken out, none of them has the eyes of Julie. She has bedroom eyes! You really ought to get to know her better!"

It took another jolt from a younger student who had been dating Julie for me to recognize her as the woman whom I should marry. Dwight Haines asked me one afternoon, "Don, what do you think about the idea of me marrying a woman five years older than I am? Do you think I can do that? I think I'm really in love with Julie King. I'd like to marry her if she says yes."

"How long have you been dating her, Dwight?"

"Since late this past summer. I really think about her all of the time. I thought maybe I should talk to her about our getting married one of these days. She's a really nice person and treats others as they wish to be treated. I can't get her off my mind."

"Well, Dwight, you really want to be sure who you marry. It's not something to do because of a sudden spark of interest. You've got to think about the long term. What kind of a wife would she make? Does she want to have children? Would she be satisfied to become the wife of a minister? Can she make her own decisions? Would she feel comfortable with a much younger husband? These are some of the questions you've got to think over before you make your proposal. Marriage should be for a lifetime."

"You're right, Don. I'll have to give this idea of marrying Julie some more serious thought. Thanks for listening."

Little did Dwight know, I was already beginning to date Julie. These questions were very much on my own mind at the time. He simply jarred me more rapidly towards Julie. She was the girl I wanted to marry!

On my birthday, December 10, 1959, she invited me over to the penthouse for a spaghetti dinner. Little did she know, this was one of my favorite dinners! She did an excellent job cooking the spaghetti and meatballs to perfection! Earlier in the week, Reg Smart had asked me if I could babysit their three sons on December 11. It was Noelene's birthday.

"I'd like to take Noelene out and celebrate her birthday," Reg asked.

When I told Julie what Reg had asked, she said, "We can babysit the boys together, Don. It'll give us a chance to become better acquainted."

We agreed we would go to their apartment while Reg and Noelene went out together. It was there that I proposed to Julie. Fortunately for me, she said yes! We made plans to tell our parents and friends over the Christmas vacation.

"We can drive out to Goshen to my parents and stop at your farm to tell your parents."

"Great! We should tell them first and our friends later."

The trip proved to be one of the most enjoyable times either of us had ever spent. My folks were duly impressed with Julie. She seemed to fit into the family very well. We made the rounds visiting the Karl Megnins, the Billy Megnins, the Richard Haussmanns Sr., Inge and Fritz Schoeck and family, Herman and Grete Weiss and daughter, and Sue and Joe Corbin. We also took a trip to Howe Jewelers in Syracuse in order to buy Julie a diamond engagement ring.

After celebrating the weekend with Pop and Mom, Julie and I drove on to Seneca, Pennsylvania, to visit Volkmar, Eva, and their family. Needless to say, she made a hit with the nieces and nephews!

"Ms. King is going to become your aunt," Eva told the girls.

Each one of them shook hands with Julie as did David and Bob. It was a brief overnight stay, but gave Julie an opportunity to become acquainted with her future nieces and nephews. Continuing our drive to Goshen the next day, Julie asked,

"What would you think of having Volkmar and Eva's youngest daughter, Kitty, as my flower girl? She would be a real pleasure to have, if her parents wouldn't mind."

"Well, that would be an excellent idea. I don't think Volk and Eva would mind. But we should also plan on having a ring bearer. Alex and Betty's son, Sandy, might be a good addition also."

"I'll call Eva and ask if she would approve of the idea of Kitty as my flower girl. You can talk with Alex about having Sandy as our ring bearer."

"Okay. When we go back to Boston, we'll call them and ask if the two kids can be in the wedding ceremony."

We arrived in Goshen late that afternoon having driven from Seneca in about five hours. When we got out of the car, Julie's parents, Inez and Bert King, came out of the hallway at the back of the house to greet us.

"Mother and Dad, this is Don Megnin. We've just gotten engaged."

We shook hands, and Mr. King helped me get our bags out of the trunk.

"Did you have a good trip?" he asked. "You were lucky. There's almost no snow on the roads."

"Come in," Mrs. King said. "I've got dinner already prepared."

It was a very pleasant evening which we spent getting acquainted.

"Don's family came from Germany. We just spent some time with his folks in New York and his brother and family in Pennsylvania, on our way out here," Julie said.

"That's interesting," Mrs. King said. "My family came from Alsace, which is a German area in France. I studied German in school, as did Julia."

Her folks told us about the Christmas party which was planned at the Lehman household on Saturday evening.

"All of my relatives will be there who live in Goshen," Mrs. King related. "You'll get a chance to meet my husband's family this next summer when you drive out again."

And so it was that Julie introduced me to her brother Tom and his wife, Flora, for the first time. She also introduced me to her aunts, uncles, and cousins on her mother's side at the Christmas party sponsored by her uncle Dike and auntie Esther Lehman in their home. During the party, Julie announced to her brother and sister-in-law, aunts, uncles, and cousins, "Don and I are getting married in the Boston University Chapel on Saturday, May 28. You're all invited to attend. Two of Don's friends are going to conduct the ceremony. Alex Carmichel, whom I've just met this past weekend, is the minister of the DeWitt Community Church, where Don used to be on the staff, and Bob Bolton, one of his best friends who is also in seminary with us. May is a wonderful time of the year. I hope as many of you as possible can come."

Upon returning to seminary, Julie and her roommates made plans to announce our engagement to the seminary community. We had already agreed to use her suggestion for the announcement. She thought an excerpt from Robert Browning's eloquent poem on love should be on the invitation to our friends and guests to attend the party at the penthouse.

"How Do I Love Thee? Let me count the ways . . ." Julie's penthouse roommates sponsored the "penthouse party" on January 28, 1960, to announce our engagement. We then announced our plan to have our wedding on May 28, 1960, in Marsh Chapel. It was a very joyous and romantic evening. With the exception of Julie's roommates, the announcement came as a surprise to the assembled guests.

"Well finally, the old man in our class is getting married!" Lamar announced. (I was one of the older members of the seminary who were still unmarried.)

The semester flew by rapidly. We studied together for our exams, had lunch and dinner together every day, and sent out the announcements to our families and friends. Towards the middle of the semester, we also sent out the wedding invitations. Julie had talked with two of her high school friends, Marilyn (Logan) Newsom, whom she wanted as her matron of honor, and Irene (McCoy) Farrand, to be members of the wedding party, plus Sally Hutton, with whom she had taught in Illinois, as bridesmaids. I asked Volkmar to be my best man and Lamar Jacks and George Carter to be my ushers. Julie had talked with Eva, and she agreed to having Kitty in the wedding as Julie's flower girl. I had talked with Alex, and he and Betty agreed; Sandy could be the ring bearer.

On Friday evening, May 27, Mr. and Mrs. Wolfskill hosted the rehearsal dinner at their home. All members of the wedding party were there, plus Mr. and Mrs. King, Mom, Ralph, and Velora McCoy (Irene's parents), Ron Newsom (Marilyn's husband), Nancy Bolton, Liz Wolfskill, the daughter of the hosts, who was going to play the violin prior to the service, and Sarah Guy, who was to read the scripture prior to the ceremony. It was an excellent dinner and a very enjoyable evening with all of the guests and participants who were included in the ceremony that next day.

Tom and Flora King flew in with Julie's aunt Mabel as a passenger on Tom's plane. Unfortunately for her, she tripped on the sidewalk in front of the guesthouse where they were staying and sprained her right ankle badly. She had to use a wheelchair and be lifted in and out of the guesthouse, the chapel, the Faculty Club, and the plane for the trip back to Goshen.

The day of the wedding was beautiful. It was a bright sunny day with the temperature in the low seventies and a gentle breeze blowing most of the day. While Alex, Bob, the ring bearer (Sandy Carmichel), Lamar, George and I stood in the front of the chapel, Julie and her dad came down the aisle. Kitty was to walk in front of Julie, but a little four-year-old is often skittish in front of such a large audience. She kept slowing down as Julie and her dad followed her. Julie had to put her hand on Kitty's shoulder and gently guide her down the aisle ahead of her. Max Miller, the chapel organist, had to play the wedding march somewhat longer until the bride, her father, and the flower girl reached the front of the narthex rail where we were all waiting. Upon reaching the rail, Marilyn lifted Julie's veil and folded it back over her head. Alex asked, "Who giveth this woman to be married to this man?"

Julie's dad answered, "Her mother and I."

He left Julie's side to sit next to Mrs. King. Alex began the service assisted by Bob. With the giving and receiving of rings, Sandy, who was holding them on the little pillow he carried, gave them to his dad. After the exchange of pledges, vows, rings, and the prayers for the success of our wedding, Alex introduced us.

"May I present Mr. and Mrs. Megnin."

I kissed Julie, gave her my arm, and proceeded to escort her back down the aisle. We headed the reception line at the door leading out of the chapel, with members of the wedding party standing in the line ahead of us. All of my relatives from Syracuse came with one notable exception. Pop chose not to come even though Volkmar and Eva wanted him to join Kitty and Mom for the trip to Boston. Inge had her two daughters, Pauline and Irene, with her. The rest of the relatives from Syracuse came: my Uncle Karl and Aunt Anne Megnin, cousin Billy and wife, Carol Megnin, Uncle Richard and Aunt Margaret Haussmann, cousin Grete and her husband Hermann Weiss, and daughters Susan, Barbara, and Kass. We greeted all of them as they came through the receiving line. Following the taking of pictures in the chapel, Julie and I and the wedding party joined the guests at the Faculty Club for sandwiches, cake, and ice cream. I was both pleased and surprised that some of my friends had made the trip from Syracuse. We were both surprised yet pleased that several of our seminary professors and their families attended besides many of our classmates. Two of our guests, Bob and Mary Anita Failmezger, drove from DeWitt that morning and told me they were driving back that evening.

At five o'clock, Julie and I took our leave for a brief honeymoon weekend in the Catskill Mountains. We stayed the first night in Springfield, Massachusetts, and drove on the next day through the Catskills. One of our favorite overnights was spent in the Martin Guest House in Saugerties, New York. It was the start of a beautiful marriage between two persons who had waited for long years until each of us crossed the path of the other and found what we desired most: a loving, tender, and understanding relationship in which to raise our future family.

We returned to Boston for the graduation ceremonies. Reg Smart and I had been appointed by Dean Muelder to be the School of Theology marshals at the Boston University commencement. Following the ceremonies, Julie and I returned to the penthouse to pack up her car for the trip to Syracuse, New York. I had been appointed to serve as the minister of the First Ward Methodist Church at 510 Bear Street, Syracuse, New York. Julie and I were beginning the long and gradual transition from one career to another following our marriage in Boston, Massachusetts.

II.

Settling into the First Ward Methodist Church

The first persons whom we met at First Ward were Ernie and Millie King and Shirley Molesky. Ernie was the church treasurer. Millie was the president of the Women's Association. Shirley was in charge of keeping the parsonage in shape for the ministers after they were appointed to the church. Millie and Ernie were very friendly and glad that a young minister had finally been appointed to their church.

"We've needed a younger man for years! We've got to give our youth an incentive to participate in youth activities. We've had nothing but older men who were about to retire in our church for too many years! We've finally got you and your wife who are just beginning instead of ending your ministry," both Millie and Ernie told us.

"My husband and I have a girl and a boy who need a youth fellowship," Shirley added. "I've told the district superintendent for years, if you don't appoint a younger minister, we're going to another church!"

For a newly married couple, the parsonage was a big ten-room house on two floors. The office was upstairs. There was a staircase going from the front door directly up the upstairs to the office. No one in the house would notice who was going up the stairs unless the door had to be opened to let in the person.

There were also three bedrooms plus a bathroom on the second floor. A back stairway left from the office directly downstairs to the kitchen. The office had built-in bookshelves on two of the walls. There was a large desk and office chair. There were two easy chairs directly in front of the desk. The downstairs had not only a large living room, but a dining room and a front parlor with very little furniture. Shirley promised us she would see to it that the house was fully furnished before the summer was over. The kitchen was a large one with a table and four chairs just off the dining room. There was also a large storeroom to the rear of the kitchen with a door leading to the backyard. A two-car garage, attached to the rear of the church, provided additional space for storage. The church was a large brick building with two front doors on each side of the front of the church. There was a stairway leading up to the sanctuary on each side. There were also two stairways on each side of the church leading to the basement. The sanctuary was in the style of a split pulpit with a lectern on one side of the chancel and the preacher's pulpit on the other. The choir sat just behind the stage next to the organist. The organist also served as the choir director. Victor Raab fulfilled these positions and had served the last three pastors before our arrival at the First Ward church. He only stayed with us for one year. After his resignation, Bill Harcourt became our organist. He was also a graduate of Fayetteville High School and the Juilliard School of Music.

There was also a small alcove in the rear of the church, behind the congregation. It was used as an adult classroom where members met for discussions prior to the service. The church kitchen was downstairs on the front end of the church. Tables and chairs were available to be set up for church dinners and special occasions such as wedding receptions. There were also three rooms on the right side of the church basement for Sunday school classes plus toilets for men and women. First Ward had been one of the leading churches in Syracuse during the early days of the twentieth century. Mrs. Eberling, who attended church regularly at age ninety-five, had grown up in this era in which the church had citywide prominence. I was amazed how she was able to climb the stairs each Sunday morning and find her seat on the fifth row on the left-hand side of the sanctuary along one of the center aisles (there were two center aisles plus an aisle down each side of the sanctuary).

Bertha Benson was our Sunday school superintendent and had been in this capacity for over thirty years. She knew all of the children by name and their parents, many of whom she also had had as youngsters in the same Sunday school when she first began teaching.

Julie and I started a Couples Club during our first fall at the church. It proved to be a rousing success with parties, bowling, swimming, boating, and cards once a month either in the home of one of our members or at the church, parsonage, or at a state park. We also started the Youth Fellowship each Sunday evening, which also proved to be very successful. We had more than fifteen young persons attending each Sunday on a regular basis. We also took a few high school seniors to visit some of the colleges in the area. They were getting ready to enroll after graduation from high school. The students attended Webster Grammar School as elementary pupils followed by Grant Boulevard Middle School and North High School.

In our first summer at First Ward (shortly after our marriage), the administrative board gave us permission to take a vacation during August. Since Julie had been a camp counselor for several years at Higgins Lake, Michigan, prior to seminary, she suggested we should go to Pokagon State Park near Fort Wayne, Indiana. It was roughly an hour and one-half from her parents' home in Goshen. We bought a small tent and set it up at one of the campsites along the lake. It was a very relaxing week where we played tennis and went swimming each day. I soon found out Julie was an expert cooking on an outdoor brazier using wood for the fire. Her years as a camp counselor were clearly evident! During our second week, we drove to Goshen and spent time with her folks and visited some of her high school friends and neighbors. It gave me an opportunity to become acquainted with some of he people of whom she spoke but had not yet met. We returned to the church after our two-week vacation to participate with our fellow ministerial colleagues on the north side, in the combined Sunday summer services at a different location each Sunday morning. I had learned from Alex Carmichel to use the summers to plan for the ensuing year's sermons. I made a studious effort to do the same before the fall activities were once again in full swing.

During the winter of 1961-62, Julie and I received information from the Experiment in International Living wondering if we might be interested in taking high school students overseas to live among foreign families for the following summer months. We were intrigued with this opportunity. We could choose our own country to visit and take fifteen high school students with us. The recruitment would be done by the Experiment. We would be the chaperones of the students while living with these local families. We would have a local counterpart who would be the official host making all of the arrangements with these families to house the American students. The American leader's costs would be covered by the Experiment. His/her partner's costs would have to be paid by the person leading the group. Couples were encouraged to be chaperones.

Julie and I were both intrigued with the idea.

"Why don't you raise the question at the next Official Board meeting, Don? Maybe they might not be against the idea," Julie suggested.

At our next board meeting, I raised the question.

"Julie and I have been asked if we would be willing to chaperone fifteen American high school students overseas during July and August of this coming summer. The Experiment-in-International Living is looking for couples to accompany students on these goodwill tours. We can choose the country we'd like to take them to and they would be housed by local families. Since both Julie and I can speak German, we thought we could be very helpful in taking a group to West Germany next summer. I'd like to ask you, members of the Official Board, if you would consider letting us do this during July and August. We've both been involved in exchanges previously and find this method of close contact on a people-to-people basis as one of the best ways to encourage better international relations between Americans and other peoples."

"It sounds like a great idea," Emerson Harsh said. "Who would conduct the summer services if you're not here?"

"I thought I'd talk it over with Dr. Cavert and Gary Hakes and see if we might have combined summer services for these two months."

"That might be a good idea. It would give us a chance to mix with our neighbors," Millie King responded.

"I don't see why the other two churches wouldn't cooperate, Don. I'm sure they'll be willing to arrange joint services for those two months," Ernie said.

"Well, why don't you talk with Rev. Hakes and Dr. Cavert and find out if they'd be willing to do that, Don," Cardie added. "You can let us know at our next meeting if they're willing to cover for you."

"Okay. I'll let you know what they say after I talk with them."

I went to see both Gary Hakes and Walter Cavert and told them about what Julie and I were considering doing that coming summer. I went to see Gary Hakes first.

"Gary, Julie and I have been asked if we would chaperone a group of high schools students overseas this summer. We'll probably go to Germany. We would be gone for two months: July and August. Would you mind having our congregation joining yours for one month? I'm going to talk with Walter Cavert of the North Presbyterian Church and find out if he would be willing to have our First Ward congregation join his congregation for one month."

"Yeah, I think we can do that. When you talk with Walter, ask him if he would mind taking July. June and I are going on vacation during August. We've bought some land on a lake north of here and I want to get started building a cabin on it. I'll be glad to cover any funerals that you might have during July. Maybe Walter can do the same in August. You'll want us to cover any funerals from First Ward too, won't you?"

"Yes. That would be a big help, Gary. I'll do the same for you when you're on vacation one of these years. Thanks, Gary. I'll talk with Dr. Cavert and find out if he'll do the same during August."

I dropped in on Walter Cavert at the North Presbyterian Church and told him about our plans for the summer.

"That's a great idea, Don. We need more of these international exchanges. That's far better than building up our armed forces because we don't really understand the cultures of other people."

"I've talked with Gary Hakes, Walter, and he's willing to have our congregation join his during July. He and June are building a cabin on their vacation up north during August. He was wondering if you would mind having our congregation and his join you during August."

"Yes. We can do that. I haven't made any plans yet for my vacation this summer. If Gary is willing to take the funerals from First Ward during July, I'll be glad to take them during August. That should be a great trip for you and Julie."

"Thanks, Walter. I'll be participating in these ecumenical services again the following summer."

After our next Official Board meeting, in which the members gave us permission to participate in the summer's exchange, Julie and I accepted the Experiment-in-International Living's invitation to become chaperones of fifteen

American students assigned to Radolfzell, Germany, during July and August 1962.

In the orientation at the Putney, Vermont, headquarters of the Experiment-in-International Living, we were briefed on what was expected of us. We were to assist the students in getting acquainted with their German "brothers and sisters" so that they would develop mutual interests and establish connections for, potentially, lifelong friendships. We also learned that the motto of the Experiment was "Expect the Unexpected" and to help students become aware of the uncertainties of life which occur in almost any experience which humans can have. No one is able to plan for every contingency. New situations require new responses which we may or may not have anticipated. We were to help the students understand the vagaries of having to make decisions even in situations which are often stressful, undesired, and most of all, unexpected from one day to the next. Can the students get along with their German counterparts? Can they adjust to new adult supervision in a different family from their own? How do they respond to new requirements taken for granted in a different culture? Can they remain "upbeat" and positive when confronted with new expectations which others may have of them in a family setting? These were some of the experiences we were encouraged to have the students encounter and surmount in a new cultural environment. Only a few of the students had studied German. Their adjustment to a German-speaking family would create difficult language stresses which they would also have to overcome.

The Experiment recruited the fifteen students from all across the United States. We met them for the first time in Hartford, Connecticut, where Capitol Airlines was based. We took off from there and landed at stops in Gander, Newfoundland; Reykjavik, Iceland; and Paris, France. From there we took a train to Radolfzell on the shore of Lake Constance, in the very southern part of Germany across the lake from Switzerland. We were met by our German Experiment leader, Herr Walter Schaeffner, who headed the group of German parents waiting to receive their American boys and girls as the "visiting brothers and sisters" of their own children. After meeting all of the German parents and students, Walter Schaeffner took us to his third-floor apartment where we met his wife, Hannelore, and son, Hartmut, for the first time.

"Donald, we only have a single bed available for you in our apartment. I've made arrangements with Frau Schaefer who lives downstairs to have Julie sleep there and come up for all of her meals with us. It's the best I could do. I hope you'll be comfortable, Julie. We're going to build a house out in the country with plenty of room, but we haven't started yet. The builder won't get around to it until this fall."

As we came into the apartment building, Walter took us to Franz Schaefer's first-floor apartment and rang the doorbell. His wife opened the door.

"Frau Schaefer, these are the Megnins from America."

"How do you do?" Frau Schaefer said as she shook hands with us. I hope you will enjoy your stay with us."

"I'm sure I will," Julie answered in German.

She ushered us into her apartment and showed us the bedroom which she had prepared for Julie to use during our stay in Radolfzell.

"I hope you like it," Frau Schaefer said.

"It's very nice."

"Frau Schaefer, thank you for hosting Frau Megnin during their stay with us."

"It's very nice to have met you, and we'll be seeing more of you, Frau Megnin."

"Herr Schaefer is a teacher in the Grundschule [Lower elementary] here in Radolfzell," Walter told us as we left to go upstairs to his apartment. "The Schaefers also have a son who's a few years younger than our son, Hartmut."

As we came in the door of this apartment, his wife and son were waiting for us.

"Hannelore and Hartmut, this is Herr und Frau Donald Megnin. Her name is Julie. She will sleep downstairs in Frau Schaefer's apartment. I've just introduced them to Frau Schaefer."

I shook hands with Hannelore and Hartmut. Hannelore hugged Julie by way of greeting.

"Come in, Julie and Donald. You don't mind if I call you Julie and Donald, do you? Dinner is all ready."

"No, we don't mind at all. We'll feel much more comfortable if we can call all of us by our first names, Hannelore."

And so our introduction to the German segment of the Experiment's program began with an enjoyable welcome and an excellent dinner which Hannelore prepared. The following days were pleasant. There were no problems with the assignments of our students with their German families with the exception of one girl. Laurie Schlanger (a Jewish girl) was placed with a family in charge of a group home outside of the city. They had a daughter the same age as Laurie. But Laurie was apprehensive at first. She wasn't sure how she would be received or how she was going to react to her German family. Some of her more distant relatives had been killed by the Nazis. After she met her counterpart, however, she accepted the location and the family with whom she was assigned.

One of the most eventful of the summer's experiences was "Die Grosse Deutschland Reise" (the Great German trip). It gave us an opportunity to travel throughout the southern part of Germany and western Austria for more than a week. We saw the ancient Roman ruins of the Laemas (fort), Speyer, Rothenburg, a medieval German city, Salzburg, Austria, and Munich before returning to Radolfzell. Walter was a very competent guide knowing the history of each stop that we made, explaining the historical significance of the cities and regions through which we traveled. There were a couple of instances where his intolerance for the conditions of our travel housing caused him to explode verbally. One instance was during our stay at an old castle on the Rhein River. We were sitting together discussing various aspects of cultural differences between American and German customs when a group of Belgian students were too loud and boisterous for Walter. He delivered a very strong message in French to them requesting that they make less noise so that the rest of the people in the dining room could also speak to each other! Needless to say, this chastising of the students drew an instant rejoinder, in German, from one the leaders telling him, in no uncertain terms, "Who are you to criticize us about being too loud? You, who were part of the invasions we've suffered in two world wars? How dare you tell us how to behave. We'll enjoy ourselves any way we like and you can't tell us how to act!"

Walter was quiet after this outburst. We knew, without his having to tell us, that he was chagrined and embarrassed not only by his outburst but by that of the Belgian leader. He also had a run in with the manager of this castle over the lack of sufficient towels in the rooms. The manager became irate and slammed down the window to his office through which Walter spoke.

"I won't tolerate your attempt to intimidate me! There are enough towels for each of the guests! If you don't like it, you can leave!"

We enjoyed hearing him tell of his experiences during World War II when he originally was in the Luftwaffe and was then pressed into service as an infantryman during the battle for Sardinia. He was captured by American troops and, after spending some time incarcerated on the island, was shipped with other captured German soldiers to Louisiana to cut timber in the swamps throughout the state. Walter was a teacher of English and had a real flourish in telling stories, not only in German, but also in English. Needless to say, he did not find the experience of cutting trees a very enjoyable way in which to spend his American captivity! Following his release from American captivity, he had to spend another year in France to help in rebuilding what "You Germans have ruined!" he heard over and over. In September of 1946, he was finally allowed to return to his family in southeastern Germany.

There was another time in which Walter got very upset with our American students. We were housed in a youth hostel on the outskirts of Salzburg, Austria, very near an Austrian army base. The curfew was 10:00 p.m. and the students had not yet returned from their evening's foray into the nearby village to eat and drink. When the ten o'clock hour arrived and the students had not, Walter was very upset. He feared they might have tangled with some Austrian soldiers nearby. He took it upon himself to walk into the village and look for the students.

"Walter, they'll come back. They know what the curfew hour is. If they're late, they'll have to ring the doorbell for admission and pay their fine [five schilling] to the director. I don't think you have to worry about them." My advice was disregarded.

"Well, I'm going over to the village and see where they are. They should have been back before now!"

Walter walked the half mile into the village only to find that the students had left. The innkeeper told him, "The German and American students were here, but they left about twenty minutes ago."

He walked back to the hostel and had to awaken the director to let him into the compound. The students had, upon their return, found the doors locked. They knocked on the windows of some of the girls who let them crawl in. By the time Walter was able to reenter the hostel, the students were all in bed. The director required him to pay the penalty for being late! Both the American and German students enjoyed their trip. It was a good opportunity for them to bond with each other as fellow travelers.

At the conclusion of our stay, we took the American students on a bus trip to Berlin. We all boarded in Radolfzell with our baggage. It would be the last time we saw our host students on this trip. The bus took us to the southern border of the German Democratic Republic, north of Bayreuth in West Germany. Upon our arrival, we were checked to make sure all of us had passports and no contraband on board. What we were not expecting was the East German government's reluctance to have any foreign travelers going through their country on the first anniversary date (August 23, 1961) of erecting the wall between East and West Berlin! Subsequently, we sat all day on the bus at the border! The East German border guards would not give us permission to pass until dark! At least they did allow us to use their bathroom facilities and their border canteen during the day to slake our hunger and thirst! It took more than eight hours until permission was finally granted for the bus driver to continue our trip to West Berlin. We spent two days visiting the Reichstag, the museum, a tour of the wall through West Berlin and visits to a few of the castles left standing at the end of World War II. It proved to be a sobering ending for the American students to experience what the Germans had to confront on a daily basis going from West to East through what had been "their country" controlled by two diametrically different political systems!

The bus took us back through East and West Germany and continued on to the Orly airport in Paris, France, arriving in time for the students to catch their flight home. Julie and I said our good-byes to them, and after seeing them off, we took a flight to Stuttgart, rented a car, and drove to Vaihingen/Enz to introduce Julie to my relatives. It was a very pleasant weekend and fitting climax to a strenuous but worthwhile summer of living and touring in Germany. We established new friendships which we have cherished ever since. While Hartmut Schaeffner came to visit us on the farm in Pennsylvania during the early seventies on his trip around the world, he lost his life in an accident as a Luftwaffe pilot in 1973. Walter is also no longer living, having died in 2005. We have kept in contact with Hannelore and Gernot, their younger son, through the years.

By our third year at First Ward, Julie was pregnant. We were looking forward to the arrival our first child. I had been taking graduate courses in the Maxwell School of Citizenship and Public Affairs for the previous three years, usually two courses a semester. Julie was very helpful in researching materials for my term papers. The reason I excelled in these efforts was due in large part to her ferreting out the books and materials which I needed to write my classroom papers. I gave her the subject matter and she researched and collected the materials from which I wrote my papers. Her research skills far exceeded mine. I could write the papers based upon what she had collected for me to read prior to writing them. I dare say, had she not helped as much as she did, I probably could not have excelled in my graduate program! Actually, I had applied to American, Syracuse, and Cornell Universities while still in my final year in the seminary. I wanted to begin my graduate program in international relations at one of these school. Cornell's program in Chinese and Southeast Asian studies, I thought, would be best to integrate my experiences in Thailand. While I was accepted in the American and Syracuse graduate programs, I felt I was not likely to gain admission to Cornell. I had had an interview with the chairman of the political science program at Cornell. He couldn't quite see why I wanted another degree since I already had one in theology and was a clergyman. He was a specialist in Italian politics and had a heavy Italian accent.

"Vy do you vant another degree? You are already minister?"

"I would like to integrate my experiences which I've had teaching in Thailand for two years and traveling throughout Southeast Asia, as the basis upon which to expand my professional expertise by getting a degree in your Southeast Asian studies program."

Sensing his reluctance to take me on as a graduate student in his program, I then talked with our Methodist district superintendent, Dr. Phil Torrance.

"Phil, I don't think I'm going to be accepted in the Southeast Asian studies program at Cornell after my interview with the political science chairman. Could I be posted somewhere near Syracuse so that I can accept their offer of attending the Maxwell School?"

"That's no problem, Don. I'll put you right in the north side of Syracuse in the First Ward Church on Bear Street."

Hence, instead of being posted to a joint Methodist and Presbyterian church near Ithaca, I was posted to the First Ward Methodist Church following graduation from the Boston University School of Theology on the first Sunday in June 1960.

The work at First Ward was challenging. Not only had the church been the final destination of ministers about to retire, but there had been little contact with the youth of the church. Julie and I started the Youth Fellowship and more than ten high school students attended our first meeting. Eileen King, Sue and Linda Harsh, Diane Lazaroff, Diane Wild, and Lynette Molesky were the real spark plugs of the organization. They were also the daughters of some of the major adults active in our church. We met in the basement of the church and played games, held pizza parties, dances, and, occasionally, held joint meetings with the Youth Fellowship of the North Presbyterian Church. Gloria and Roger Reid were the advisors of this group, and the joint meetings reflected the common interest both of our churches had to further opportunities for the youth of the area. The Presbyterians had a summer camp for their youth at Vander Kamp, north of Oneida Lake. We enjoyed swimming parties and picnics with the combined groups at this camp.

Some of the excellent resources of the First Ward were members of the Women's Association, neighbors, and friends who attended the church as often as they could and Mrs. Julia Whitehead. She and her committee prepared Manhattan clam chowder each month as a money raiser for the church. The chowder was so popular; as soon as the word was out that the ladies were making it, it was sold out! It was one of the chief moneymakers for the church.

One of the ideas we had was to mix the ladies' circles periodically so that new members could become acquainted with the older ones. It was a bit of a struggle to have the concept accepted, but most of the ladies did. Only one long-standing old-timer refused to participate. She was well into her eighties.

"You're trying to break up our old friendships! You're doing nothing more than trying to gain control over the membership of this church! I'm not going to participate in your plan! I've been a member of this church since the turn of the century, and I want to meet with whomever I please, not with people I don't know! You're just like Alex Carmichel! I've heard he did the same thing in DeWitt when he first came there. We don't want to change just for the sake of change. We want to stay with the women with whom we're comfortable!"

Needless to say, she never attended any of our services. Even though some of her best friends joined in a new circle for that next year, she did not. In fairness to her, it may have been a matter of living on the south side of Syracuse. She really should have become a member of a church near where she lived, but she did not. She wanted to keep her membership in the First Ward Church.

Another of the problems which I created for some members was when I asked in a sermon, "Are you asking our youth to do too much?" I was referring to a member of our Youth Fellowship who was involved in a variety of activities and groups because her parents were so socially active. I was trying to suggest the youth didn't have to be involved in everything their parents were doing. I thought it was unfair to our youth. I used the example of a woman who recognized herself as the target of one of the points I was making. After the service, she came storming into the parsonage and said, "Who are you to tell us what we should or should not be doing? It's none of your business!"

"What I was trying to suggest was that it's not fair to our youth if they are overwhelmed with responsibilities which their parents have taken on. They should focus, first, on doing well in school, second, school activities, and third, on developing friendships with their classmates. I think, quite frankly, you are expecting your daughter to do too much by getting her involved in each of the groups of which you and your husband are members."

"That's for us to decide, not you!"

She turned around and left as angry as she was coming in. While she did not attend church for several weeks, she allowed her daughter to come to our weekly Youth Fellowship meetings. What I tried to say each Sunday morning to the congregation was we need to develop the talents that each of us has. We can't find out what these talents are if we continue to waste our time on peripheral and meaningless activities simply for the sake of participating. Life has meaning, and we need to focus on finding out what best applies to ourselves.

Julie was an absolutely indispensable part of our joint effort in the life and work of the church. She helped prepare the weekly church bulletin, sang in the choir, was a cosponsor of the weekly Youth Fellowship, met with the Women's Association, cleaned the parsonage, did the weekly shopping, and answered the telephone and doorbell while preparing our meals every day. In addition, she was invaluable to me in conducting research on the topics which were part of my graduate courses at the university. We had to follow a very tight schedule from one week to the next. Sundays were set aside for church and youth activities. Mondays were used for attending class and writing my papers. Tuesdays I spent calling on our members, including those hospitalized and attending meetings in the evening. Wednesdays were spent in research, reading, and writing papers for my classes. Thursdays were spent on sermon preparation during the day and counseling sessions in the evening, if there were no meetings. Fridays continued with sermon preparation. Saturdays were used to complete my sermons in the morning followed by driving out to the farm to spend time with my parents. I usually walked up the hill behind the house to a huge rock. I would stand on it and preach my sermon to the birds, trees, and grass. I wanted to become as familiar with it as possible so that I would not be too dependent upon my notes in the pulpit. After supper, Julie and I played cards with Pop and Mom for a couple of hours before returning to the parsonage. The only variation to this schedule was to conduct funerals, emergency hospital visits, and weddings with rehearsals on Friday evenings and the ceremony on Saturday afternoons. On occasion, Julie and I met with some of our friends on a Friday evening to attend a movie or go out for an evening meal. We had made friends with fellow clergy of the Central New York Conference. There were also several of my friends from high school who still lived in the area with whom we got together.

Bob and Nancy Bolton, with whom I had gone to high school and seminary and with whom Julie had also become acquainted, returned from their two-year stay at the International Church in Rio de Janeiro, Brazil. They were posted at the Marcellus Methodist Church and we got together with them occasionally. I was pleased when Bob and Nancy asked me to baptize their oldest child (Jimmy) in their church shortly after he was born. In the following spring, Julie was pregnant with our first child.

At the beginning of our third year at First Ward, I had applied for the Cokesbury Award for College Teaching which the Methodist Church gave out yearly. I discovered I really was more interested in teaching than continuing in the pastorate. To our surprise, I was fortunate enough to win the award. It very likely helped that the chairman of the Awards Committee, a professor of education at Syracuse University, was a friend of Alex Carmichel. He also had known who I was as an intern at the DeWitt Community Church during the early 1950s. The combination of excellent performance in my graduate work plus knowing me and one of my leading sponsors (Alex), I'm sure these attributes were shared with the Cokesbury Awards Committee by the chairman. The award enabled me to study full-time with all of my graduate expenses paid by the grant. It was now that we had the most difficult part of the task to complete. We had to inform the First Ward Church that we would be leaving after conference at the end of June 1963. At the Official Board meeting, I told them what had happened.

"I almost hate to say this to you. Julie and I will be leaving at the end of conference time to begin full-time graduate study in the Maxwell School of Citizenship and Pubic Affairs. I just received the letter of congratulations for having won the Cokesbury Award for College Teaching. It means that all of the costs of graduate study will be covered by the grant, but I have to be a full-time student. I know this is hard for all of us. Julie and I have really enjoyed getting to know all of you. We've had some really great times together these past three years. I hope my successor will continue working with all of you to keep the church alive and prospering through the years. I'll submit my formal letter of resignation just prior to conference time in May."

The shock was palpable. No one said anything for some time. Millie finally said, "And you and Julie are going to have your first child too! We won't be able to see it if you're not here anymore."

"I'll bring him or her over for you to see, Millie," Julie responded. "After all, we're still in the same city."

The ladies were dabbing their eyes. The men stood and shook my hand.

"At least you've gotten something started with our youth, Don," Emerson said.

"I just hope whoever comes after you will keep up the good work you and Julie have done here at First Ward."

"If there's an older minister who comes here, I'm afraid we'll be right back where we were before Don and Julie came," Millie sighed. "We're not a growing community in a suburban area. We're in the oldest part of town!"

Her sentiment was echoed by several of the other board members. "Well, let's wait and see who's appointed," Esther Vine suggested. "It may not be as bad as you think. The conference appointed a young minister at the Woodlawn Church. Maybe we'll be lucky enough to have the same here again at First Ward."

To the dismay of members of First Ward, an older minister who was to retire in three years was again appointed. After the last two appointments (my successor and one other), the Methodist Conference decided to close First Ward Methodist Church. There were simply too few persons still attending. Most of the congregation either affiliated with churches closer to where they lived or joined the North Presbyterian Church or the Woodlawn Methodist Church where Gary (also a recent seminary graduate) and his wife, June Hakes, were assigned.

Pop and Mom bought a house for us at 559 Columbus Avenue (around the corner from Westcott Street) which became our home during our time in graduate school. It was only about a twenty-minute walk to the university in the winter. I rode my bicycle to and from the classes during the rest of the year.

Shortly after our move, Julie talked with Dr. Donald Adams, professor of comparative education, about enrolling for a master's degree in this field. She was getting bigger and bigger in her pregnancy but felt she could transfer some of her hours from Boston University while taking additional courses at Syracuse. She had more than sixty graduate hours toward her sacred theology bachelor's degree only to find out she could transfer in six of these hours toward her master's degree, but no more. Nevertheless, she decided to transfer these hours and began her studies for the MA degree. It was the beginning of a new life for both of us especially since we were awaiting the birth of our first child in late October 1963.

III.

Full-Time Graduate Study

The house my parents had bought for us was a two-story frame house with an upstairs and a downstairs apartment. The Mr. and Mrs. Mansfield lived upstairs with a young son. Julie and I lived downstairs. We preferred this arrangement because it gave us access to the basement which had been used by the previous owners as a combination office and workstation. We had a living room, dining room, two bedrooms, and a kitchen in our apartment plus a hallway leading downstairs and outdoors.

Julie and I completed two courses over the summer. The temperature in the basement was a bit damp and cool, but I thought nothing of it. Surely when winter comes, the furnace will keep it quite pleasant. By the time I enrolled for full-time study in September, I was beginning to cough ever so slightly. I kept going to class but the coughing continued. On October 21 I drove Julie to the hospital because the water sack had broken. After I saw her in her room, she suggested, "Why don't you go see Dr. Ayer about your cough, Don. It seems to be getting worse."

"Okay. Dr. McLean said it would be some time yet before the baby comes. I'll go see Dr. Ayer and come back afterwards."

I went to see Dr. Ayer, our family doctor from the DeWitt Community Church days.

"Don, you've got a fever and what's called walking pneumonia. I want you to check into Syracuse General Hospital so that we can keep an eye on you for a few days. With the fever you have, it's too dangerous to have you wandering around not only for yourself but for your wife and neighbors."

I drove to the hospital and checked myself in. I was put into a private room and heavily medicated. Before I fell asleep, I called Julie to tell her where I was.

"Dr. Ayer told me to check myself in at Syracuse General. I've got a case of walking pneumonia and a fever that he doesn't want me to spread around, Julie. What a time to land in the hospital! I guess you'll have to go through the birth of our baby by yourself. I couldn't have been with you at any rate, but I had planned on seeing you right afterwards."

"That's okay. Gloria [Reid, not only a friend but a nurse] was just here and she's going to stay with me through the birth. I'm sure she'll let you know whether it's a boy or a girl."

"Keep up the good work, Julie. I love you and take care of that little baby!"

Between medications, lunch, supper, and sleeping, I found out the next morning that our baby was a little boy. We had decided on the name of Martin King Megnin long before his birth. In fact, we had picked out all of the names of the children we thought we would have. The next morning, Gloria came to visit.

"Guess what, Don! You're the father of a little boy! He was born last night around five minutes after nine o'clock. Julie did a great job through the birth. She handled it very well for a first-time mother. You can be real pleased with both of them. If your fever disappears, I wouldn't be surprised if the doctor releases you and you might even be able to take them home. Julie and the baby will be in the community hospital for another three days. I would guess once your fever has broken, Dr. Ayer will release you. If he doesn't, I'll take Julie and Martin home."

Julie and Martin were released before I was. Gloria took them home. I arrived shortly thereafter. I had left my car in the hospital parking lot. It was a joyful reunion! I didn't want to get too close to Julie and Martin in case I might still be infectious.

"Isn't he a nice little boy, Don? He drinks very well too. I give him the nipple any time he wakes up and begins fussing. Once he is through, he falls asleep again."

"He's a very nice-looking baby, Julie. He takes right after his mother!"

With a baby in the house, our lives were to change radically. No more just going out to visit friends. We had a baby to care for. Julie fed Martin almost every time he awoke. Between caring for Martin, washing diapers, cooking, and going shopping, Julie didn't have many hours available for activities other than watching television in the few minutes she had between feedings. She postponed taking any more courses until the following spring semester. By then, she thought she would have a better idea of what her schedule was going to be like.

At the end of October, Julie's parents came to see their new grandson. Since he was in his crib located in our bedroom, we had one spare bedroom for them to use. Grandmother King enjoyed holding him and talked with him after each of his feedings. After our evening meals, we sat and talked, drove out to visit my folks and some of the other relatives in Syracuse. Whenever it was time to feed Martin, Julie excused herself and went into a bedroom to let him drink until he fell asleep. Before Julie's folks left, they promised to visit us over Christmas. They wanted to see their new grandson as much as possible.

On November 22, 1963, the killing of President John F. Kennedy by Lee Harvey Oswald changed the course of history in the United States irrevocably.

I had just walked over to Maxwell after lunch and was going into our research methods classroom when the professor came in and announced, "The president's been shot. We won't be doing much in class today. You might just as well go home and watch what happens on television."

We left the classroom very quickly and returned to our homes. We literally spent the next four days glued to the television watching the swearing in of Lyndon B. Johnson as the new president; the return of Kennedy's body to Washington and the accompanying entourage on Air Force One of Jacqueline Kennedy, Bobby Kennedy, President and Mrs. Johnson, and the Kennedy advisors. We followed Mrs. Kennedy as she selected the grave site for her husband in the Arlington National Cemetery, planning the funeral service and watching the horse-drawn hearse bearing the president's body to Arlington Cemetery on television. The entire country watched if a television was available. It was only by chance Julie and I had one. When we were about to leave the television which Shirley Molesky had provided us as chairperson of the Parsonage Committee, she said, "Take it with you. I'm sure the next minister who is assigned here will have one!"

Fortunately for us, we took her advice. Otherwise, we wouldn't have been able to follow these tragic events in our nation's history!

Our professors were somewhat more tolerant than usual after the tragedy. They gave us an extra day to write our papers.

Dad and Mom King came out to visit us over Christmas. The weekend before, we spent with Mom and Pop on the farm, together with the Schoeck family. It gave us an opportunity to celebrate two Christmases for the first time. Needless to say, Julie showed off our son to his cousins, aunt, and uncle.

"He sure is a handsome little boy!" Aunt Inge said. "He takes right after his parents!"

Everyone laughed. But they did agree Martin was a very handsome little boy.

Before Dad and Mom King left, to return to Goshen, Dad King proposed, "Julia, why don't you, Don, and Martin join us next summer when we take our vacation on Birch Lake? We're renting a cottage and there's plenty of room for all of us."

We both thought that was an excellent idea and agreed to spend a week with them during early August.

I continued with my course work and was making progress towards finishing my master's degree in international relations. At the beginning of my second year in graduate school, Dr. Frank Munger, chairperson of the Political Science Department, asked me if I would be willing to work as an assistant to Professor Arthur Osteen. He was the director of the Africa-Asia Public Service Fellowship Program. The Ford Foundation had given the Maxwell School a grant to oversee the recruitment, selection, and placement of recent graduates from law and graduate schools across the United States to work as advisors to the governments of newly independent countries. These governments were glad to have such assistants help in setting up their departments and agencies to administer the new programs being undertaken by their governments for the first time. Dr. Fred Burke, director of the African Studies Program, had started the teaching of Swahili and other African languages at Syracuse. This program aided in making Syracuse a natural base to train specialists for service overseas in a variety of countries. I agreed and spent twenty hours per week working for Arthur. Most of my time was spent organizing the files of each candidate. The applications, transcripts, and letters of recommendation had to be complete before they could be considered for participation in this program. It was my job to make sure each file was complete before giving it to Arthur and his committee to make their yearly selections. I was particularly intrigued by one candidate from Stanford. He had been a student of Bob Textor, whom I had known in Thailand. Bob had written a letter of recommendation for him as the director of the Stanford University Research and Computer Center. Since I knew Bob very well, I wrote him a letter and told him what I was doing and how I had gotten his name from a letter of recommendation he had written for one of our candidates for public service overseas. Unfortunately, I never received a reply. I suspect Bob didn't want his past to become a part of what he was now doing.

Another of the interesting experiences of working in the program was trying to get used to the cordial blonde secretary whom Arthur had hired. While she was a very competent and thorough secretary with whom our candidates got along very well, she used an enormous amount of perfume each day. I felt it was overwhelming. I mentioned this to Arthur.

"Arthur, could you ask Juanita to put on less perfume? It's really overwhelming."

"I can't do that, Don. She's a very competent secretary. If it bothers you, why don't you tell her to use less perfume?"

It was obvious Arthur wasn't going to say anything to Juanita. Since I was only his graduate assistant, I didn't think it was my place to tell her what to do. I simply opened the windows in the office. Invariably, if the temperature was rather cool, Juanita closed them. Fortunately, as the day wore on, her perfume fragrance gradually wore off!

In addition to the courses I was taking, I also worked on writing my master's thesis. The subject was "West Germany's Relationship to the Common Market, European Integration, and the United Nations from 1953 to 1963." By the end of the fall semester, I had completed writing it. Dr. Bishop, my thesis advisor, scheduled the defense for the later part of October. After a two-hour session, in which they asked all kinds of questions, they approved it with certain minor changes to be made in the table of contents and bibliography.

"You can complete it by December 1, can't you?" Dr. Bishop asked. "It has to be finished by then in order to have it conferred in the January commencement."

"I should have it finished within a few days, Dr. Bishop. There's nothing major that needs rewriting."

"As soon as you complete the changes, bring me the thesis and I'll have it signed by the committee and sent to the graduate school."

The graduate courses in the Maxwell School were uniformly interesting and usually presented in such a way that the enthusiasm of the professor came through. In talking with my fellow graduate students over lunch occasionally (in one of the conference rooms of Hendricks Chapel), we all agreed if the professor was fascinated with the subject matter, we were much more likely not only to learn the concepts, but it would have an influence upon our own capabilities to teach the subject in the future. The seminars were especially interesting. Comparative politics, international organizations, political theory, and the legislative process were among the best that I had. There was one problem, however. In the seminars in which not only the faculty member smoked but many of the graduate students, the rooms were often so thick with smoke we only saw our classmates across the room through a blue haze! In Dr. Fisher's political theory class, those of us who were nonsmokers sat next to the windows and kept them open as long as possible. Unfortunately, in the winter we were asked to close them because the room had gotten so cold! It may have caused me to have pericarditis (an inflammation of the outer lining of the heart). Dr. Ayer put me in the hospital for a few days in order to control the inflammation. He was surprised when I told him I've never smoked.

"Your condition is one which I've noticed smokers sometimes have."

"I sit in seminar rooms in which there's a lot of smoke, but I really can't control it."

"Well, sit as far away from the smokers as possible, Don. Otherwise you could have it again," he told me as he discharged me. "You don't want to take this suggestion too lightly. You've got a family to think about and their future as well as yours."

Martin was a real joy for Julie and me. He liked to sit on my lap, and we would rock back and forth in the rocking chair. On one occasion, I rocked so hard we literally went over backward when one of the rockers broke. Fortunately, the wall behind us kept us from falling completely on the floor!

During the warm summer days, we took him out into the backyard and filled a plastic tub with water for him to play in. He had a plastic whale which he liked to splash around as Julie washed him. She got almost as much water on her as on him but did succeed in giving him a bath. Whenever we went out to the farm, we took his playpen along. After supper Julie put on his pajamas and placed him in it. He usually fell asleep after his supper.

During the summer of 1964, we drove out to visit Julie's folks and went with them to Birch Lake in Michigan. Martin spent a lot of time in his playpen, which we set up on the dock in front of their cabin. It was a safer place for him than to let him wander around as he was beginning to do. We sat on the deck next to the playpen and watched him play with his toys while we adults were having something to eat and drink. It was also the summer in which I went fishing with Dad King. He and I went out in his boat, and we caught several bluegills, which he cleaned and Mom King cooked for supper. Once Martin fell asleep, we played cards before going to bed ourselves. During this trip to Goshen, Martin also became acquainted with his cousins Cindy and Mike King. Cindy was two years older than Martin and Mike was almost three months younger. It was the beginning of many pleasant summers which we've spent with Tom, Flora, Cindy, and Mike, not only in Goshen, but also at Lake Wawasee, our Pennsylvania farm, and Butler, Pennsylvania.

Among my professors, Dr. Donald G. Bishop, whom I had also had as an undergraduate, was definitely the most influential in making it possible for me to complete the doctorate. He knew the intricacies of European governments as no other professor whom I had. He was my master's thesis advisor. I took every course which he taught; he was influential in obtaining graduate assistantships, passing my oral comprehensives, and obtaining a research grant which enabled Julie, Martin, and me to travel to Germany and India in order to conduct research for my dissertation. He was truly what the Germans called "mein Doktor's Vater" (the father of my doctorate.) It was only after he had died that we found out from Iona Bishop (his wife) that he had been a CIA agent through his years of teaching at the university. I often wondered why Dr. Bishop would be gone for a semester or two during the course of his years at Syracuse. I knew sabbaticals usually were granted after seven years of teaching or some arrangement might be made because of a professor's ill health, but to be gone so often was novel indeed. Not only was he sent to Europe, but also to the Far East. After completing all of my requirements for the doctoral degree (courses, comprehensives, and orals), he asked me what I planned to use for my dissertation research.

"It'll probably be on the common market, Dr. Bishop. I'd like to know how the decision-making process is determined throughout this system. I can use my German in conducting some of my research in Europe, since I speak it."

"Why don't you research some topic in one of the developing countries, Don? The Shell Foundation pays everything from airfare to housing rentals and internal travel in the country being researched. The Maxwell School has been selected by this foundation to grant two fellowships for an entire year of research abroad if it involves some developing country. Bob Palmer, Arthur Osteen, and I think you'd be the ideal student to receive one of these awards. You've spent time overseas in a developing country as our Syracuse-in-Asia representative to Thailand. You shouldn't have any problem being selected. We've got one student who we're going to send to East Pakistan. He's been there as recently as two years ago."

"Let me think it over, Dr. Bishop. When do you have to know?"

"The deadline is next Wednesday. Do you think you can come up with a topic by then?"

"I'll give it a try. I've been doing a lot of reading about the common market. I'll see if I can dig up a topic that might apply to a developing country."

"You might want to explore why West Germany has spent so much money giving aid to India. It's in the tens of millions of dollars from what I've heard. You could spend as equal amount of time in each country doing your research."

"Thanks, Dr. Bishop. I'll do that. I'll work on a topic over the weekend."

The result of changing my topic which then became the name of my dissertation was "German Economic Assistance to India: An Analysis of Its Principles and Effects on Indo-German Relations." The grant was for more than six thousand dollars for one year including airfare and local expenses in each country.

Before we could embark on our research and travel overseas, however, I had to complete my written comprehensives and oral examinations. There were fifteen questions covering the four fields which I had chosen as my major areas of concentration: comparative politics, international relations, political theory, and American politics. To my great satisfaction, I received twelve As and three Bs on my written comprehensives. Marion Borst, Dean Bailey's secretary, told me after the test results had been posted, "The dean wants to sit on your orals committee, Don. He's impressed with how well you did on your comps!"

The old adage "Pride goeth before a fall!" could not have been truer. Steve Bailey was, indeed, on my orals committee. It was chaired by Dr. Robert Palmer, with Dr. Margarete Fisher and Dr. Oliver Clubb comprising the committee. The orals are usually two hours in length covering questions from each of the areas of expertise represented by these faculty inquisitors. I did very well with the three nonadministrators, but Steve Bailey nailed me on some issues for which I had not really prepared related to Southern politics in the United States.

"What types of voting patterns have you found existing among members of Congress from the Southern states?"

"I think they reflect the interests of their Southern constituents, but I'm not sure who these senators or representatives are. I know a few of them, but I'd be hard-pressed to name even most of them."

"Haven't you been following what's going on in the South these days?"

"I've read the newspapers, Dr. Bailey, but I haven't really studied the voting patterns of the members of Congress."

"What are you going to tell your students when they ask what you think about Senator So-and-So in your class and why he votes as he does? How can you presume to be prepared in American politics when you can't answer such a simple question?"

These were a few of the questions he asked me on voting patterns and behavior in various parts of the United States. I really didn't know the answers. It soon became apparent that of the four fields we graduates were supposed to prepare for our orals, I was not up to par in American politics. Dr. Palmer and Dr. Fisher asked me about the structure of our political system and how it is organized. I had no problem answering these questions. Dr. Clubb raised the question about how our government had performed over the centuries to which I gave a rather lengthy answer from my survey of American politics. After two hours, Dr. Palmer said, "That's it for now, Don. I'll let you know what the committee decides about your performance."

I left the room deflated, to say the least. I knew my performance was not satisfactory from Dean Bailey's point of view. I thought the other members were sympathetic, but his vote would be crucial in determining the outcome. I retired to the office I shared with Dr. Palmer. It was Dr. Bishop's desk which I had been using since he had left to go to Taiwan that year. After several minutes, Dr. Palmer came in.

"I've got some bad news for you, Don. The committee has to be unanimous in approving the performance of a candidate, and Dean Bailey wasn't satisfied. After considerable discussion, he agreed you could take the orals over later on this summer. I'll get the committee together when Dr. Bishop comes back in August. I'll have him on your committee instead of Dean Bailey. I'm sorry you didn't pass it this time, Don. But you may want to bone up on American politics, particularly voting behavior."

I gathered my briefcase and papers together and left the office. Julie was outside with Martin waiting for me in our second Plymouth, which Julie's folks had given us. She could tell right away from my depressed demeanor something was wrong.

"What's the matter, Don? How did the session go?"

"I didn't pass. I couldn't answer Dean Bailey's questions about American politics. Dr. Palmer says I'll have to take the orals over again later on this summer. He told me to read as much as possible about American politics. I did fine on the other three areas, but not on Dean Bailey's favorite topic: Southern politics."

"I'm sorry it went that way, but at least you can take them again later on. They didn't have to vote that way, did they?"

"I don't know . . . After doing so well on my written comps . . ."

I was really exhausted. Martin slept through the entire discussion and only woke up when we returned to Columbus Ave. It took me several days to recover and return to the library to read as extensively as possible about American politics, particularly on voting patterns.

When Dr. Palmer reconvened the committee in early August, Dr. Bishop had returned from the Far East. It was the same committee as in the spring, but Dr. Bishop had replaced Dean Bailey. As the committee gathered, Dr. Palmer said, "Dean Bailey's on vacation." He told the committee as we were about to start the second orals. This time I passed, and each of the professors shook hands with me and extended their congratulations. We could now prepare for our departure in early September to begin my research on German economic assistance to India.

During this year of preparation, Julie had finished writing her thesis in comparative education. The title of it was "Increasing the Understanding of Other Cultures" for upper elementary teachers. She wrote it under the direction of Dr. Don Adams. He had wanted her to continue on for a doctorate. But with Martin as a baby, she felt she couldn't take the time to continue her studies. Her name did appear, however, in the Syracuse University's commencement bulletin (1965) listing master's degree candidates who had completed their degrees. My name was not among those listed even though I had also completed my master's degree in international relations that previous December. I took Mom and Pop to the graduation exercises (May 1965) in which she received her master's degree. Gloria Reid volunteered to look after Martin so that we could all go to her graduation.

IV.

Dissertation Research

The major requirement of the Shell Foundation's grant was that the research had to involve a developing country. Dr. Bishop's suggestion about looking at the West German government's interest in India via its economic development aid was intriguing and ideal for me to use my German fluency. I had been to India on my return from Thailand in 1956 and felt somewhat familiar with what we could expect of our stay for the second half of the year's research. I drew up a series of questions which I wanted to use for my inquiry of both German and Indian governmental aid and development personnel. Since I thought my German should be flawless, I had Walter Schaeffner, our friend from the Experiment-in-International Living program, look over my questions and improve them, if necessary, to ask the German officials.

Julie, Martin, and I arrived in Germany in early September 1965 and spent a few days with my Tante Luise Luipold and her family in Vaihingen/Enz. We bought a used VW for our stay and travel in the country. My cousin Liz Grossmann and her husband, Hans, had a little boy, Hans Joerg. He was a few months older than Martin. They played together during our stay at Tante Luise's house and also in the Vaihingen/Enz community sandbox. Hans Joerg was a big boy for his age, but seemed to enjoy playing with his younger American cousin, Martin. They got along very well with each other. After a few days, we drove down to Radolfzell in order for Walter to look over my questionnaire. He made some changes and improved the quality of the questions so that he said, "You can easily ask the German officials these questions. I'd like to know how they answer them, Donald."

"If I ever have the results published, Walter, I'll send you a copy."

We spent a couple of days with the Schaeffners in their new home. They had moved from their apartment in Radolfzell to the new house which they had built on a hilltop just outside of the little village of Moeggingen. It was a very pleasant stay. We also were treated to excellent dinners which Hannelore prepared during our visit. After spending the weekend, we drove north again and stopped briefly in Vaihingen before continuing on to Bonn, Germany, to find a place to live. We were planning to spend one-half of the year in Germany and the other half in India gathering the research data for my dissertation. We looked for apartments in and around Bonn for a few days. There was nothing available in Bonn, but we did find an apartment house in Roleber, just across the Rhein River, not far from Beuel, Bonn's sister city. The owner and builder of the apartment house was Herr Fassbinder. The interior was complete, but the outside was a builder's mess. The yard was nothing but dirt all around the house. The only way into the apartments from the street was by several planks planted end to end through the dirt. So long as the weather was sunny, it was possible to enter without too much of a problem. Each time it rained or snowed, however, the dirt turned into mud. If you slipped off the planks, you were sure to be covered with mud! I usually carried Martin into the apartment. He would have preferred to go through the mud!

Our second-floor apartment faced the street. There was a pianist living below us who spent a great deal of time in his apartment. Opposite our apartment was another apartment facing the backyard rented by a man, his wife, daughter, and a friend from Saarland. The two men were studying at the University of Bonn. There was another apartment under them facing the musician's apartment that was still empty. The owner was in the process of trying to finish the work around the entranceway. The workmen would often be gone for days working on other projects. As winter came and snow fell, the yard was really a mess. It was impossible to take Martin outside. He wanted to tramp around in the mud with his boots. On one occasion, I slipped off one of the planks and almost fell into the hole left near the foundation wall. When Herr Fassbinder came to pick up his monthly rent, I really let him have it. I cursed the slow pace with which he was building the units.

"Wie koennen Sie so einen Schlumberei bei bringen? So einen Schumtz hab ich schon seit meiner Zeit auf dem Hof nicht gesehen! Sie muessen doch selber sehen das diesen grossen Loch zugemacht wird! Wie lang muessen wir noch in diesem Schweine Stahl wohnen bis Sie as fertig gemacht haben?" (How can you allow this mess to continue? I haven't seen such a mess since I left our farm! You must see to it that this big hole is covered. How much longer are we going to have to live in this pigsty before you're finished?)

Needless to say, Herr Fassbinder was not too pleased with my description of his construction! I didn't wait for his response. I went into our apartment and slammed the door. The wife of our neighbor from Saarland agreed with my comments. She heard me talking to him and had looked out of her window.

Actually, we were lucky to have found a place so close to Bonn. Roleber was just a fifteen-minute drive from the Bonn University library and the various ministries in which I conducted my interviews. My questionnaire was twenty questions in length and covered the gamut of the information I needed to sustain my original hypothesis: the West German government was supplying India with an enormous amount of financial aid for some political advantage. My dissertation was to spell out what this purpose was.

The basic data for the dissertation was to be derived from the questions which I asked of government officials in both Germany and India in addition to the materials which I received from them. The questionnaire dealt with some of the following issues in setting up and beginning economic aid programs sponsored by the German government in behalf of the Indian government. Questions such as how the aid programs began, the types of aid, how much money and equipment were given, the types of relationships which developed between German and Indian personnel, the problems and personnel issues which were confronted, the types of evaluative criteria used to assess the programs, where records and figures could be found for each of the projects, what additional sources might provide an objective assessment of the problems and interactions encountered by these cross-cultural development programs, where I could find data to verify what I was being told in my interviews, how were the projects selected for development, what types of interpersonal problems had to be overcome by each government in order for the programs to be continued, how were the priorities for development set and by whom, would the governments continue to work cooperatively in future projects, why or why not?

One of the persons whose name arose as a consequence of my interviews in the German Foreign Ministry was Jan Bodo Sperling. He was the former director of the German Sports Club in Rourkela, India. He lived in Aachen and taught at the Aachen Institute of Technology. The official with whom I spoke strongly suggested I talk with him about some of the interpersonal problems which were encountered between German and Indian personnel at the Rourkela Steel Works in Orissa province. His insights helped me to clarify which questions were paramount to have answered in the course of my interviews with officials from both countries dealing with the cultural differences which each side brought to the development table. His book *Die Rourkela Deutschen* (The Rourkela Germans) gave a unique insight into the influence of religious, cultural, and social distinctions between personnel coming from such differing cultural contexts.

The three most important ministries in Germany pertinent to my research were Foreign Affairs, Economic Cooperation, and Development and Economic Affairs. My hypothesis was that Germany was giving an enormous amount of aid for political purposes. The German government was giving vast sums for India's economic development with a particular objective. The West German chancellor, Konrad Adenauer, had visited the Soviet Union in early September 1955 to discuss the issue of German reunification. Nikita Khrushchev was not at all interested in discussing this issue. He flatly refused to discuss reunification. He did agree to release the last five thousand German prisoners of war still held by the Soviet Union which Adenauer had also requested. To reunification, Khrushchev is said to have replied, "I'll never discuss this issue. I'm going to keep the fifteen million East Germans in the German Democratic Republic on my side! That way, I'll be certain they'll never oppose me!"

With Adenauer's failure to secure even a discussion of possible German reunification, he looked to others to try to convey his interest in this crucial foreign policy goal. Jawaharal Nehru was greatly respected the world over. Adenauer knew he was slated to pay the Soviet leader a visit that next year. He thought Mr. Nehru might be able to talk to Mr. Khrushchev about this issue. Nehru was a world-renowned and respected leader in the nonaligned movement among the newly independent third world countries.

"If anyone should be able to encourage discussion of German reunification with the Soviet government, Nehru should be that person!" I was told by the director for foreign policy issues in the Ministry of Foreign Affairs of the West German government.

In the meantime, the Indian government was interested in expanding its industrial and technological infrastructure. The Soviet government was funding the construction of a new iron and steel plant in Bihar, India. The Indian Ministry of Industry had conducted a nationwide survey of its natural resources and found enormous quantities of iron ore and coal in the state of Orissa, west of Calcutta. Since the Soviets were building this steel plant in Bihar, the Indian government approached the West German government about doing the same in Orissa. The German Ministry of Economic Development reviewed the Indian survey and thought there were plenty of natural resources, including water from the river, to make such a project feasible. Through the efforts of personnel in the Ministry of Economic Cooperation and Development, the Ministry of Economics, and the Ministry of Foreign Affairs, a consortium of twenty-nine German corporations was formed to undertake the construction of a first-class steel-making plant second to none in the world at Rourkela. The West German government promised to underwrite the financial outlays of these corporations if they would send their personnel, equipment, and provide financial support for the construction of this gigantic project literally in the wilderness of Orissa. The only connection to the rest of India was the rail line built by the British which ran through it to Calcutta. The West German government spared no effort in reviewing other projects which the Nehru government wished to undertake. Three other projects were highlighted by the Indian government. The Okhla Production-cum-Training Center in Delhi was the second project. It was to train Indian workers in the use of basic industrial tools and equipment in an industrial environment. The third project was the creation of an institute of technology in Madras in order to train Indian students to become proficient in an industrial society by training engineers, theoreticians and researchers, industrial development specialists, and managers of the new businesses and industries which would develop as India became more and more industrialized. The fourth project that the Indian government wanted the German government to undertake was the creation of an agricultural experimental station in Himachal Pradesh. An experimental agricultural station had been successfully established by the University of Illinois, for example, in Allahabad. The Indian government wanted to start other stations around the country and the project in Himachal Pradesh was suggested to the Germans. The rolling countryside and mountains seemed somewhat similar to the landscape of Bavaria. After reviewing the site, this project was also approved by the West German Ministry of Economic Cooperation and Development.

With the involvement of German corporation personnel, financial resources plus guarantees, upwards of more than three hundred million deutsche mark were allocated to undertake these projects, recruit staff personnel, and begin to build these various facilities around India. Prime Minister Nehru came to Bonn to thank, personally, Chancellor Adenauer for undertaking and underwriting these four projects.

"These projects will help us enormously to transform my country from an agricultural country to an advanced industrial society."

It was during this meeting that Chancellor Adenauer asked Jawaharal Nehru if he would broach the subject of German reunification when he met with Nikita Khrushchev later that year. Nehru promised he would speak to Premier Khrushchev about this issue when he paid him a visit in July 1956. With the outright rejection of any interest in this issue when reported by Nehru to Adenauer after the visit, German economic experts wanted to reduce the German commitment to these projects. They were overruled by the chancellor. The funding, staffing, supplying, and heavy investment continued unbated for the next decade. The Rourkela Steel Works alone was to cost more than 660 million German marks before it was able to produce a profit for the Indian government.

After five months of interviewing German government officials, reading classified documents and written reports from on site German personnel, my research in Germany was complete. It was now a matter of going to India to see the outcomes of these efforts.

Julie, Martin, and I said good-bye to the Tante Luise, Marianne and Michael, Liz, Hans, and Hans Jeorg, and Tante Lina before flying to Munich where we were to meet my cousin HermannLuipold, his wife Kuni, and their son Thomas for lunch. Before we left Vaihingen/Enz, however, Hans had agreed to take us to the Stuttgart Airport for our continuation flight eastward. We had sold our car to the same dealer from whom I had purchased it that previous September. We had a lot of baggage for the three of us because it had to last for the whole year. The station wagon Hans had borrowed from his boss was full. Hans and Liz's son, Hans Jeorg, wanted to go along to the airport.

"Hans Joerg, du kannst nit mit fahren. Das Auto ist voll. Es gibt nur platz fuer mich, deine Mutter, Unkle Donald, Tante Julie und Martin." (Hans Joerg, you can't go come along. The car is full. There's only enough room for me, your mother, Uncle Donald, Aunt Julie, and Martin.)

Hans Joerg said plaintively, "Die Luija kann dobleiba!" (Julie can stay here!)

Needless to say, this broke the tension of departure as his father and mother explained to Hans Joerg, "Die Julia muss doch mit Martin und Donald mitgehen. Sie kann nicht hier bleiben. Martin will doch das seine Mutter mit kommt nach Indien. Du musst hier bleiben mit deine Oma." (Julia has to go with Martin and Donald. She can't stay here. Martin wants his mother to go with him to India. You have to stay here with your grandmother.)

We said good-bye to Hans and Liz at the airport and went into the terminal with our baggage for our flight to Munich. It was a relatively short flight. We had a two-hour layover before our flight continued. The Luipolds met us at the gate, and we went into one of the airport restaurants for lunch. I returned the overcoat which I had borrowed from Hermann for the winter. When we left the States in September and were going on to India, we didn't think it was necessary to take one along. As the weather got colder in November, however, Hermann offered his overcoat. Since we were approximately the same build, I gratefully accepted. It had really gotten cold in Germany. It was an enjoyable time to reminisce and recall our previous visits.

Our next stop was Beirut, Lebanon. We rented a car and drove into the Bekaa Valley to visit the ruins of Baalbek as well as some of the cities along the Lebanese coast. We spent the night in the international hotel right on the beachfront. Julie and I were awakened in the middle of the night to Martin's sobs, "Bye-bye, car car! Bye-bye, car car!"

Evidently, selling our blue VW was too much for Martin! He had grown very fond of it! We succeeded in calming him down by promising him a ride in another VW. Hence our car trip in Lebanon before continuing our air trip to India. We also made a brief stop in Tehran before flying into the Delhi International Airport.

We stayed at a large international hotel on Janpath Road for the first few days while I looked for more permanent housing. We were on the fourth floor of this hotel. The Indian staff cleaned the rooms daily and the carpets about once a week. As Martin and I were taking a walk around the hotel yard one morning, a rolled-up carpet came flying down from the fourth-floor balcony. It landed right next to us. If we had moved one foot closer to the hotel, we would have been hit by the flying carpet! I looked up at the workers on the fourth floor and they were laughing as they saw us. I shook my fist and called them all kinds of names! It could have resulted in a real tragedy had the carpet hit us . . . It did stimulate me to find other housing as soon as possible.

I walked around the neighborhood and found a very pleasant estate which had been converted into an apartment rental compound. There were individual cottages with two bedrooms, a living room, bathroom, and porch for each one. The meals were provided by the compound kitchen staff. I talked with the owner of the compound and found out he was an ex-Portuguese citizen who had grown up in Goa. This colony of the Portuguese had been taken over by the Indian government in 1961 and his citizenship then changed to Indian from Portuguese.

Mr. Fonseca was very cordial and showed me what one of his apartments looked like. I was suitably impressed and told him I would rent it on a monthly basis.

"I'm doing my research on German economic assistance to India," I told him. "I'll be traveling around India, but my wife and son will be here most of the time."

"That's fine with me. You'll find this place is a very safe environment for your family. They shouldn't have any problems. We have a real international clientele living here, and we have a guard at the gate day and night. Your wife won't have to cook. She can take her meals in our dining room three times a day, if she wishes. Most of the foreigners seem to eat one meal out each day. But she can have all of her meals here with your son, if she likes. I do require that you pay me each month that you stay at the beginning of the month."

"That's fine with me."

I gave him Rp1,000 (approximately $125) for the month. It proved to be an enjoyable stay for Julie and Martin. There were other foreign children from the United States (the Levys) from the University of Chicago. He was also doing his research for his doctorate. There was also a Dutch boy and girl near Martin's age who were the children of the second secretary of the Dutch embassy. Other foreigners came through and stayed a month or two before moving on. Martin enjoyed his stay in the compound. There was a large sandbox similar to the one he had played in with Hans Joerg in Germany. There was one drawback to this environment which we only discovered after being there for a few days. Each evening the lawns were flooded with the sewage water from the compound in order to keep the lawns green and growing. Unfortunately, it did cause Martin to have dysentery a few times. Fortunately, medical care was available, and he did not seem to suffer any long-term ill effects from it. He was exposed to the sewage water because he liked to walk with the Indian groundskeeper who cut the lawn each week. He helped to push the lawn mower, and the Indian groundskeeper seemed to enjoy having him help.

Each month an Indian barber came around and cut the children's hair. He placed a chair on the porch in front of the cottages and a large dictionary on top of it so that the child was high enough to cut his hair. Martin seemed to enjoy this experience especially after watching the other boys getting their hair cut. There was only one time when I felt uneasy about our stay at I Man Singh Road. Julie was taking a bath and I said, "Julie, I'm going to take Martin over to the dining room for breakfast. We'll see you when you get there."

"Okay. I want to wash my hair anyway and it'll take a little time for it to dry."

I took Martin by the hand and we walked over to the dining room. The Indian staff was always dressed in formal serving attire with the folded and starched headdress from the colonial times. The headwaiter was a very distinguished and formal elderly gentleman who spoke with a flawless British accent. He had served several diplomatic families prior to Indian independence. He kept the waiters attuned to the needs and desires of the guest as he walked around the dining room. If someone had a problem, he was there in an instant to find out what was required. He then conveyed the message in Hindi to the staff member even though most of the staff knew some English. The headwaiter greeted us as we came in and helped place Martin in a high chair. He asked what we wanted for breakfast.

"I think we'll try some porridge [oatmeal] this morning. We usually have eggs and toast, but I want to try something else."

"Certainly, Mr. Donald!"

He instructed one of his Indian waiters to bring us a pot of porridge and set it on the table. I opened the lid and began stirring the oatmeal. As the spoon came to the bottom of the pot, I noticed the dark brown residue of rat droppings. I didn't want to upset Martin since he liked oatmeal. I lifted the spoon quickly to the top of the pot and spooned out a bowl of oatmeal for him and then one for myself. I was to learn later, on another visit to India, rats are prolific in kitchens. That's where the food is. That's also where they are most likely to leave their feces everywhere. If the staff is not careful and fails to wash out the containers that are open in the kitchen, they are likely to pour their steaming hot porridge directly into the dining room containers! Hence, the feces get mixed in with the food! When I told Julie this after breakfast, we did not eat oatmeal again in India!

My visits to the Indian Lok Sabha (the equivalent of the House of Representatives) library and to the various government ministries proved very helpful in gathering data for my dissertation. By and large, the Indian staff was as polite as the Germans, except they were somewhat more reserved in answering my questions regarding German economic assistance. I soon learned I was to ask about "cooperative programs." As I asked my questions, similar to those I had asked German aid personnel, I was told, "The German personnel are assisting us in carrying out programs which we wish them to undertake. They do not tell us what we should or should not do! They work with us on these cooperative programs. We're glad to have them here, but we choose what we want. It's not a matter of them telling us what we need!"

My interviews were usually shorter with the Indian personnel than with the Germans. It probably was because I spoke German but did not speak Hindi. I was also impressed with the ease with which birds flew in and out of the various government ministries. The seat of the Indian government is located in the massive sandstone buildings built by the British in 1911. The offices were open for the wind to blow through. The access to the outside kept the offices as cool as possible in the summer. It reminded me of Thailand. The only difference was the Thais did not allow birds to nest in their offices! Several of the officials whom I interviewed seemed oblivious of the fact that birds were nesting over their windows or the doors of their offices. Each Indian official had one or two men whom I would call "runners" at their disposal. These men not only made the tea which each official served his guests, but who would also keep the office clean and the bird droppings cleared out each day. Whatever the official wanted, these workers would provide.

The official government reports, which I read in the Lok Sabha library, were helpful in giving the Indian perspective on the projects largely funded by the German government. There was no mention of the amount of aid given. Rather, that the two governments were jointly cooperating in undertaking the construction of the Okhla Production-cum-Training Center, the Indian Institute of Technology in Madras, the Rourkela steel plant, and the Himachal Pradesh Agricultural Experimental Station. When I asked for the amounts being spent for each of these projects, I was given the amount in Indian rupees not German marks. When I asked how much the German contribution was, I was told, "They have sent personnel and equipment, but we are paying for whatever they have contributed. It's their know-how that we want. We pay for what is being done. You have to understand the Germans are not doing this for altruistic reasons. They know that whatever is being done will mean that they will have a vested interest in the outcomes in terms of trade and further business being promoted with these contacts."

The difference in perception of what each government was doing was remarkable. The German personnel viewed their efforts and expenditures as aiding in the development of an underdeveloped country. The Indian personnel, on the other hand, were more realistic and recognized the long-term benefit to both countries with these cooperative projects.

As the months passed and the temperatures in Delhi rose, we thought of moving to the mountains for the summer. I had come across Bill Jones in my journeys into the mountains. He was the principal of the Woodstock School in Mussoorie to which the missionaries sent their children from not only India but from all over Southeast Asia. The classes were from first grade through senior high and staffed by Indian and foreign teachers.

"Bill, are there any hill stations available where we might be able to rent a room for a few months?"

"Sure. Here's the address of Dr. and Mrs. Rip Moore from the University of Wisconsin. They run a guesthouse in Landauer, which is just above us on the ridge behind Woodstock. Their apartment house is called 'Cozy Nook.' I'm sure they still have some apartments available."

I went to see the Moores. Fran was the hostess. Her husband was a Hindi and Indian specialist at the University of Wisconsin. He was on sabbatical leave for the year.

"We have four apartments in Cozy Nook," Fran said. "You can rent one of the apartments on the second floor which has a staircase down the outside, if you like. I'm sure we'll have all of them rented before the summer is over."

I noticed she also had a daughter probably slightly older than Martin.

"What's your name?" I asked the little girl.

"This is our daughter, Mona. She's three years old," Fran offered.

"We have a little boy named Martin. He's just a little younger than she is."

"That's nice. She'll have a playmate right here in Cozy Nook," Fran offered.

The apartment consisted of a large bedroom with a double and a single bed, plus a bathroom. There was only a hot plate for cooking. The meals could be provided by the staff, if we so desired. I thought it would be best to let Julie make this decision.

"Can I rent the apartment on a month-to-month basis? I really don't know how long we'll be in India. I've got to visit the four projects for my case studies yet in the different parts of India. I'm not sure how long it's going to take," I explained to Fran.

"That's fine. Your wife and son will have plenty of company while you're traveling. I have all of my guests paying their rent at the beginning of each month."

"That's what we've been doing in Delhi ever since we got here."

Since I had completed my interviews with Indian government officials and researched all of the documents available in New Delhi, it was now time to make on-site visitations. We took the overnight train from Old Delhi to Dehra Dun in an air-conditioned compartment. The temperatures were already in the nineties. In Dehra Dun we took a taxi up the mountainside going from switchback to switchback all the way to the top. We had the driver stop a couple of times in order to get out and avoid getting carsick from the constant turning back and forth. Once we arrived in Mussoorie, we still had more than two miles to go to reach Cozy Nook. We hired a pedicab for the rest of the way on the dirt trail. The driver had to stop occasionally to push his tricycle up the slope of the trail. With all of our baggage, plus Julie and Martin, he had a heavy load. I walked behind and helped push as the situation required. Upon our arrival, Fran gave us a drink of cold lemonade and Coke with ice cubes she had frozen herself in their refrigerator. Ice cubes were not usually safe to use. The water was not purified. Fran made sure all of her guests had plenty of fresh boiled water to drink while we were her tenants. Julie had the use of two hot plates in our apartment if she wanted to cook herself. Without a refrigerator, however, she couldn't keep any leftovers. Hence, most of the time we ate in Fran's dining room.

With Julie and Martin well cared for in Cozy Nook, I began my traveling around India to visit the four sites of my case studies. We had only been in the mountains a short time when Julie discovered two of her Mennonite friends from Kansas were just down the mountainside near the Woodstock School. They had an apartment during the three-month summer vacation during which time they spent visiting their son and daughter who were students at the school. Wendell and Norma Weins were stationed in Allahabad where he served as a doctor in the local hospital. Norma was a teacher in an Indian school. The Weins became my friends as well as Julie's. We've kept in touch with them ever since our chance acquaintance on the mountainside near the Woodstock School.

While I traveled around India visiting the various projects, Julie decided it would be a good idea to start a nursery school for the young children in the Landauer community. The Woodstock School was only for children from first grade through senior high. There were no classes for preschool or kindergarten children. She organized a group of mothers, both foreign and Indian, who had preschool children. They arranged to use the local church basement and yard for their classes. The mothers divided up the responsibilities themselves of who was to do what during the course of each day's activities. They took turns reading stories, supervising playtime, doing physical exercises, and suppling snacks and drinks for the children. Martin took to this new routine with alacrity. Since our apartment was the farthest from the school, Julie talked with Fran about what she should do to get Martin to nursery school at eight o'clock each morning.

"I could have our Chakidar [the Cozy Nook guard and caretaker] take Martin on his shoulders to school each morning, Julie. He could then pick him up after school at noon. If you could give him a tip each day for his help, I'm sure he wouldn't mind."

"Excellent. I'll be glad to pay him each day. How much do you think I should give him?"

"Two rupees would be enough. We're paying him very well as it is."

From what Julie told me later, Martin enjoyed interacting with the other children very much. On one occasion, the teacher for playtime suggested they form a train using their chairs to set them in a row and pretend they were riding in it. One little boy pushed his chair in front of a little girl and an argument broke out between the two of them. Since both children had pigtails, Martin pointed at the one and said, "She started it! She pushed right in front of Mona!"

What Martin didn't know was that the little girl was actually a Sikh boy whose hair is never cut. He didn't know it was a boy with whom Mona was arguing about breaking into the line ahead of her! The staff got a big kick out of the mix-up. Even the little boy's mother was not offended that her boy had been called a girl.

"She told me," Julie continued, "without a turban it is hard to tell the difference. He's too young yet to wear one. When he goes to regular school, he'll have his own turban."

The Indian farmers have a practice of burning off their fields after the crops have been harvested. While I was at the Himachal Pradesh Agricultural Station, the local farmers on the mountain across from Cozy Nook set their fields on fire. The fire raced over the mountains near Mussoorie and Landauer. The entire mountainsides were set ablaze, and the smoke drifted up to Cozy Nook. Units of the Indian army were called in to fight the fire. With only shovels, axes, and baton sticks, the fire quickly got out of hand. It raced across the neighboring mountain and into the valley just below where Cozy Nook was located. Rip Moore went with a group of missionaries to reconnoiter. As they approached the fire wall, Rip walked out on a fallen tree which hung over the fire below. Tragically, the tree broke and Rip fell into the raging fire. He was consumed almost immediately. There was nothing any of his colleagues could do. They couldn't even retrieve his body from what Julie told me later. She filled me in on the details upon my return.

"The entire community was shaken by Rip's death," Julie said. "Fran's decided she's going to continue to run the guesthouse until the end of the summer season. She'll go back to Wisconsin in September. There was a memorial service held for Rip at the local Landauer church. It was filled to overflowing," Julie continued. "We didn't have to evacuate. The fire continued up the other side of the valley where the Indian army finally succeeded in putting it out."

Rip Moore was a brilliant young linguist. The profession lost a good man when he took his life in his hands to survey the fire!

The visit to the agricultural station was another of the interesting case studies for my research. The Germans were attempting to improve the local dairy cattle by shipping some of their best types of German cows. They brought in twenty of the best Simenthaler cows and a bull. They hoped that the bull would be useful for interbreeding with the local Indian cows to improve the quality of the Indian cattle. Simenthaler cows are very heavy animals. For those who do not know the breed, they would think the cows are actually a variety of beef cattle. They are very heavy and give the same heavy appearance of well-fed American Herefords. Imagine the shock among the Indian personnel when these cattle arrived!

"You can send them right back to Germany! We don't eat beef in India! We don't want to breed beef cattle! Our religion forbids eating cows! We can't have this bull interbreeding with our cows!" The German project leader told me. "We had to show them the volume of milk these cows produced, which was more than twice the amount their cattle gave at each milking. I told my Indian counterpart this cow is the best for this mountainous region. They came from Bavaria, which has a very similar mountain terrain as you do here. You don't have to eat them!" I said. "If you interbreed them with your local cows, the next generation of cows will give you twice the amount of milk which yours do now." "Begrudgingly", the German director went on, "The Indian personnel accepted what they knew they couldn't change: our government had paid for the cows and shipped them here. We weren't about to send them back again!"

What the story illustrated was but another example of how cultural differences can influence the perception and behavior of peoples from differing social, religious, and cultural environments. The introduction of new seeds, fertilizers, and agricultural machinery were also helpful in overcoming the initial reluctance to continue the project.

I rode back to Delhi with the German assistant project director in his Unimok (the German equivalent of a jeep). He was looking forward to returning to

Germany within the next two months. He had been in India for more than two years and sorely missed his family.

"I'll be glad to get back home again. We've had nothing but a series of problems getting the local farmers to allow our bull to be used to breed their cows. Their cows are so thin and emaciated compared with ours. It was hard for them to bear the weight of our bull! We couldn't get them to fence in their cattle. They either let them roam where they wanted, or had them tied to a post behind their dwellings. The concept of fencing can only be employed on government-owned land."

He went on to say, "It's going to be a long time before Indian agriculture achieves the success required to feed its population on a diet comparable to what we have in the West. There's only one area in India that I know of that produces food on a modern agricultural basis. That's the Punjab. That's where the farms are larger, tractors and machinery are used to plant and harvest crops, and the use of fertilizers is pretty much standard. But from what I've seen in much of the rest of India, that's an exception."

From Delhi, I flew to Madras to visit the Indian Institute of Technology. After coming from the northern mountains, the temperatures of Tamil Nadu were overwhelming. From my hotel, I called the institute and asked if I might have an interview with the Indian director, Mr. J. Gupta. He agreed. I took a pedicab to his office and was taken into a conference room where I asked him the same questions I had been asking all of the Indian and German project personnel. He was very proud of what had been accomplished thus far. Most of the fields of technology were staffed.

"We only need additional staff in our Aeronautical Department. I'm hopeful a German professor from Wiesbaden will be coming soon to fill this void in our curriculum."

His answers were short. I got the distinct impression he was eager to have my interview end as soon as possible. He gave me the institute's bulletin.

"I don't have any current figures about the costs in setting up the program. You'll have to get these figures from the German government. They are underwriting all of the costs of creating this institute."

I looked up the German counselor official in Madras. He gave me the names of the German staff members then current on the staff. I visited them in their offices, and one Austrian professor, a specialist in thermodynamics, invited me to dinner with his family. We had an interesting evening comparing notes on what was being achieved in India. When I told him of the various programs which the German government had set up, he was completely unaware of the scope of any of these other projects.

"I'm only familiar with what's going on here at the institute. The students are exceptionally intelligent. There's never a problem with their intellectual capability. It's just after they graduate, they seem incapable of solving common engineering problems. If an assembly line breaks down, there is a reluctance to get dirty by going into the machinery itself to ascertain what's not functioning. Most of the students here are from the upper Hindu castes, and they still think of themselves in these terms. They should be getting into the machinery to find out what caused the problem in the first place. But they don't. They usually tell a worker (lower caste) what to look for instead of examining the problem themselves. They need to learn how to use even the most basic tools of an industrial society. Come over to the institute, tomorrow, Herr Megnin. I'd like to show you around."

My host showed me around the institute that next day.

"The equipment which we have is first-rate. The German government has spared nothing in supplying us with the best there is. Even the computers are the latest models" (these units were similar to the huge ones we had in graduate school).

"The syllabus is what you would find in any technological institute in the West. Except for their reluctance [he used this phrase repeatedly], Herr Megnin, to get their hands dirty, our graduates can compete with any engineers in any industrialized society!"

My next stop was the Rourkela Iron and Steel Works in Orissa province. This is a huge industrial complex literally built in one of the poorest provinces in India. The German Ministry of Economic Cooperation and Development personnel thought they had studied the details of the planning and research manual which the government of India had produced prior to undertaking the project. There was an ample supply of coal and iron ore in the vicinity. The railroad passed through four times daily. It was on the direct route from Delhi to Calcutta. The shipment of supplies and personnel would pose no problems. There was an ample water supply in the local river for the industrial and human needs of the new complex. The only real shortage, according to the Indian report, was a lack of local personnel who had the experience, training, and know-how to work in an industrial setting. The Indian Ministry of Industrial Development thought this would pose no problem. Calcutta was not too far away. Once the project got started, the report cited, Indian workers would flock to this new enterprise.

Much to the dismay of the German personnel assigned to the project, it was only after the commitment of money, equipment, and German engineers that the Ministry of Economic Cooperation and Development discovered the manual was formulated during the rainy season when the river was overflowing! During the summer's dry season, the river virtually dried up except for a little stream flowing amongst the rocks at the river bottom! The Germans had to drill wells to tap an adequate water supply for such a huge plant and to supply the human needs required to staff and operate this industrial complex. Workers did not flow from Calcutta; they had to be recruited from all over India and then trained to use modern tools and equipment. Housing also had to be built for the workers.

A special depot had to be constructed to receive the sophisticated equipment being sent to India from Germany.

By the time I arrived, the plant had been built; housing for the workers, for the German engineers and German consortium personnel, and a social club with all of the amenities of a country club (swimming pool, tennis courts, guest apartments, and dining facilities) were completed. In contrast to my other case studies, the Indian director refused to grant me an interview. He dismissed my request with the comment "Rourkela is not a subject for a case study. This is a highly important factory for the defense of India. It is, therefore, off-limits to nontechincal personnel."

As a result of this denial, I could only interview German personnel on all levels of expertise and management. If it were not for a team of German workers from Thyssen-Mannesmann, I would not have gained entrance to the plant itself. I got acquainted with two of the German workers who were living in the same guesthouse during my stay. When I explained what I was doing and how my interview request had been rejected, one of them said, "Why don't you join us tomorrow morning when we go to work? You can become one of our workmen for the day."

I took his advice and joined them after breakfast for the ride into the plant. As the driver drove up to the gate, the Indian army guard looked into the van and asked, "Who is he?" as he looked at me. "He doesn't have an official badge."

Franz explained, "He's a conveyor specialist. He has just arrived."

This explanation seemed to satisfy the guard. He counted the number of us in the van and let us pass through the gate.

Franz, a technical specialist from Duisburg, directed the driver to drive around the plant and pointed out the various components. He explained the role of each in the production of steel. As we were driving around, huge billows of smoke seemed to be pouring out of the smoke stacks.

"Why is all of that smoke coming out of the chimneys, Franz?" I asked.

"That's not smoke. Every hour more than five hundred tons of ash is emitted from the chimneys, Herr Megnin. The dust and dirt is everywhere! The wind takes a lot of it away, but a lot stays here in the yard, which has to be removed when it gets too thick."

I wouldn't have believed it if I hadn't seen it! What it did to the surrounding countryside, I caught only a glimpse. Depending on the wind, most of the ash and dust blew away from the inhabited quarters of the workers and staff personnel working at Rourkela. The plant was using the latest steelmaking system known as the "Linz-Donau" system. It originated in Austria (Linz) and was the best system devised for making high-quality steel. Unfortunately, the plant had numerous breakdowns after it was turned over to the Indian personnel. During my time in Bonn, Herr Solveen, the chairman of the group of German specialists who had investigated why the plant had broken down, gave me his official report.

"Herr Megnin, read over the report very carefully. The plant broke down in only nine months after the Indian government assumed full control. The Indian government blamed us for "shoddy equipment and workmanship." Our investigation, however, revealed the reasons for the breakdown were due to the failure to carry out routine maintenance and servicing of highly technical equipment. The breakdowns would not have occurred if maintenance had been routinely undertaken on a regular and systematic basis. To expect the machinery to continue producing without maintenance was the major reason for the shutdown of the plant!"

The German companies had to replace key parts of the highly sophisticated equipment at an enormous cost in time and product because of nonmaintence of the sensitive parts of the plant's machinery. The question of who was to pay for this additional cost was bandied back and forth between the Indian Ministry of Industrial Development and the German Ministry for Economic Cooperation and Development for several months. The German government, reluctantly, had to reimburse the German firms for their replacement of key elements to get the plant producing again. The stipulation to which the German and Indian governments agreed was German maintenance would be a cooperative arrangement until the Indian staff had been sufficiently trained to take over the complete operation of the plant. The German aid personnel felt they had to replace the broken equipment. If they did not, it would blemish their industrial reputation if they did not repair what had broken down even though it was not their fault.

I returned to Delhi to visit my last case study project. The Okhla Production-cum-Training Center was located just outside of the city. Its purpose was to train Indian workers in the use of basic industrial tools and equipment. The training also included the instructors, who would give their student workers the know-how to become employed by the expanding Indian industrial system. The instructors had to learn how to produce simple tools such as hammers, wrenches, screwdrivers, drill punches, files, lathes, drills, and hundreds of other basic tools needed in any industrial system. Walking through the center, it was interesting to observe how the students were learning simple tasks such as how to file chisels and scrapers to give them a sharp edge. Once the basic skills were learned, the students were allowed to move to the next level: learning how to produce the items they were using. The basis of an industrial system was being taught by German technical personnel who weren't interested in cultural excuses.

As one of the German instructors told me, "Our purpose is to train competent workers to develop the necessary skills to avoid similar situations such as what occurred at Rourkela from ever happening again. The students have to learn that an industrial system requires a modicum of dirt as a natural part of their training. If they don't accept such a requirement, they are dismissed from the program!"

With my studies completed, I returned to Cozy Nook and spent the rest of June enjoying the vagaries of hill-station living, as the British called it. We took hikes along the trails, visited our friends, did some shopping for souvenirs, and gradually made our plans for the return to the United States. We were impressed with the fact that all of the goods sold in Landauer and Mussoorie had to be portaged up the mountainside on the backs of Sherpa carriers. They carried upwards of six hundred pounds on their backs with a carrying cloth strung over their foreheads and around the articles they were expected to carry. The elevation was over 7,200 feet. They carried everything from kitchen tables to beds, sofas, sinks, nails, tools, whatever would be needed on the mountaintops. After bringing up the loads, the Sherpas could be seen stretched out along the roadside sleeping to regain their strength. There were no cars or trucks on these mountaintops. There were no streets, simply trails they had to follow. Usually the trails coincided with the electric lines that were strung from the valleys to the mountaintops. This area was an extension of the jungle terrain on the lower levels inhabited by wild animals. We often heard tigers growling on the outside of our guesthouse at night as they also walked along the same paths used by people. On occasion, a Sherpa was killed by a wild animal which the local people assumed was from either a tiger or a mountain lion.

Julie, Martin, and I said our good-byes to our friends in the mountains and returned by train to Delhi to prepare for our trip home. After we flew into Calcutta, it reminded me that little had changed since I was there ten years earlier. The streets were still crowded with people on foot, asleep on the roadways, trishaws still being pedaled through the crowds, and two wheeled carts still pushed or pulled by men bearing huge loads of everything imaginable. There were thousands of refugees from East Pakistan (now Bangladesh) literally living on the streets. Huge bulls lay next to banks on the busy roadways just as unconcerned as they were in 1956. Of all of the cities I've visited in over seventy countries, I've never experienced another city like Calcutta. There were still stately buildings from the British era, a renowned library and museum, an exclusive country club with its own racetrack and restricted membership. The contrast between the old era and the new was still beyond imagination. The abject poverty was and still seemed to be as extensive then as it was forty years earlier. It was a sight we shall never forget.

Air India was the airline we took to Calcutta. The stewardesses were very gracious. We had bought Martin a plastic tricycle in Germany for Christmas. He rode around on it in the terminal as we waited for our flight to depart. I carried it on board, and the stewardesses allowed us to store it behind the first-class seats. Our stops in the international airports were a pleasant time for our almost three-year-old. We could always tell where Martin was. The plastic wheels made a distinct sound on the concrete or marble floors. He enjoyed riding around, and when something struck his fancy, he stopped and watched. Whenever we went from one country to the next, the stewardesses did the same with his tricycle. He seemed to know each time he got off the plane, he would be able to ride his bicycle around the terminal.

In Calcutta, we stayed at the Christian Women's School headed by Ms. Karuna Lee. Her name and address had been given to Julie by a couple of missionaries in Landauer.

"You really should stay there, Julie. All of the missionaries stop there on their way home. She's a great lady and an excellent hostess."

We spent an overnight at the college. Ms. Lee seemed genuinely glad to have a little boy in her school. After she showed us around, we returned to her office on the third floor. She gave her keys to Martin, who enjoyed shaking them. They made a very pleasant ringing noise. The window of her office was open. Martin walked over to it and looked out as he walked behind her desk. After he looked out for a short time, he suddenly threw Karuna Lee's keys out the window.

"You shouldn't have done that, Martin!" Julie scolded. "Now we'll have to go down and find them!"

It took Karuna, Julie, the janitor, the secretary, and me some time until we found the keys. They were among the trash cans behind the school. Fortunately, we found them. All of the keys to the school, the apartments, the gates, and the school van were on the keychain!

From Calcutta we flew the next day to Bangkok, Thailand. We spent two days there in order to visit Nopakhun Tongyai and Chulalongkorn University. She was the vice chairperson of the Modern Language Department when I taught there from 1954 to 1956. She also had stayed with us initially when her husband was first admitted to the Upstate Medical Center in Syracuse, New York, to be treated for a brain infection. As the Thai minister of agriculture, he had been in an automobile accident in Greece a few months earlier and the infection had never been completely removed. Hence, they came to Syracuse for his medical treatment. They were familiar with the Syracuse area since both she and her husband were graduates of Cornell University in 1936.

We stayed at the Oriental Hotel, which is situated next to the Chao Phraya River. It gave us a fascinating view of river traffic and floating markets along the canals bordering the river. We also watched a classical Thai dance performance in the hotel garden for a while until it became too much for Martin to sit any longer. It was the last time we saw Nopakhun. She told us that there were no longer any colleagues with whom I had taught in the midfifties.

Our next stop was Tokyo, Japan. We spent two days there visiting the highlights of the city. We toured a series of cottage industries on the outskirts. One was a doll maker who made dolls which could not be knocked over. Martin tried and tried to knock it over, but each time it popped up again. He tried and tried, but each time it righted itself.

"These dolls can't be knocked over, Martin. We'll take one home with us so you can try it again when we get home," Julie said.

We stayed at the Imperial Hotel, one of the world's most famous. I had stayed there on my first visit to Japan in 1955. The wartime destruction of homes, businesses, and infrastructure which I still saw then had been completely rebuilt. The traffic was once again one of the biggest concerns of the city government.

While waiting for our flight to the Hawaii, Martin rode his tricycle around the marble floor of the Narita Airport. We could hear him at some distance away from us. He continually stopped to observe what people were doing. He was concerned about a little boy who was obviously lost. He couldn't find his mother.

Martin rode back to us and said, "The little boy is lost. He's running up and down the room looking for his mommy!"

"Keep an eye on him, Martin. Maybe he'll find his mother," Julie suggested.

Sure enough, Martin came back and told us, "He found his mommy. He was crying very hard."

What Martin didn't know was the fact that this is an important method used by Japanese parents to help their children to understand it is very important for them to learn to stay close to the family. The parents will seemingly allow their child to wander off and explore the world around him/her. When the child can't see his/her parents, the child becomes anxious and wanders around frantically looking for his/her parents. The parents know where the child is, but let the child struggle to find where the parents are. Once the child discovers his/her parents after crying and searching everywhere, the reunion is a joyous one for the child.

Our next stop was Hawaii. We took Japan Airlines from Tokyo and stayed in a hotel on Waikiki Beach, Honolulu. The weather was ideal for swimming. We spent most of our time playing in the sand with Martin. We were supposed to leave the next day on a United Airlines flight for San Francisco. An airline strike by United workers, however, prevented the airline from continuing their service. We had a two-day layover courtesy of the United Airlines. By the fourth day, United arranged with Japan Airlines to take American passengers to the mainland. When we arrived in San Francisco, Julie contacted her cousin, Mary Jane Baker. She and her husband, Gene, came and got us. We spent a day with them in their new home along the American River. Since they had not attended our wedding, it gave me an opportunity to become acquainted with them.

Our next stop was Chicago. We rented a car and drove to Goshen, Indiana, to visit Julie's folks. We spent a few days with them, visiting Tom and Flora, Dad King's relatives, and friends of Julie's still in Goshen. Dad King told us he had had a call from the president's office of Widmar College in Ames, Iowa, asking if he and the dean could stop by and interview his son-in-law. They had a teaching position open. Since Dad knew when we were going to be there, they agreed to stop by that next evening. It was an interesting interview. Widmar College is a Methodist college. Since I was a Methodist minister, they took it for granted I would say yes. I declined their offer. I remembered Dr. Bishop's admonition during my graduate studies: "Finish your doctorate before you become obligated to teach classes. Unless you do, you won't have time to write and teach at the same time. I've seen too many graduate students fall by the wayside, Don. Finish your dissertation before you accept even a part-time appointment."

Upon our return to Syracuse, Arthur Osteen asked me, "Don, there's position open to teach a course in American government at Colgate. Would you be interested? One of their faculty members is going on sabbatical leave. It pays very well."

Again, I declined. I was offered a position to teach full-time for one semester at Hamilton College with the possibility that it might lead to a full-time position. Dr. Bishop's admonition, however, stayed with me.

After almost a year overseas, we returned to Syracuse to take up our residence again at 559 Columbus Avenue. Frank Munger, the political science chairman, asked me if I would like to work for John Lindeman for the next year. John was an economist and adjunct faculty member who was the director of the South Asian Studies Center.

"The job takes roughly twenty hours a week. It would give you plenty of time to work on your dissertation, Don."

I accepted his offer. It also helped to cover my expenses in paying for the sixty credit hours which completing my dissertation entailed.

V.

Candidating, Buying Farm, and Writing My Dissertation

Upon our return to Syracuse and our subsequent visit to the farm, we found out Pop had incurable cancer of the esophagus. Inge had taken him to the Upstate Medical Center (where she was a lab technician) and the growth was confirmed through a biopsy. The doctor recommended radiation, but Pop refused. Hence, he could not swallow any solids. Mom made a variety of soups for him which seemed to sustain him for a while. He gradually lost weight. He had rented some of his fields to Warner Durfee as he had done with Warner's father. There was one field which was not included.

"Pop," I suggested, "why don't I plant winter wheat on the seven-acre lot and the one just behind it? I could do it in a short period of time."

"Ja, that would be a good idea, Donald. I'll buy the seed and fertilizer. You can rent a tractor and equipment from the Mabie Brothers to prepare the field and plant the crop."

It meant I had to take time off from my job as an assistant to John Lindeman and working on my dissertation. I thought once the seed is planted, there was nothing further that had to be done. Warner had promised Pop he would rent the entire farm that next year. He agreed to harvest the wheat if I planted it. It took me about three days to complete the project. While I was planting the wheat, Pop walked down to the first field to see how I was doing. He seemed satisfied with the progress I was making. Shortly after Pop walked back up to the house, Jack Benson drove his Chevrolet coupe down to the field next to ours.

"What are you going to plant?" he asked from his car after I stopped the tractor across the fence from him.

"I'm going to plant winter wheat, Jack."

"Is your father still living?"

"Yes. But he has cancer of the esophagus. He probably won't last much longer."

"What's that?"

"It's cancer of the throat."

"I always had a hard time understanding him. He was wounded in the First World War, wasn't he?"

"Yes. He had a field operation. The surgeon cut the nerves to his vocal cords as he was removing polyps from his throat. He was never able to speak louder than a whisper after that. Are you checking your fences, Jack?"

"Yes. I thought it would be a good idea this fall now that silo filling is over. I'm going to start plowing this field next spring, and I want to keep my heifers out of the crop."

"At least you won't have to worry about our bull coming over to your heifers anymore, Jack," I laughed.

He smiled knowingly, but said nothing. It had always been a problem. Our bulls just wanted to go over to his heifers in the worst way. If they broke down the fence to do so, they did! Since Jack's cows were Holsteins, he didn't want them impregnated by a Guernsey bull! The female offspring wouldn't produce as much milk as a Holstein!

Since I still had the tractor running, I excused myself. "Well, I've got to finish getting this field ready. Good-bye, Jack."

He rolled up his window and waved as he drove off. Our paths never crossed again.

After plowing, disking, and dragging the fields, I rented a grain drill from the Mabie Brothers and planted the wheat. It took all of four full days to complete the project. John Lindeman was very gracious about it. I missed a week of work in his office.

"Should I come in for a couple of weekends to make up the time I've spent planting wheat on our farm, Dr. Lindeman?"

"No. There'll be other times when you've got something to do. In my position, I'm glad to have a graduate student working here."

On one of the nicest days we had in October, Julie, Martin, and I took Pop and Mom on a trip through the Adirondack Mountains to see the beauty of the fall foliage. It was a brilliant, sunny day. Mom had prepared a bag lunch for us and soup for Pop. We drove to Old Forge, Raquette Lake, and Long Lake before heading south to Glens Falls on our way back to Chittenango. I sped along between Old Forge and Raquette Lake at about sixty miles an hour in a forty-five-miles-an-hour zone. A local policeman stopped me and issued a speeding ticket. I tried to explain what I was doing but to no avail. He looked inside the car and told Pop, "Better tell your son to slow down. These roads are not the straightest ones here in the Adirondacks!"

It wasn't a very small fine either. It cost seventy dollars, which Pop paid.

I started outlining my dissertation each afternoon after working in the morning at the South Asian Studies Center. The only place I had to work was in the cellar. When I went down there, Martin wanted to come along with me. After a few times of going out the back door and then back into the house to go down cellar, he heard the door open.

"I want to go down to Daddy," and down the back stairs he came.

After a week of trying to sneak back into the house without him hearing me, Julie suggested, "Why don't you find another place to work. As long as you're here in the house, Martin's going to try to go downstairs."

Rada Lynn, the director of the DeWitt Community Church's preschool program, lived on the corner of the street running at right angles with Columbus Avenue. She and her husband had a two-story garage behind their house with a kerosene stove to heat it. When Julie and I talked it over of where I might find a place, she said, "Why don't you talk to Rada, Don. Martin's in her program at church. They may be interested in renting it. It doesn't seem to be used for anything right now."

I went over to the Lynns to talk about renting the upstairs of their garage.

"Rada, would you be interested in renting the room upstairs in your garage so I can write my dissertation? I can't do it at home. Martin wants to be with me all of the time, and I can't really do any work when he's around."

"I'll talk with my husband, Don. Why don't you stop over Saturday morning and talk with him about it?"

I went over to the Lynns with my briefcase. With Martin standing in the window, I waved to him and walked around the corner. I doubled back and knocked at their door. Rada invited me in, and I had a chance to meet her husband for the first time. He was an engineer at General Electric who grew up in Great Britain. He had also spent some time in Switzerland where he met Rada and married her. She was a teacher in Zurich at the time. When they came over to the United States, she applied for the position in DeWitt and was hired by Bill and Alex.

"Rada tells me you're working on your dissertation?" Richard asked.

"Yes. That's why I need a quiet place to work. We've got a three-year-old who wants to be with me whenever I'm home," I laughed. "I don't get much writing done that way!"

"Yes. I can understand that. As you can see, Ian is our young son, and we know he wants to be with us wherever we are."

"Don wants to rent the room over our garage, Richard. Don't you think we could rent it to him? We're not using it right now."

"That's not a bad idea. What do you think it's worth on a weekly basis?"

"I don't know, Richard. That's for you to decide," I replied.

"How about a dollar a day and you buy the kerosene for the stove when it gets too cold up there."

"Okay. I'll take it."

And with that conversation, a deal was struck. Richard helped me carry a large folding table and two chairs upstairs from their cellar. There were electrical outlets which proved invaluable. On our next visit to the farm, Pop asked, "Donald, wouldn't it be faster for you to use a Dictaphone than a typewriter in writing your dissertation?"

"It probably would, Pop, but I don't have a Dictaphone."

"If you find one you like, I'll buy it for you."

I was intrigued by this possibility. That was the way Bennie typed up Alex's sermons each Sunday morning. The sermon was taped, and Bennie listened to it that next week and wrote it up. I thought Pop's idea was excellent. Now all I'd need is someone who could type up what I would dictate from the Dictaphone discs. I looked at several Dictaphones, and after talking with Bill Cummins, I went to an office supply store and bought the one he recommended. My next move was to go to the German Department at the university and ask if they could recommend someone who was fluent in German who might be willing to type my dissertation from my Dictaphone cassettes. Fortunately for me, the chairman of the German Department told me about one of his students who was looking for work. She was a master's degree candidate who was recently divorced and needed employment. He told me where she lived. It was only three blocks from our Columbus Avenue address. I stopped in to talk with her. She agreed to type my pages as I dictated them for fifteen cents a page. It meant I had to dictate several cassettes and then let her use my Dictaphone to type the material on the nine-by-eleven-inch paper required by the graduate school. The dissertation had to be in written form. It could not be a series of Dictaphone cassettes. It had to be in written form so that not only my the dissertation committee could read it, but anyone else who might want to do so. I dictated a chapter at a time on the cassettes and then took the Dictaphone over to her to type the written copy on her typewriter. She did an excellent job in preparing the dissertation for Marion Borst, Dean Steven Bailey's secretary. Marion had agreed to type the dissertation in its final form. Each morning I left with my briefcase and waved to Martin as he stood at the window. I walked around the corner as if to go through Thornden Park on my way to the university. I then doubled back to the Lynns' garage to work during the day. When I returned at noon for lunch, Martin was glad to see me again. I waited until he lay down for his afternoon nap before heading back to the garage.

While my dissertation was being typed, I took advantage of the time to candidate at various colleges and universities during March and April of 1967. The first campus visit was to Ohio Northern University in Lima, Ohio. The College of Liberal Arts was looking for someone to teach in the fields of comparative government and international relations, two of my favorite subject areas. I was met at the airport by the chairman of the Department of Social Sciences, who drove me to the campus. His field was history. He told me the vice president for academic affairs was the former chairman of the Music Department and knew little about the social sciences.

"But he's a good man to work with. You should get along well with him."

"Who's been teaching comparative and international relations?"

"We really don't have anyone at present. I teach a course in American government and try to fill in as much as possible in the international fields. Probably American foreign policy is the closest I come to these fields."

In other words, I thought to myself, I'll have to develop these subfields of political science myself. The more I talked with him and then the vice president, it looked as though they really wanted someone who would also teach political theory. The chairman asked me, "In what subfields of political science did you take your comps?"

"International relations, comparative government, political theory, and American politics. I'd like to teach comparative and international politics mainly. I could teach each of the other subfields, but they would not be my preference."

"Well, we'd expect you to teach a course in American government each semester. Then maybe alternate teaching courses in comparative and international relations. There are three of us teaching courses in political science. You have to be rather versatile to teach in this college."

The more we discussed what I might teach, the more I discovered they were really interested in law. The law school had an abundance of students, the chairman told me.

"Have you ever taught a course in international law?"

"No, I haven't. I've only had one course in this field, and that was a seminar with a mixture of students from political science and the law school. I don't think I'm really qualified to teach a course in international law."

"I'm not saying we would expect you to teach such a course, but don't be surprised if the vice president asks you if you could teach it. He's been looking for a specialist in international law for the past semester and still hasn't found one."

I very much appreciated the chairman's openness and honesty. I might have been tempted to accept their offer as an assistant professor had it not been for the vice president's comment after my interview.

"If you accept our offer, Mr. Megnin, we'll pay the entire amount of your costs for coming here. If you don't, we can only pay for half of your expenses."

Needless to say, this comment was the finishing touch which helped me to turn down his offer after I returned to Syracuse. Both Julie and I could not believe he would have even suggested such a condition for the reimbursement of my expenses!

My next visit was to Bradley University in Peoria, Illinois. I was also met at the airport by the chairman of the Political Science Department. I might have accepted their offer had the chairman not said, "We're looking for a political theorist. I've been teaching the course for this semester because the man who had taught it has retired. But public administration is really what I like to teach."

"I suppose I could teach it, but it wouldn't be what I'd prefer."

"We can use someone to teach international relations, but you might have to teach theory occasionally."

"Who teaches comparative politics?"

"We have a man who comes over from Northern Illinois who has taught it for several years as an adjunct professor. I don't think we can ask him to give it up. You'll probably teach two or three sections of American government and a course in political theory."

As I was leaving, the chairman, at the airport, I said, "If you can find someone who's a theorist, I won't be disappointed if you hire him. I really would prefer to teach comparative and international politics."

When I wrote him a letter of thanks for this hospitality, I received one back two weeks later informing me they had hired a political theorist from the University of Chicago.

My third visit was to Muskingum College in New Concord, Ohio. It's located in an attractive setting with a mixture of hills, plains, and shade trees. It's a relatively small liberal arts college. I was housed on campus in the college's guesthouse. The chairman squired me around campus and took me to his home for breakfast the next morning. The other professor (there were only two) was unable to meet with us. He was an adjunct professor at a nearby community college and had to teach that morning.

"You should know, Mr. Megnin, we would expect you to teach American government, comparative, theory, and international relations on a ratio of two to one each semester (two American government sections, comparative, theory, and international relations alternating each semester). Before I left, I told the chairman, "I don't think I'm interested in teaching this kind of a schedule. You better find someone else."

My fourth trip was to Slippery Rock State College. It was actually tied into my visit to Muskingham College. Julie had picked me up at the Pittsburgh Airport. We were staying with Volkmar and Eva in Seneca, Pennsylvania, and were driving past the exit that said Slippery Rock State College.

"Why don't we take a look at Slippery Rock, Julie. We're going right through the neighborhood."

"We might just as well. It'll give us a better idea of what it looks like and where it is."

Julie turned off Interstate 79 and drove into Slippery Rock. I had written to the chairman earlier indicating an interest in applying for their position in international relations which had been posted in the Political Science Department's job list in Syracuse. The chairman wrote back indicating they had already filled that position.

We were both very much impressed with the college. The older part of the campus had the traditional Old Main building from the nineteenth century. The other buildings were from the early twentieth century and a few new ones were under construction. It looked like an expanding state college with new buildings being added to the campus in the fields to the east of the main campus.

"It's too bad they've already filled the position," Julie said. "It looks like they're really going to increase their enrollment."

"Yeah. I just applied too late."

Upon our return to Syracuse, I wrote a letter to the chairman complimenting him on what we saw in Slippery Rock. I'm only sorry I hadn't contacted you sooner when the position opened in your Political Science Department. Should you ever have another position opening in the comparative-international fields, I would appreciate being contacted.

Two weeks later, I received a letter from Dr. Donald Hayhurst, the chairman, asking if I were still interested. The candidate whom they thought they had hired had decided to take a position at the University of Georgia. I wrote back immediately I was still very interested. Dr. Hayhurst wrote back and asked if I could come for an interview with the vice president and president that next week. We'd like to fill this position as soon as possible.

Julie called Volk and Eva and asked if we could come down that next Monday for a visit.

"Don's going to be interviewed at Slippery Rock State College, Eva. Would it be possible to stay with you for a couple of days?"

"Certainly. Why don't you come down on Friday and stay over the weekend? You can stay longer if you like. It'll give us a chance to visit with you and have the girls play with Martin. He doesn't have many children to play with, does he?"

"Thanks, Eva. We'll be down on Friday evening."

We drove down to Seneca and spent a very enjoyable weekend with the Megnins. We played Wiffle baseball in their yard. Tony and Greg Schill, the children next door, also participated. Even Martin had a chance to swing the plastic bat with some help. We played card games in the evenings.

"How's Pop doing?" Volkmar asked. "Is he eating anything solid?"

"No. Mom still has to make soups of various kinds. He can't swallow anything else. You probably ought to come up for a visit. I don't think he's going to last much longer."

"It's even hard for him to play cards," Julie added. "One of us has to mix the cards for him."

"We'll go up for Easter. I should have my taxes finished by then," Volk said.

Monday morning we got up (we slept on the living room couch which pulled out into a double bed), and I drove to Slippery Rock after breakfast. Eva and Julie decided they were going to take a drive to Butler, Kittanning, and Whitesburg where Volkmar had his cooperage mill.

"Julie, Martin, and I can look over the area while you go to Slippery Rock, Donald. She ought to see what the area looks like if you may locate here," Eva said. "The reason we've stayed in this area is because of the good Catholic schools in

Oil City. You'll want to do the same, Julie, if Donald decides to teach at Slippery Rock. There was no good school near the mill. Venango Christian is about the best school in the area."

I made the visit to Slippery Rock alone. When I suggested Julie might want to go with me, she said, "I didn't go with you to any of the other campuses. I've seen Slippery Rock."

Hence, I drove to Slippery Rock by myself. The new Malibu station wagon Pop bought us earlier in the spring was running very well. It was less than an hour's drive. I took the shortcut over the Bradensburg Road then Route 322 to Route 8 south in Franklin. Route 8 was a winding road running through Franklin and the little towns of southern Venango County. The region passes through farming and forested areas as well as a few scattered houses along the way. The villages of Polk and Wesley are soon followed by crossing Interstate 80 and continuing through Harrisville, past the Critchlow farms, to the sign indicating Route 108 to Slippery Rock. I drove in the village and up Main Street to the campus on Maltby Drive. There were several parking spaces next to Old Main. Don Hayhurst had said his office was in this building. I parked the car and went into the side door nearest the parking lot and asked in the Registrar's Office, "Could you tell me where Dr. Hayhurst's office is?"

"It's on the third-floor landing," the secretary said. "If you go up these stairs just outside of this office, you'll find Dr. Hayhurst just before you reach the third floor."

"Thank you."

As I walked up the stairs, I noticed there were classrooms on each of the floors. Reaching the third floor landing, I saw the glass door with the name of Dr. Donald Hayhurst written on it. I opened the door and was greeted by Dr. Hayhurst.

"Hi. I'm Don Hayhurst. Are you looking for someone?"

"You're just the man I'm looking for. I'm Don Megnin."

"Oh yes. You've come for the interview for our new position in political science."

"That's right. I understand your previous candidate decided to go somewhere else."

"That's his loss. I'm glad he's not coming. Let me show you around, Don. You don't mind if I call you by your first name, do you? You can call me Don too."

We shook hands as he stood up.

"This is my office. Yours will be on the first floor just as you come into the building from Maltby. This is only temporary. They're building a new classroom building for us on the lower campus. When it's finished, we'll move in there. Excuse me a minute, Don. I'll call the vice president's office and see if he's in."

He turned to his phone and called, "Hi, Ruby. Is Jim in? I've got a candidate for our position in political science whom I'd like to have Jim meet."

"He's free just now, Dr. Hayhurst, but he's got a meeting in about half an hour. Can you come down right now?"

"Okay. We'll be right down."

As we walked down the stairs, Don told me about Jim Roberts.

"Jim's a great guy, Don. You'll like him. He's spent some years in Arkansas at Ozark State College before coming here. He's from Michigan originally."

Jim's office was on the first floor just across the hall from the president's office. The stairs creaked as we went down them.

"They're going to revamp Old Main once the World Culture Building is finished. The State has lots of money that they're going to invest in the state college system. The president wants to double our enrollment in five years, and we have to hire a lot more faculty in order to do that."

"Do you teach in this building?" I asked.

"Yes, we do. Let me show you one of the classrooms on our way down."

We stopped on the second floor and opened the door after listening to see if a class was in session. There was none. It was a large room with more than forty seats in five rows across. The windows gave a view out to the parking lot, the School of Education and the street leading down the hill into the village of Slippery Rock. There was a lectern in front of the room and plenty of chalk for the blackboards in the front and sides of the classroom.

"Your classes won't be this large, Don. You may have about half this number of students in your sections. "It's only in American government that our classes are really large. American government is required of all of our students by state law. The legislature thinks it's necessary to have an educated populace in order to live in a democracy. Actually, it's not such a bad idea."

"This is the first college that I've heard it's required of all students. Has this been a requirement for a long time?" I asked.

"It probably has, but I don't know when the law was passed by the legislature. It's been in effect at least since we've become a state college in 1962. I was hired to teach American government when I first came here at that time. I'll find out from the president how long it's been a requirement. I wouldn't be surprised if it was required even when Slippery Rock was still a normal school in the twenties and thirties."

We walked down the stairs to the first floor and went into the office to the left of the staircase. In one corner was another door with the sign Registrar's Office. The room next door was the Office of the Academic Affairs. Don led the way and introduced me to the secretary, Ruby Thompson, sitting just inside the door, and Jim Roberts.

"Dr. Roberts, this is Dr. Megnin, who's applied for our position in political science. Dr. Megnin, this is Dr. Roberts, our vice president for academic affairs."

We shook hands and Don introduced me to Jim's secretary. We shook hands.

"Come on in," Jim said. "Does he know what he'll be teaching, Don?"

"I've sketched out a possible schedule for him, Dr. Roberts. After you've had a chance to talk with him, we'll go over the courses we'll want him to teach."

"Okay. Have a seat, Dr. Megnin. You're finishing your doctorate at Syracuse University?"

"Yes."

"What's your dissertation on?"

"I've written on "German Economic Assistance to India: An Analysis of Its Principles and Effects on Indo-German Relations." I should have it completed by around July 1."

"Then you'll be defending your dissertation this summer?"

"Yes. I don't think I'll have any problem doing that."

"How did you happen to select this topic to research?"

"Actually, I was going to study the decision-making process in the European Economic Community when a professor of mine asked if I might be interested in doing a topic related to a developing country. He knew I had spent time in Thailand and had also visited India. He thought I might want to consider going in that direction. He told me that the Shell Foundation had just offered the Maxwell School two dissertation research grants if the topics were related to a third world country. All expenses would be paid by the foundation. He thought, since I spoke German, I might be interested in finding out why the West German government was giving so much economic aid to India. Needless to say, I redirected my interest in order to apply for the grant. I wrote up a proposal after reading Chancellor Adenauer was hosting Jawaharal Nehru in Bonn in July 1956. My research led me to believe Adenauer thought Nehru would have a great deal of influence with Nikita Khrushchev over the issue of German reunification. That's how the research interest got started. I got one of the two dissertation research grants given out by the Shell Foundation in 1965."

"That's an interesting story. I see from your resume you spent two years teaching at Chulalongkorn University in Bangkok, Thailand. You have an excellent background to teach in the international field."

He turned to Don Hayhurst. "That's the area you want him to teach, isn't it?"

"Yes, it is, Dr. Roberts. He's had more international experience than anyone I know."

"Well, let me take you over to see President Carter. He likes to meet all of the new candidates for positions in the college."

Jim led the way across the hall. As we walked in the door to the president's suite, Dr. Roberts asked the president's secretary, "Lorraine, we'd like to have Dr. Carter meet Dr. Megnin, who's a candidate for the position in political science."

Lorraine dialed his number. "Dr. Carter, Dr. Roberts and Dr. Hayhurst are here to introduce a candidate for the political science position. Can I send them in?"

She escorted us into the president's office. He was seated at a large desk on the right-hand side of the room. He could look out into the courtyard and observe whoever came up the steps to enter Old Main from the south side of campus. He stood up and Jim introduced us. He shook hands with Dr. Hayhurst and me.

"So you're the new candidate for the position in political science?"

"Yes, he is, Dr. Carter," Don Hayhurst answered. "He wrote me a letter that he had been on our campus earlier this spring and was very impressed with what he saw. He had seen our ad in the *Chronicle of Higher Education* listing our position and was sorry it had been filled by the time he had applied. He wrote me a letter telling me if there should ever be another position open in political science, he would like to apply. And here he is. As you know, our previous candidate has gone off to the University of Georgia."

"Have you defended your dissertation?"

"No. I'm planning on doing that this summer. I've just given my last chapters to the typist who is getting the five copies ready for submission to the faculty committee. As soon as I get back, I'll arrange for my defense."

"You understand you have to have completed all of the requirements for the doctorate in order to come in as an associate professor. Has Dr. Roberts made that clear to you?"

"Dr. Hayhurst told me. It shouldn't be a problem."

"Well, there'll be a problem for you if you haven't finished by September 1. If your dissertation is completed and approved by your committee, we'll hire you as an associate professor at the $10,200 annual salary. If you don't complete it by then, we'll hire you as an assistant professor at $8,800 annual salary. I just want you to understand these are the conditions for employment. We're trying to get as many PhD's on our faculty as possible. This is the only way we can do it by putting these conditions on our faculty. It's the way to raise our teaching standards."

"Thank you for telling me."

We shook hands and left. Jim had already gone off to his meeting. Don escorted me to the door.

"We'll have an office for you here in this building, Don. You'll be teaching on the second and third floors. Is there anything else I can help you with?"

"Are there any houses or farms for sale in the Slippery Rock area?"

"You shouldn't have any problems finding a place to live, Don. Grove City is just seven miles down the road. You might just be lucky and find a place out in the country, I see for-sale signs occasionally as my wife and I drive around the area. Housing shouldn't be a problem."

We shook hands and I drove back to Seneca. By the time I arrived, Eva and Julie had returned from their trip to Butler and the mill. Eva was cooking supper as I gave them a resume of my day's experience at Slippery Rock. By the time Volkmar came back, I had told them all about my visit. The girls had had an enjoyable time playing with Martin. I filled in Volk about what had taken place at the college.

"If I defend my dissertation before September 1 and pass, I'll be hired as an associate professor for political science. If I don't, I'll be hired as an assistant professor."

"How much of a difference in pay is there between the two ranks?" Volk asked.

"Fourteen hundred dollars. If I complete it by then, I'll get $10,200. If I don't, I'll get $8,800."

"That's quite a difference, Donald. But being appointed as an associate professor is the highest rank you've been offered by any of the colleges, isn't it?"

"Yes. But as the Slippery Rock president said, they're trying to get as many PhDs as quickly as possible. That's why they're offering such an incentive."

We had an enjoyable dinner of shrimp casserole which Eva had made. It was preceded by a glass of orange juice for everyone and a toast from Eva.

"Here's to many enjoyable years of get-togethers with your family and ours, Julie and Donald."

"That means we can play with Martin when he comes to visit," Mary said.

"Where are you going to live, Aunt Julie and Uncle Donald?" Liz asked.

"We'll have to find a place somewhere between here and there, Liz," I said.

"We'll find a place, Don't worry, Liz. Then you and your sisters can come to our house and stay overnight," Julie promised.

"We'd like that, Aunt Julie," each of the girls responded.

Our conversation turned to Pop and how he was doing with his cancer.

"He's getting very weak. Mom still has to make him only soups. He can't swallow anything else. We even have to mix his cards for pinochle," Julie offered. "I don't see how he's going to survive much longer."

"Well, I should have my taxes finished pretty soon. We'll come up as soon as we can," Volk said.

The next day, Julie, Martin, and I drove back to 559 Columbus Avenue. I wanted to make sure I finished my last two chapters to take to Marion Borst. Ironically, she was Dean Bailey's secretary and had offered to type up the final copy for the committee. I had told the Slippery Rock president I wouldn't have any problem completing my dissertation before the beginning of the fall semester. I still had the final two chapters to complete. I was continuing to work my obligatory twenty hours a week for the South Asian Studies Center. Basically, Dr. Lindeman wanted me to keep the files up-to-date for the graduate students going to the East Pakistan Administrative Center in Dacca, East Pakistan. The graduate students were to spend a year working for the district officers throughout the country in setting up schools and training centers for administrative staff officers. The Syracuse students were mostly from the Department of Public Administration.

Volkmar, Eva, and their girls came up to the farm over Easter 1967. Bob was attending the University of Pittsburgh after spending a year in the College of Forestry at Syracuse University. He didn't like the living arrangement (on the farm), nor was he too enamored with the Syracuse environment. He transferred to the University of Pittsburgh's Titusville branch. David was finishing his studies in political science at Pittsburgh. He had dropped out of West Point after two years finding the military customs too onerous for his taste. Why should a sophomore salute an upperclassman, whom he doesn't even know, just because he's a year ahead of him in the academy? The growing list of demerits for such infractions were more than he wished to take. Pop barely got up during the day. He had become so weak; he slept most of the time. He'd get up to sit and drink his soup, watch the news, and then retire to his bed. While Pop was in the living/dining room having his soup and coffee, Volkmar and I went into his bedroom. We knew where he kept his loaded Luger (under the mattress) below his pillow. I told Volk, "Pop says when it gets too unbearable, I'm going to shoot myself."

"I don't think we should allow him to do that, do you, Volk?"

"I agree. Let's unload his pistol."

He lifted the mattress and I took the pistol out and unloaded the last two bullets he had in it.

"Let's put it back under his mattress and he won't know the difference," I said.

Volk put the mattress down and made sure the sheet was tightly down over it. We left the bedroom before Pop came back to go to bed. We learned later from Mom that Pop had tried to use his pistol and was very upset when it didn't fire. He checked the chamber and found the bullets had been removed.

"Volke must have done it! I was all set to shoot myself and the gun didn't go off!" he complained to Mom. Little did he know I was the one who had taken the cartridges out, not Volkmar. Pop probably didn't think I could do something like that! After all, I was the one who was inserting the pain suppositories into his rectum whenever we were out on the farm in the last few months of his life. He didn't think Mom put them in far enough!

The girls dutifully shook hands with their grandfather. They gave their grandmother a hug and kiss as she tearfully said good-bye. She knew it wouldn't be much longer before they saw each other again, but without their grandfather. It was to be the last time that they saw their grandfather alive.

Towards the end of June, I finished the last two chapters of my dissertation and gave them to Marion Borst to type in final form for the committee. Julie and I decided we needed to return to the Slippery Rock area and begin searching for a place to live. Julie called Eva and asked if we could come down during the last week of June, stay overnight, leave Martin with them while we went house hunting.

"Certainly, Julie. You can stay as long as you like. We'll have the beds ready for you."

We drove down to Seneca in about five hours. We spent the late afternoon and evening discussing not only what was going on in the family, but Volk's business, what kind of place we were going to try to find, and whether or not they were coming to Syracuse for the Fourth of July.

"Yeah, we'll come up. We usually close down the mill for the holiday. Since it's towards the end of the week, we'll probably take the rest of the week off too. If not, Pat can run it. I don't have to be there all of the time."

"I'd like to find a place like yours, Eva. You have a large yard and a place for a garden with plenty of room for kids to play," Julie told her.

"Why don't you buy a farm?" Volkmar asked. "You'd have plenty of room and you could raise beef cattle on it. They wouldn't take up much of your time. You could just keep them on the pasture for the summer and fall and then sell them before winter."

"That's not a bad idea," I agreed. "How would you like to be a farmer's wife, Julie?"

"I wouldn't like that," Eva said scornfully. "Those of us who grew up in the city don't think much of farm life, do we, Julie?"

"Well, I've spent some time on my uncles' farms in Illinois and Michigan. I've sort of liked it. I wouldn't want to make it a full-time occupation, but it does have its appeal."

"It's probably not a bad place to live," Eva agreed. "But be sure you have indoor amenities that we take for granted in the city. I wouldn't want to go back to our in-laws' farm and live. It's just too primitive!"

"I agree. They should have done something long ago to bring it up to date. I don't see how Mom put up with it as long as she did!"

The next morning, Julie and I left to reconnoiter the Slippery Rock area. We looked at town houses, single family houses in the Grove City area, looked around the Harrisville and Slippery Rock area for farms. We decided to stay another day and look between Franklin and Slippery Rock to make sure we had at least seen everything that was available. We also contacted Lional Stevenson, a realtor from Harrisville who took us to look at several places, including farms, in the wider region between Slippery Rock to the south and Polk to the north. Some of the farms were really out in the country with dirt roads leading to them. I didn't think I would like shoveling a half mile of snow in the winter!

On our way back from Harrisville, we saw a for-sale sign on a farm between Wesley and Barkeyville. We stopped and knocked on the door. The owner's wife opened it. We introduced ourselves. I asked, "We noticed the for-sale sign. Does it refer to both the house and the farm?"

"The sign is for the house and farm. My husband isn't here just now. He can tell you about the farm. But if you want to look over the house, I'll be glad to show it to you."

"Thank you. I'd like that," Julie said.

As we entered the front door, we noticed the stairs directly in front of us; the room to the left was the living room, and the door to the right was the family room. We walked through the family room to the archway leading into the kitchen. There was a kitchen table with four chairs, a gas stove, a kitchen sink under a window directly over it looking out into the garden, a refrigerator, and another window facing the washhouse, garage, and barn, and a door leading out to a small porch. There was also a doorway on the north side of the kitchen leading into the dining room. There were two windows in this room; one looked out into the apple orchard on the north side of the house, and the other looked out into the garden to the rear of the house. There was an archway leading from the dining room to the living room. Mrs. Surrena took us back into the kitchen and opened the door leading to the basement. It was directly under the staircase which we saw coming into the house through the front door.

"The basement is only half-finished," Mrs. Surrena said. "It could be dug out if you wanted to do so. We never thought we needed the extra space down here, so we left it as it was when we bought it in 1925."

There was a fuel oil tank next to a window on the northwest corner of the basement, a furnace, hot water heater, two washtub sinks in front of the window looking out towards the garden next to a washer, and a dryer and a door leading out of the basement into the backyard. There was also a water outlet leading to a pipe in the northeast corner of the floor with a metal screen to prevent rodents from coming into the basement. As we looked at the unfinished part, she said, "It's really a convenient place to store potatoes and vegetables. My husband placed these shelves on the dirt where I can store these things."

The crawl space between the floor and dirt was narrow and only partially excavated.

"It's a good place to store things keeping them cool in the summer and warm in the winter."

She led us back upstairs to the kitchen.

"Let me show you the upstairs. There are three bedrooms, a bathroom, and additional storage space for our clothes and other items we seldom use," she told us as we proceeded upstairs. At the top of the stairs to our right was the door leading into the bathroom. Directly in front of us were sliding doors into the storage areas. There was a window looking out from the left storage room into the yard facing the barn and other outbuildings. Directly behind us was the bathroom tub and toilet on the west side of the bathroom. The sink and mirror were on the east side of the room. There was also a window looking out into the garden to the rear of the house.

She led us across the top of the stairs into a large bedroom. There were windows on both the north and east side. A sink and faucet were built into a counter with storage shelves directly over and under the countertop. The shelves were used for storing linens, towels, pictures, games, etc. She led us to the master bedroom through a door on the northwest corner of this first bedroom. The master bedroom faced the highway to the west. There were three windows in this room, one on the north side and two facing west.

"In the evenings we often see a really beautiful sunset from this side of the house. From up here, we can see it even longer than from below."

She then led us through the door on the southwest corner of the room which went across the top of the staircase into a smaller bedroom with a window looking out over the back porch into the yard to the south and another window facing the west. There was also a closet on the eastern end of the room. Mrs. Surrena then took us back downstairs.

"I'm sorry my husband hasn't come back yet. You probably want to look over the other buildings. Could you come back tomorrow? He can show you around the farm."

Julie and I talked it over.

"All right. We'll stop in tomorrow. Thank you for showing us your house."

"What's in the little house just outside the kitchen, Mrs. Surrena?" Julie asked.

"That's where I used to do my wash. It's called the washhouse. I haven't used it since we put in running water in the house in 1940. I'll have my husband show you tomorrow when you come."

"Okay. Thanks again. We'll see you tomorrow."

We drove back to Seneca and spent another night at the Megnins. After supper, we played cards and talked about what we had seen.

"We saw an excellent place near Wesley this afternoon. The woman showed us the house, but her husband wasn't home. She wants us to come back tomorrow to talk with him and have him show us the rest of the buildings and farm. The house has real possibilities," Julie said.

"There's also a barn, a pigsty, and sixty-five acres which we haven't seen. It's right on Route 8 about a quarter of a mile north of Interstate 80," I added. "It's only about a fifteen—or twenty-minute drive from Slippery Rock. It would be a very convenient place to live, as I see it. It's only another half an hour or so from this place."

"It sounds great, Donald," Eva said.

After breakfast that next morning, Julie and I drove down to Wesley to look over the farm. Upon arrival, I knocked on the door and Arvil Surrena answered.

"Hi. We're Don and Julie Megnin and we told your wife we would stop by today to talk with you about your farm."

"I'm Arvil Surrena. My wife told me you stopped by yesterday, and you want to see the farm today?"

"Yes. We were very interested after your wife showed us the house."

"I hear you're going to teach at Slippery Rock?"

"Yes. I start September 1. We'd like to be settled in before then. Mr. Stevenson showed us several places. We just happened to see your sign as we drove past."

"Well, you're lucky. You're the first ones who've noticed the sign. I'm sure there'll be a lot of people who would like to buy it once they know it's for sale."

"I understand you've lived here since 1925?"

"That's right. My dad and I used to dig coal for a living in the late twenties and early thirties. There's lots of coal in the hill just behind these front fields. If I don't sell my farm, I'll have it stripped."

"Aren't you farming at all?"

"I rent my hayfields to some of my neighbors and one of them plants corn on the back lot. But I'm too old to do any of that anymore. I've sold my machinery. I don't even have a tractor anymore. Let's start with the washhouse."

He took us behind the house and pushed open the door of the little building to the south of the house. Inside was a concrete floor, with a water outlet in the center also with an iron grate over it as we had seen in the cellar. There were two windows: one on the south side facing the garage and barn and one on the north side facing a grill and the garden. There were two electrical outlets: one by the door, the other on the wall at the eastern end of the room. The rest of the interior was unfinished with rough boards covering the walls. The outside was shingled. Directly behind the building was an attached doghouse.

"This is where our dog, Cinder, sleeps. We keep her chained up most of the time. She likes to chase cars. I take her into the woods when I go hunting."

There was also a large concrete grill with an iron grating over it for cookouts on the concrete apron which connected the grill with the washhouse and the sidewalk leading to the back porch of the house.

"My wife doesn't use the washhouse anymore. She has her washer and dryer in the basement of the house. I use it mostly for storage."

There were several chairs, tables, and garden tools in it.

"Let's take a look at the garage."

He led the way to the large building between the washhouse and the barn. He opened the door, and there was enough room in it to keep two cars, I thought. One car could be kept in the side facing the house. The other facing the barn since there were two doors in the garage. There was a stairway leading to the second floor where he had stacked boards, tools, oil, and gas cans, window frames, doors, and other odds and ends. Next to the large garage was a smaller one. It had a garage door which swung open into an overhead position. Inside he had his tractor lawn mower, sickles, scythes, oil, and gas cans.

"You have a big yard to mow. How long does it take you?" I asked.

"I can do it in about two hours if I stay with it. But then I have to trim around the trees and house. That takes another hour or two, depending on how tired I am. While we're here, let me show you my pigsty."

We walked down to the little building next to the gate leading into the field to the east. There was a wooden picket fence surrounding the entire yard which connected the pigsty and the barnyard.

"This is where I used to house my pigs. I haven't had any for years, but the building could still be used if you wanted to raise pigs."

"Your pig yard is a lot bigger than what we had for our pigs on our farm. We had a shed slightly larger than yours, but the yard was only about a quarter of the size you have."

"You wouldn't want to raise pigs anyway," Julie said. "You'll have enough to do with your teaching."

"Let's take a look at the barn."

He led us around behind the garage and over to the barn. Arvil opened the sliding door.

"I used to keep cows on the east side. [There was a runway through the middle.] I kept my horses and calves on the west side."

We walked through the barn, and I counted fifteen stanchions with a wider manger in front. There was a hay shoot in the center, which made it easy to feed the hay to the cows. The aisle in the center was different from anything I had ever seen in a cow barn. A tractor and wagon could drive through the middle, just as I remembered we had done in our barn. But in cleaning the gutter in this barn, the farmer stood on the concrete aisle behind the cows and pitched the manure down into the spreader. There were also four windows on the east side of the barn looking out into the barnyard and fields beyond. On the western side of the barn were two stalls for horses and a holding pen for a cow who was calving and another pen in which to keep the calves. There was a stairway to the second floor leading into the hayloft. There were two large haymows on each side of the center aisle running from west to east into which the hay was pitched. A tractor and wagon could be pulled completely into the barn to unload. The only reservation I had about the barn was the ramp leading into the hayloft. It was getting old and the planks were cracking. There was a three-inch gap between the barn door and the ramp. It can still be used, I thought to myself, but the ramp will have to be replaced in the next few years.

"Do you want to see the rest of the farm? I can drive my truck down the fields and show you the farm boundaries and the woodlot."

"Yes. We'd like that."

We got into his truck and he drove down through the fields showing us the fence lines bordering his property. The trees in the woodlot were large and hadn't been harvested in many years, I thought. There were several white oaks that Volk might be interested in one of these days. As we came to the road bordering his farm on the eastern end, Arvil said, "I've had several people ask me if I'd sell lots along this road. I want to sell the whole farm, not just pieces of it. If you drive up Route 8 to the interstate, you'll see where people have built houses on farmland along the roadside. I haven't been interested in doing that, but there are people who do."

As he drove us back to the house, I asked, "What are you asking for your farm, Mr. Surrena?"

"Twenty-three thousand dollars."

"Ouch. That's a lot of money, Mr. Surrena. Would you take eighteen thousand for it?"

"No! That's not enough! If you give me eighteen thousand five hundred, I'll sell the house, barn, outbuildings, and forty-five acres to you and I'll keep the back twenty acres along the road."

"That sounds reasonable. Let us check and see if we can get a loan and get back to you. How would that be?"

"I'll give you one month from today. If you haven't raised the money by then, the deal's off."

"What about the twenty acres along the back road? Could we have first option buying them if you should decide to sell?"

"Okay. I'll give you one year in which to decide if you want to buy the back twenty acres. After that, the deal's off!"

"Fair enough."

Julie and I shook hands with him and left. As we drove away, Julie said, "All we have to do now is get a loan from a bank. We could stop in Franklin and see if the bank will loan us the money. We're going right past the First Federal Bank on our way back to Seneca."

"Good idea."

We stopped at the First Federal Bank and introduced ourselves to the woman manager. She had us fill out a loan application. After completing it, Julie gave it to her.

"You're going to be teaching at Slippery rock this fall?" she asked.

"Yes. I should have my dissertation finished and defended in another month or so," I responded.

"You're going to put down two thousand dollars towards the purchase price of this farm?"

We both said, "Yes."

"I don't think you'll have a problem getting a loan from our bank. Check back with me next Monday and I should have an answer for you, Mr. and Mrs. Megnin. It'll have to be surveyed and checked to make sure the title is clear. Do you have an attorney here locally?"

"No, we don't. But I have a brother in Seneca who can recommend one to us. I don't think we'll have a problem finding one."

We thanked her for her help and shook hands. As we drove back to Seneca, Julie said, "I didn't think Mr. Surrena was willing to make a deal. I don't think we can afford to buy the whole farm. I'm glad he was willing to sell us the front forty-five acres."

"Yeah. I'm glad too. It's an excellent location and so close to Interstate 80. That'll be a good connection to drive out to Indiana to visit your folks."

We returned to Seneca and sat down for an excellent dinner of shrimp creole Eva had prepared. She poured everyone a glass of orange juice and proposed a toast.

"Here's to Uncle Donald and Aunt Julie's new home! While it's not Seneca, at least it's not far away!"

We all drank the toast when Mary said, "It's at least in Western Pennsylvania!"

Everyone laughed in agreement. "Just think, Martin, we'll help you celebrate your fourth birthday!" Liz said. "And I'll go down the slide with you," Kitty added.

"Do you know anyone who's a surveyor, Volk?" I asked.

"Yeah. Alan Longtine has done some surveying for us. If he's not too busy, you can probably hire him. I'll give him a call tomorrow and find out what his schedule is."

"What about a lawyer? Could you recommend one for us for the closing, if we get the loan?"

"Sure. Max Gabreski is our lawyer. I'm sure he would be able to help you with your closing. I'll give him a call tomorrow too, and see if he would be available."

The calls Volkmar made to Longtine and Gabreski did, indeed, prove to be successful. We stayed one more day in order to meet these two gentlemen and to make sure the work would be done while we went back to Syracuse. That evening, on the thirtieth of June, Mom called to tell us Pop had died during the night. His body had been taken by the Tyler Funeral Home in Chittenango. Since Pop wanted to be cremated, Mr. Tyler recommended a less elaborate and less expensive coffin for the viewing and the service.

"I told Mr. Tyler that my two sons were in Pennsylvania," Mom told Volkmar.

"When do you think the funeral should be, Volke?"

"We'll come up tomorrow, Mom. Wait until we get there to make that decision."

"Papa was also angry when he found out his gun was unloaded. He was going to use it and it didn't work. I'm glad you unloaded it, Volkmar."

"I didn't unload it, Mom. It was Donald's idea, and he did it. Well, we'll be up tomorrow. Thanks for calling. Good night."

Volkmar turned toward us and reported what Mom had told him.

"Pop died in his sleep last night. I guess he thought I had unloaded his pistol. Mom said he wanted to use it and it didn't work."

"And she thought you had unloaded it?" I asked.

"Yeah. That's what Pop thought. He was really angry at me, Mom said."

"Well, we can't change that now. He's been sick for more than a year with his cancer. He literally starved to death. And he held the wrong man responsible for unloading his pistol! It's too bad, Volk, he accused the wrong man. Unfortunately, we can't change that now," I said.

"I'd better get our things packed tonight, Pete. We'll want to leave first thing in the morning," Eva counseled.

"Yeah. We should get up there by tomorrow afternoon and check in with the funeral home."

It was a sobering evening. We all went to bed early. Eva got their clothing packed for the girls and themselves. We wanted to leave after breakfast in order to arrive at Tyler Funeral Home before closing time. It seemed ironic to Julie and me. Here we were going to my first full-time job since leaving First Ward, we had agreed to buy a farm, and now Pop dies. It was, indeed, the end of one era and the start of another. His life had been a hard struggle almost from the beginning. It was difficult for him growing up as a boy with a father who had been the victim of his own illegitimate birth. A bastard growing up in Germany in those days (early nineteenth century) was the constant victim of abuse, ridicule, and torment from the townspeople and young boys. The early life of his farther didn't give him any empathy or understanding of the needs of young children for protection from abuse! Pop's father must have been the constant victim of the pranks of his peers. Pop didn't have much of a model to follow in his formative years. He patterned his life, unwittingly, upon what he saw and how he was himself treated by his father. While Pop suffered greatly from his war wounds, he never got over the experience of losing his voice. He treated his siblings as he had been treated as a boy. He then treated his children as his father had treated him and his siblings: with almost a harsh cruelty for his older children, but with a great fondness and favoritism for his youngest child. Pop's father had treated his younger brother, Karl, the same way Pop treated me: with kindness, generosity, love, and encouragement to do the best in whatever situation I was in.

We drove through Oil City and into Rouseville that next morning following Volkmar, Eva, David, Bob, Mary, Liz, and Kitty in their station wagon. As we were going forty-five miles an hour in a thirty-five-mile-an-hour speed zone, the local motorcycle policeman stopped Volkmar. He was about to issue him a ticket for speeding when I stopped behind him. I explained why we were going faster than usual.

"Look, Officer, he's my brother and we're going up to Syracuse because our father died last night. My brother lives in Seneca. He wouldn't be speeding if we weren't in a hurry to help take care of the funeral arrangements. Can't you excuse him this one time? This is a real emergency."

"Are you on your way to make funeral arrangements for your father's funeral?"

"Yes," Volkmar agreed.

"Well, I'll let you go this time, but don't let me catch you speeding through Rouseville again! I won't be so generous next time!"

"Thanks, Officer. If this hadn't happened, I wouldn't be speeding," Volkmar assured him.

We continued our journey to Syracuse and arrived around three o'clock. Mom was glad to see us. She gave all of us a big hug and a kiss.

"It's been a long, hard time for you, Mom. But at least it's now over. You can start to relax again," Eva told her.

"It's been a hard time for Papa. He didn't get up much these last few days. He said he didn't feel like getting out of bed. He just drank a little water, but that was all."

"Have you talked with Bob Bolton about doing the service, Mom?" I asked.

"No. I thought it would be best if you talked to him. You know Papa didn't want Mr. Carmichel to have the service."

"Yes. He made that quite clear before we went to Pennsylvania. He must have known it wasn't going to be too long before he died. I'll give Bob a call and find out when he can do the service. You said Tyler's left it up to you when you wanted the service?"

"Yes. Mr. Tyler thought probably it would be the day after the Fourth of July. He didn't think anyone would come on the holiday."

"Okay. I'll see what Bob thinks."

I called Bob.

"Sorry about your dad, Meg, but it's probably a lot better for him now. Alex is just leaving for Maine. He said he was going to stop and talk with your mom. He knows your dad didn't want him to do the service. So I guess we can set it whenever it's convenient for you, Meg. How about the fifth? Then those people who want to celebrate the Fourth can do so and come the day after."

"That sounds okay. We'll have calling hours on the afternoon and evening of the third. You can conduct the service in the funeral home on the fifth. That should be enough time for anyone who wishes to come from the neighborhood and relatives."

"That sounds good. Nancy and I will stop by tomorrow afternoon at the funeral home, Meg. I'll see you then."

"Okay, Bob. Thanks for doing the service."

On the afternoon and evening of July 3, we greeted friends and relatives at the Tyler Funeral Home. Since Pop was going to be cremated, Mom and Inge had picked out a simple casket covered by a gray felt material. There were several flower arrangements from the relatives and even one from the Mycenae neighbors. There was also one from the First Ward Methodist Church. Some of the members of the Couples Club had gotten together and sent a flower spray. There was also one from the DeWitt Community Church which Mom attended as often as she could.

Following the Fourth of July picnic, which we had together with the Schoecks, the service Bob conducted the next day was well attended. Those who attended were mostly from the family and relatives from Syracuse. There was no graveside ceremony since Pop's body was going to be cremated. We thanked Bob for his services. I handed him an envelope with money in it. Bob handed it back.

"You don't have to pay me, Meg. I wouldn't think of charging you!"

"Thanks a lot, Bob. If my dad were alive, I'm sure he would have appreciated what you had to say."

We left and returned to the farm. Mom prepared dinner for all of us after the service. Volkmar and his family left shortly thereafter to return to Pennsylvania. Julie and I talked with Mom, Inge, and Fritz for a while.

"We're going to buy a farm not far from Volk and Eva. We'll have to go back to Pennsylvania to finalize our loan and arrange to have it surveyed," Julie and I told them.

"What? Another farm, Donald? I thought you had given up farming?" Fritz asked.

"He's not going into farming, Fritz. It's just a nice place to live," Julie assured him. "He's going to be tied up getting his lectures ready. He won't have time for farming!"

Mom, Inge, and Fritz were interested in what we had found. "We'll have to come down and visit you one of these days, Donald," Inge said. They all agreed it sounded like an ideal place for us to live.

Before Volk and Eva left, we had agreed as soon as Pop's ashes came back from the crematorium, we'd inter him in the Woodlawn Cemetery. Julie and I had already made arrangements with Woodlawn to purchase the grave sites for Pop, Mom, Julie, and me on one side and Inge and Fritz on the other. We also picked out a gravestone from the Waltzer Monument Company and had them carve our names into the stone. We then had them place it directly in the center of our six grave sites. Pop's name was the only one which had his date of birth and death recorded in the stone. The rest of us had only our names and dates of birth listed.

I checked with Marion Borst to see how she was coming along with typing the final copy of the dissertation.

"I've already finished it, Don. I'll have the five copies run off by the middle of July. You can go ahead and arrange to defend it with your committee. It's about one of the most interesting dissertations I've ever read! I'm sure your committee will find it very interesting too. You made good use of the Shell Foundation Research Grant."

"Thanks, Marion. I'll see when I can schedule the committee. I hope it can be before the first of September. You probably don't know, but if I can defend it before September 1, I'll be hired as an associate professor. If I'm not finished by then, I'll be hired as an assistant professor. There's quite a difference in salary between these two categories."

"I hope you can get your committee together in time, Don. Everyone should be back from their summer travels by then."

Unfortunately, I was unable to get the committee together until the ninth of September. Two of them were still in Europe on September 1, and Dr. and Mrs. Bishop had just arrived from Taiwan on August 30. I think actually only three of my committee members read the dissertation in its entirety. The other two must have skimmed it at best from what I could determine from their questions.

Julie, Martin, and I returned to Pennsylvania after checking the progress being made by Marion. We wanted to finalize the purchase of the Surrena farm in Wesley. Volkmar had arranged with Dick Longtine to do the surveying. He had also talked with Max Gabreski about handling the closing. Since Max was an attorney, he discovered that Longtine was not a fully licensed surveyor. Hence, he told us we didn't have to pay the full charge for the survey. I'm sure Max, as Volk and Eva's attorney, gave us a special reduced rate for his services. By the end of July, the purchase of the farm was completed. The Surrenas moved out by the thirty-first of July and we prepared to move in by the middle of August.

Mom called us after she received Pop's ashes. I called Volk and Eva and we decided to inter them on the third Saturday in July. We would all gather in Syracuse and I would conduct the interment service in the Woodlawn Cemetery. Prior to the graveside service, we brought a shovel from the farm, and Volkmar dug a hole and placed the two canisters in it. For the two o'clock service, Mom, Volkmar and Eva, Fritz and Inge, Julie, Tante Gretel, Grete, Tante Elise, and Wally were in attendance. I gave the traditional last rites, and Pop was buried. Within the next decade, most of the members of the original families immigrating to America were also buried in the plots nearby.

On August 15, David and Bob drove up to Syracuse and helped us move. All of our furniture, books, household items, toys, crib, etc., were loaded into a U-Haul truck. It took most of the morning to empty the apartment on Columbus Avenue. After lunch, we all drove down to Pennsylvania. David and Bob traded off driving the truck and their car. Julie, Martin, and I drove in our Malibu station wagon. David was finishing his undergraduate studies at the University of Pittsburgh. He had dropped out of West Point. Bob had started at the College of Forestry in Syracuse, but since he didn't get along very well with his grandfather, he decided to transfer to the Pitt campus at Titusville, Pennsylvania, to complete his degree in biology.

Arriving in Wesley late in the afternoon, we unloaded the truck. David then returned it to the U-Haul distributor in Franklin on their way home. Julie, Martin, and I spent our first night at R. D. # 3, Grove City, Pennsylvania 16127. It was the start of a seven-year stint on our farm commuting to Slippery Rock to teach undergraduate and graduate students in political science.

Before we left Syracuse, I had arranged for my dissertation committee to meet at 10:00 a.m. on September 9 in the Graduate Salon of the Maxwell School. Marion suggested it would be good to have the committee meet for coffee and cake prior to the defense.

"If you don't mind, Don, I'll arrange it for you."

"Thank you very much, Marion. Is that what these committees usually expect?"

"This is usually what happens. It helps to sweeten the temperament of the committee."

On the ninth, Dr. Oliver E. Clubb, chairman (recommended by Dr. Palmer); Dr. Bishop; Dr. Lindeman; and Dr. Agananda, the graduate school representative, met for the coffee and cake. After a fifteen-minute period of coffee and cake, Dr. Clubb said, "You all know why we're here. Don's going to defend his dissertation. I must say, I knew nothing about German politics, but I thought he did an excellent job presenting the reasons why the West Germans have spent so much money on aid to India. Who would like to open the questioning?"

"Why don't you tell the committee how you started this research, Don?" Dr. Bishop suggested.

"I was intrigued by the amount of money the West German government had provided India in its economic package. They've given more than one billion dollars in aid between 1955 and 1965. I wondered why. The initial reason, I've decided, had to do with trying to prevent the Indian government from extending diplomatic recognition to the German Democratic Republic. The Bonn government wanted to ensure that the Indian government understood the East German regime was an illicit creation of the Soviet Union and, therefore, did not represent the best interests of all Germans. Since the East German government had been imposed by the Soviets and not freely elected, the Adenauer government felt if recognition were withheld from the GDR, then the West Germans' claim as the only real representative of all Germans would be accepted in the international community. The federal republic would then be recognized as the only true representative of the German people. Furthermore, Adenauer believed Jawaharal Nehru had such an enormously favorable international reputation and was so highly respected by all of the world's leaders, he might become a spokesman for German reunification in his projected meeting in Moscow with Nikita Khrushchev. By the time the meeting took place, however, the West German government had already committed itself to supporting one of the biggest construction projects ever undertaken by a foreign government in India: the construction of the Rourkela Steel Works in Orissa, India. Nehru's inquiry in behalf of the West Germans was bluntly turned down by Khrushchev.

"I will keep the fifteen million Germans whom I now control in East Germany rather than have eighty million united Germans who would be opposed to what I want to accomplish in the world! German reunification is out of the question!"

"So that's how the German economic assistance got started in India?" Dr. Bishop asked.

"Yes. That's what propelled the infusion of German marks into the Indian economy originally. The Indian government had also asked for aid in setting up a production-cum-training program for industrial workers in Okhla [Delhi], a technological institute in Madras, and an agricultural experimental station in Himachal Pradesh."

Each of the professors asked questions pertaining to each of these case studies. I used them for my documentation and argument of why the Germans had become so heavily involved in supporting Indian economic development.

After two hours of questions and answers, Dr. Agananda said, "I want to thank you, Mr. Megnin, for a most informative and insightful presentation of your dissertation. Unless anyone else has any other questions, I think we can ask you to leave us for a short while so that we can discuss your candidacy among ourselves. Mr. Megnin, would you step out for a while? Don't go too far."

"Certainly. I'll wait out in the hall."

I sat on the bench in the hall opposite the door and waited. I was too far away to hear any of the comments especially with the door closed. After an interval of fifteen minutes, Dr. Agananda came out and said, "Dr. Megnin, could you come in and let the professors thank you for your presentation?"

It was the first time I was called Dr. Megnin. I felt thrilled by being addressed with this title and knew the committee must have approved of my dissertation. Each man stood and shook my hand. They also thanked me for the coffee and cake.

"Actually, you should thank Mrs. Borst, the dean's secretary. It was her idea to have the coffee and cake for you."

Dr. Agananda said, "I've had each committee member sign this copy of the dissertation which goes to the graduate school. I think that takes care of all of our business. Congratulations again for doing such an excellent job in writing and defending your dissertation."

"I'll sign your dissertation, Don, that you'll keep for yourself. We just have to give the graduate school the one Dr. Agananda has with all of our signatures," Dr. Clubb said.

And with those words of endorsement and a few changes which the committee wanted in the structure of the document, I was told to rewrite two short sections of the dissertation and bibliography to have it ready for submission to the graduate school in time for the December deadline. It had to be completed by then so that I could be listed under the January 1968 graduates.

Needless to say, since I hadn't conducted my defense before the first of September, I became an assistant professor for political science at Slippery Rock State College. Dr. Hayhurst, knowing the conditions under which I was to be hired, promised, "You teach a course this next summer, Don. It'll make up for the difference in your salary."

Unfortunately, too few students enrolled in the summer political science courses in 1968. Hence, I had to wait until the following year before I could do so.

VI.

Settling in on the Farm

I started teaching on September 10, 1967. I was assigned three sections of American government and one section of international organizations. Since I had not taught these courses previously, I had a great deal of preparation to do to keep ahead of my students. Since we had three bedrooms upstairs, I used the one looking out into the garden and field behind the house as my study. Julie and I used the master bedroom facing the road and to the north for our bedroom. Martin had the smaller bedroom looking out into the backyard. I set up a card table and chair next to the sink that was in the bedroom. It had been used in previous years by Mrs. Surrena's mother when she lived with them. It was a convenient room in which to do my work. The bathroom was just next-door. These days of preparation set the stage for the rest of my teaching career at Slippery Rock. After devising the syllabus for the semester, I had a guide for my lectures, which was convenient not only for the students, but also for the professor.

The American government classes were taught in a large lecture room on the third floor of Old Main. The room held approximately fifty students. I made up a seating chart in order to learn the names of the students more quickly. American government was mandated by the Pennsylvania legislature requiring every student to take the course. Therefore, it was the course which had a built-in following. There were so many students taking it the department had to teach American government during each of the summer sessions. One of the interesting features of this classroom was the need to place buckets in three different places during heavy rainstorms. Fortunately for the students, the rain dripped in over the aisles and not on the students! By the next year, not only were we installed in the new classroom building (World Cultures) for our offices, but for our classrooms as well. Within the next two years, Old Main was completely renovated and housed only administrative offices and conference rooms.

With Pop's death, Volkmar thought it would be best for Mom if she came to Pennsylvania to spend the winters. She was getting along in years, and shoveling snow was out of the question for her. It was bad enough when Pop was still alive. She had to shovel the path from the house to the mailbox or road to catch the bus. She had been able to call in for their grocery needs to Mayers Food Market in Chittenango and the groceries were delivered. It was the start of Mom's yearly visits in Pennsylvania during the winters. She spent time with both of our families. With the vacant washhouse right next to our farmhouse, I decided to convert it into my study. I bought plywood for the walls, ceiling tiles, and boards to cover the floor. Volk helped me on a couple of Saturdays, and we completed the job before winter. I installed an electric heater and a new door which I could lock. Julie and I then bought two three-by-three-foot filing cabinets and a door to place over them to use as my desk. We bought an office chair and I was in business! By the end of October, I was able to move all of my books, cabinets, and notebooks into this new study next to our house. Cinder, the dog whom we inherited with the farm, slept in the little shed just behind the study. She was a very gentle dog and got along well with Martin. She did have a very bad habit, however, of chasing after cars if she were near one of our entrances. Just before we were about to leave to teach a summer course in Salzburg, Austria (1969), Cinder ran out into the road to chase a car going south. As she was coming back across the road, she was hit by a truck. She dragged herself into the yard but was unable to go any farther. We put her into the station wagon and took her to Dr. Richards's office in Harrisville. After examining her, Dr. Richards suggested, "The best thing to do for her is to euthanize her. She's got such extensive external and internal injuries, I don't think she would survive anyway. She has three broken legs, internal injuries, and is barely able to hold up her head."

"Okay, Dr. Richards. It's probably just as well. We're going to Austria in another couple of weeks anyway."

We petted her for the last time and left.

During the winter of 1967-68, Werner and Anne Marie Meyer-Koenig and their three daughters Martina, Andrea, and Danielle came over Christmas for a visit. Werner was Mom's cousin. He was a visiting mathematics professor at the Milwaukee branch of the University of Wisconsin. Between our home in Wesley and the Megnins in Seneca, we hosted them for a few days during their midwinter vacation. Earlier that previous summer, I had arranged for Werner to buy Hermann Weiss's Mercury sedan. Werner had asked me, shortly after they arrived in the States, "Donald, can you help me find a car to buy for us to use for the year we're here in the United States?"

"Certainly, Werner. I talked with Hermann and Grete Weiss, she's my cousin, earlier that summer and they're interested in getting a new car. I think they would be willing to sell it to you very reasonably."

Werner did, indeed, buy their Mercury sedan. Following the purchase of the car, Mom, Volkmar, Eva, and family, together with the Meyer-Koenigs, Julie, Martin, and me, drove to the Chautauqua Institute to stay for week living in the Ministers' Union. I was filling in for Dr. Bishop for a week at the institute teaching American government. He had to go overseas during the last week of his class and he asked me if I would fill in for him.

During the Christmas holidays, while the Meyer-Koenigs were visiting us on the farm, we took them to Slippery Rock and showed them around our campus. Werner was amazed at the size of our campus.

"Stuttgart University is small compared with what you have here, Donald. We have a couple of blocks of buildings in downtown Stuttgart, but you have room for a score of classroom buildings, dormitories, a field house and track, all kinds of playing fields, and tennis courts. Slippery Rock is much bigger than our university. You have room for expansion. We don't have that in Germany."

"We're trying to become a university from what I'm told, Werner. We have the room, now all we need to do is build up our academic departments to accommodate such an expansion."

During that first winter on the farm, Saturday mornings were the times I used to clear out some of the wild apple trees, berry bushes, and underbrush from the north slope of the hill that had been used as a pasture behind the woodlot. I thought it would be an excellent place for a toboggan run down the slope. When the snow began to fall, Julie, Martin, and I went down to the slope with our toboggan to try it out. It worked perfectly. I gradually widened the slope so that more and more open space was available for sliding. We invited Larry, Peggy, Michael, and Cheryl Cobb to come and join us for tobogganing parties. Larry had become the chairman of the political science department with Don Hayhurst's relocation to Auburn University. Julie was instrumental in setting up a nursery school for preschoolers in Slippery Rock for the college community's children. As a consequence, she became acquainted with Jean Severance, the wife of the local Protestant chaplain at the college. They had three children, two of whom were in the preschool program with Martin. Since they were also good friends of the Cobbs, we invited them also to join us for tobogganing parties. After these outings, Julie served hot chocolate and cookies. It was a delightful way to spend the winter.

On Easter 1968, Julie's parents drove out from Goshen, Indiana, to visit us. It was their first visit to our farm. They stayed with us for several days and enjoyed getting reacquainted with their grandson, Martin. They used our spare bedroom that had previously been used as my office until we moved my office to the rebuilt washhouse. They enjoyed their stay. Dad King was impressed with the layout of the farm. He thought the coal under the fields would one day prove of value should we ever decide to have it strip-mined. When I showed him around the farm, he noticed one of the best fields was the one not part of the farm which we had purchased from Arvil Surrena.

"What did you have to pay to buy the farm, Don?"

"Eighteen thousand five hundred dollars for these forty-five acres, Dad. We didn't think we could afford to buy the entire sixty-five acres. Mr. Surrena has given us a year's first option to buy the remaining twenty acres that abuts this back road."

"It's too bad you didn't buy the whole farm. How much did he want for the sixty-five acres?"

"He wanted twenty-five thousand dollars. We didn't think we could afford that much."

He didn't say anything as we drove back to the house. When we got back, he again said to Julie, "It's too bad you didn't buy all sixty-five acres, Julia. The lot in back along the road is going to be valuable one of these days."

"We took out a fifteen-thousand-dollar loan, Dad, from the First Federal Savings Bank in Franklin. Between what Don's dad had originally given us, and what we had left over, we made a twenty-five-hundred-dollar down payment and borrowed the rest from the bank," Julie explained.

"You've got a really nice place, Julia. Don tells me you've got a one year's option to buy the rest of the farm."

"Yes. It'll be up this coming August. I don't know if we can afford to borrow any more from the bank, but it's possible. Do you think we should have bought the whole farm?"

"Yes. Maybe you can get a local farmer to rent the land from you, Julia, to help you pay for it. Are there any dairy farms around here?"

"Yes, there are, Dad," I chimed in.

"Why don't you talk to them about renting your farm? You might be surprised what you can get for it."

"My mom does that in Upstate New York. She doesn't get much. Five dollars an acre, but at least it's something she wouldn't have otherwise."

Grandmother King enjoyed reading to Martin during their stay. The last time they were together with us was at Christmas. "He's really growing, Julia. He pays good attention to the stories."

One week after Grandmother and Grandfather King returned to Goshen, they sent us a letter addressed to all three of us.

> Dear Julia, Don, and Martin,
>
> Your mother and I, Julia, want to thank both of you for the very enjoyable time we had with you and your son, Martin, on your farm in Pennsylvania. Martin's a real nice boy and already asks many questions which is very unusual for a child of his age. He's going to be a really bright young man when he grows up.
>
> Your mother and I have decided to send you this check to help you pay off your mortgage on your farm and also to buy the remaining twenty acres to complete the purchase of the sixty-five acres. We're sure you will be able to put this money to good use as you settle in at R. D. 3, Grove City, Pa.
>
> With best wishes to the three of you. Hugs and kisses to our grandson.
>
> Love,
> Mom and Dad King

The check was in the amount of ten thousand dollars. We did, indeed, buy the remaining twenty acres!

We got acquainted with our neighbors in Wesley and Barkeyville. Kate and Wayne Phipps were among the nearest neighbors. They lived across from our farm down the first road to the left after leaving our driveway heading south. Wayne's father lived next door to them and raised young stock. That first summer, he cut our hay on shares, bailed it, and put our half in our barn. Unfortunately, he was well into his seventies and by the next summer he was no longer able to carry on with his farming. Among other members of nearby farms and homes with whom we interacted were the Millers (owners of a gas station just down Route 8 from our northern driveway entrance), the McDougals in Barkeyville, Greg and Chris Miller, the Voguses, the Sterritts, the Corys, Smiths, and the Muellers. Each of these families had children roughly in the age of Martin or baby sat for us while we attended a function at Slippery Rock. We attended dinners at the Wesley Grange, and while we were invited to attend one of the local churches, we preferred to drive to Franklin to attend the First United Methodist Church. It not only gave us a wider range of people with whom to interact, but the church was also between our farm and Volk and Eva's house in Seneca. Since the farm was located in the Franklin Area School District, when a vacancy occurred on the school board, I was asked by Dr. Judson Hill if I would consider being appointed to the board to fulfill the term of a former member who had moved out of the district. Jud was a sociologist at Slippery Rock. He also received his doctorate in 1968. I agreed and spent the next four years serving on the board at its monthly meetings. What I did not know was the fact that often these meetings would not be concluded before one or two o'clock in the morning! Usually teaching an 8:00 a.m. class meant pushing my physical tolerance levels to heights they had not known before. I had to overcome a bout with ulcers before my time on the board had ended.

As I've indicated earlier, during the summer of 1969, Julie, Martin, and I went to Salzburg, Austria, to teach a course for Slippery Rock titled Problems in European Politics. Henry and Linda Lenz had been conducting a German language and literature program there since the early 1960s. Henry thought if our college could begin a study abroad program, it could dovetail nicely with his Cultural Studies Academy. Ever since Albert Watrel became our president (replacing Bob Carter, July 1, 1968), I had been asked by Jim Roberts if I would be willing to work in Academic Affairs with a special focus on international education. I had agreed, and Henry's suggestion seemed just what we needed to get such a program under way. We had successfully recruited ten students (the usual number needed to offset the cost of the air ticket for the faculty member) from Slippery Rock and neighboring colleges. Volkmar and Eva's oldest daughter, Mary, a student at Villa Maria in Erie, was among these first students for study abroad in Salzburg under the Slippery Rock program. As so often was the case, Volkmar and Eva took us to the Pittsburgh Airport together with Mary for the trip with Henry's Cultural Studies Academy. We used the same system which Henry had been using ever since his program got started (1962) to house the students and faculty with different families in and around the Salzburg area. Our designated "homestay" was with the Graggaber family in Groedig, a small town just outside Salzburg. This family not only had a dairy farm (father and son) but took in tourists during the summers. We had a second-story room overlooking the main street in this little town with two beds, a small eating area, and bathroom. It proved to be an ideal setting for all three of us. Martin made friends with the Graggaber brothers, Helmut and Hermann, and often went with them and their father out into the hayfields on the hay wagon to bring in the hay. It proved to be a very auspicious time for Julie and me. We had time to ourselves which we used to full advantage. In fact, it was so successful we had another little boy that following spring! We had tried, unsuccessfully, to have more children, but it took the summer in Groedig to produce the result which both of us very much wanted.

After the eight weeks of classes, Julie, Martin, Mary, and Gaye (a friend of Mary's from Wisconsin) and I took a trip through Austria, Switzerland, and Southern Germany in the car I had rented. We then also visited our relatives in Vaihingen/Enz before returning to Munich for the flight back to Pittsburgh with Henry's group.

On the following May 10, 1970, Daniel F. Megnin was born in the Greenville Hospital, Greenville, Pennsylvania. With a new baby in the house, Julie had more than enough to do. She had to care for our baby, run our household, and take care of our garden. In spite of the work she had to do, she wanted us to go to Goshen that summer to show off the newest addition to our family. We visited Goshen and made the rounds of family and friends. We stayed with Grandfather Bert in the new house he and Grandmother Inez had purchased just a few months prior to her death on November 8, 1968. During the day, we visited family and friends. In the evenings we played cards with Grandfather Bert. Julie learned, once again, traveling with a baby is hard work.

During the following spring (1971), Dan was one year old. Grandfather Bert suggested it might be better if he came to visit us over Dan's birthday.

"I'll come and visit you, Julia," he said on the phone. "It's a lot easier for me to drive out to Pennsylvania than it is for you to come way out here."

"Okay, Dad. We'll expect you on the weekend of the eighth of May."

Bert King, second oldest son of a farmer in Southern Michigan, decided he didn't want to become a farmer. After high school, he enrolled in the Elkhart Business School which enabled him to become employed by a bank for a number of years during the 1920s. He married Halsie Simmons, a girl from Goshen, Indiana, and settled down to what he thought would be a lifetime of banking. He and Halsie had one son, Thomas O. King, who, at the age of four, was determined to have tuberculosis. It soon became apparent he had contracted it from his mother. While Tom was placed in a sanatorium for the next two years, his mother died soon after. Her early death left Bert King with a son to raise by himself. In the course of the next two years, he became acquainted with Inez Lehman, who was from an old, established family in Goshen. She was a kindergarten and first-grade teacher. She and Bert King were married on January 5, 1930. During the previous year and one-half, Tom had been discharged from the sanatorium and lived with his grandmother King and aunt Stella King, near the family farm in Michigan. After Bert and Inez were married, Tom returned home and was raised by his stepmother Inez. Before the year was up, the family was joined by a baby girl, Julia Mae King, born on November 1, 1930.

With the onset of the depression, Bert lost his banking job and became an independent insurance agent. He remained as an independent agent for the rest of his career, later being joined by his son, Tom, who went into the insurance business with him. Bert King was the father of my wife, Julia Mae (King) Megnin. In her professional career as an upper elementary teacher, she became known as Julie, which is the name I've called her ever since we met. To her mother, childhood friends, and Goshen neighbors, she was known as Judy.

We had a very good time together with Grandfather King at Dan's first birthday. We have a picture of his grandfather holding him out in our yard on the farm. Grandfather King spent almost two weeks with us during May of 1971. Since we had so many apple trees in our yard, he thought they needed to be trimmed in order to produce more apples over the summer. While I was teaching, he took my ladder, placed it against one apple tree after another, and literally cleaned them all out! That summer, these trees hadn't produced so many apples in years! What neither he nor we realized was the strenuous exercise was just too much for a man of seventy-six! Upon his return to Goshen, he had his first heart attack which placed him in the hospital. Since I was in India leading a group of teachers on a study program during the summer, Julie asked Liz Megnin to go with her, Martin, and Danny to Goshen to help celebrate Grandfather King's birthday on August 18. They had an enjoyable visit. After their return, he refused to limit his activities as his doctor advised. As a consequence, he had another more serious heart attack in late August and died in early September 1971.

As an assistant vice president for academic affairs and director of international education, I had written a grant proposal to the United States Department of Education requesting counterpart funds (Indian rupees) to take two groups of teachers (ten from Slippery Rock and ten from Clarion) to India for two months. The purpose was to expose American secondary school teachers and college professors to Indian society and culture through travel in India and hearing lectures conducted by Indian professors at various universities. The grant was funded, and from the third week of June until the third week of August, our groups traveled extensively throughout India. I took three faculty members from Slippery Rock with me: Narciso Gamberoni, professor of second education; Robert Davis, geography professor; and Clare Settlemire, professor of history. Unfortunately, we had some problems with Mohammad Iqbal Khan, professor of history and leader of the group of ten from Clarion. At each of our stops where the students were encouraged to buy books or items for display in their classes, Mohammad demanded a 10 percent gratuity be paid to him for bringing the teachers to the shop. He also demanded it from the travel agency, the hotels, or anyone else having to do with making the arrangements or in any way connected with our program. When Narciso and I made a formal complaint before the Clarion administrators that following fall, nothing was done about what we called the unscrupulous behavior of one of their faculty members!

After we bought a Cub Cadet tractor and mower from the Morrison Brothers International Harvester Agency in Seneca, Pennsylvania, Martin became our main operator. He mowed not only our yard inside our picket fence but also the adjacent end of the hayfield bordering our garden and backyard. It was a big yard and took him more than two hours to complete the job. We had set up a campfire near our backyard Northern Spy apple tree for hot dog and marshmallow roasts. The end of the mowed part behind the pigsty was used as our burning pile: newspapers, magazines, branches, and burnable trash were consigned to the weekly fires. The nonburnable items were hauled down and dumped into the pit where the Surrenas had had their coal mine entrance.

When Danny was about three years old, he wanted to see Martin mowing the grass. We walked out together, and while talking with Martin, Danny put his hand on the exhaust pipe! His screams reflected the serious burns he had suffered from touching the hot metal. We took him to the emergency of the Grove City hospital where the doctor smeared his hand with a salve, bandaged it, and told us not to let him try to take it off for the next week.

"After two weeks, take him to your doctor. It should be okay by then. Just be sure it's kept dry. Don't let him put it under water."

"Thank you very much, Doctor," we said and left. Two weeks later, we took Danny to Dr. Anderson Donan, our family doctor in Grove City.

"Have you been a good boy and kept your hand dry?" he asked Dan.

He nodded. Julie and I assured him he had kept it dry.

"Let's see what it looks like," he said as he unwrapped Danny's bandaged hand.

"It's coming along very nicely. I'm going to bandage it up again for another two weeks. It should be all healed by then. You're not going to touch the exhaust pipe again, are you, young man?"

Danny shook his head in agreement.

"The next time you come, it'll be all healed, Danny. It'll be as good as new."

We thanked Dr. Donan for his services, paid our bill, and returned to the farm.

Our farm became a favorite place for the two Megnin families to get together on Sunday afternoons during the summer and fall months. One of the real highlights was to go down to the woods or old coal mine shaft and have target practice with our twenty-twos and pistol. We could shoot directly into the hill with no fear that we would hit anyone nearby. There were plenty of targets available from the trash which we had dumped into it.

During the winters, the snow was often deep around the garage. I bought a blade for the front of the Cub Cadet. It worked very well in pushing the snow into large piles between the garage and house in the turnaround behind the garage. Martin and Dan enjoyed digging in the piles and making snowmen and snow caves. Since the driveway ended at the front of the garage, I decided it would be better to have a drive-through from the south end of the yard and exit on the north end in front of the house. It would be much safer since the northern end took the driver to the top of the hill instead of at the southern end, where the driver could not see the cars coming up over the hill from the north. I had the owner of a dump truck bring me a load of gravel and had him dump it gradually from the garage to the northern exit. Using our Cub Cadet with the snow blade, I was able to spread the surplus gravel over the grass so that we now had a semicircle driveway from one end of our yard to the other. It proved to be very helpful for guests also who could line their cars one after the other down the entire length of the driveway. If someone had to leave early, he/she simply pulled out of the line and drove over the grass to one of the exits.

With Pop's death in 1967, as I mentioned earlier, Mom came to Pennsylvania each winter. She sent most of the time with Volkmar and Eva's family and a few weeks with us. She seemed to enjoy these visits very much. She had her own bedroom since Martin and Danny shared one using the bunk bed in their bedroom. There was only one time when we had a problem during Mom's visit. She had gotten a dog to replace Max after he died. The new dog was a combination of a Labrador and beagle. Mom had named him Heine and brought him with her to our farm to spend a couple of weeks. The arrangement didn't work out very well. The boys and I had found a cluster of baby rabbits whose mother had evidently been killed on the road. I had constructed a rabbit hutch out of chicken wire and boards and placed them inside the garage thinking we could raise them until they could fend for themselves. They were sitting in the hutch out in the sunlight behind the house when I brought Mom and Heine to the farm. When Heine saw the rabbits, he immediately went after them. So long as they stayed in the center of the hutch, they were safe. As soon as they hopped to the side, Heine grabbed them through the chicken wire and wouldn't let go. I dragged him away, but as I did so, he almost pulled the leg off the little rabbit. As I tried to pull him away from the cage, he went after me. I let him have a stick across his head.

"Oh, Donald, you might hurt him! Don't hit him."

"To hell with him! Look what he's done to that little rabbit. It already has a broken leg!"

The leg hung and dangled through the chicken wire.

"If you think I'm going to let him kill our rabbits, then you've got another thought coming! That bastard is going to be tied up in Cinder's doghouse! He's not coming into this house!"

"But, Donald, he's only a young dog! He's been a very good watchdog for me!"

"I don't give a damn! He's not coming into our house! He's going to stay outside! Cinder stayed in her doghouse all winter! I don't see why your dog can't do the same!"

Needless to say, it was not a very good beginning for Mom's stay with us. After two weeks, Volkmar came and got her and Heine. They had dogs in their house all of the time. Heine made the adjustment fairly well with the change of venue. The rabbit whose leg had been broken, I killed. I set the other two free to fend for themselves. We never saw them again.

With the purchase of the back twenty acres, it gave us more than fifty acres of good farmland. I thought I should buy a tractor and farm equipment. If we couldn't rent the farm, I thought we should at least keep the fields mowed. The two ponies which the Cobbs put in our care on the farm kept our pastures in good shape. The little black pony had been given to Martin with the understanding that we would house both of them on our farm. We had a barn and pasture; the Cobbs did not. In talking it over, Julie agreed we should buy our own equipment and do limited farmwork should it become necessary.

Martin and I drove to Franklin to an International Harvester dealer who was interested in selling whatever used equipment he had sitting in his yard. We bought a model C Farmall, a two-bottomed plow, a mower, and a posthole digger which ran off the tractor's power take-off. The total cost came to seven hundred dollars. I thought it was a fabulous buy! The dealer delivered the tractor first and then the rest of the equipment that next week. We parked the equipment in the lower part of the barn in which Surrena had kept his cows and horses. We used the mower to keep the fields cut each summer. Martin used the tractor and plow on the field where the mine had been. It was the only time the plows were used. We did drive the tractor and posthole digger up to Jim Roberts's farm to drill the holes for a new fence he wanted to put in. Overall, the equipment sat mostly in the barn. We did use the tractor occasionally, to park our sailboat in the barn. It was easier to use for that purpose than the station wagon.

Julie has long been a very creative and active woman. She had set up a preschool program not only in India but also in Slippery Rock and formed the Wesley Cub Scout Den on the farm. She had eight young boys in weekly attendance. The meetings were held either in our basement or in our yard. The boys were all classmates of Martin in the Victory School, the local elementary for grades kindergarten through eighth grade. (It was the southernmost school in the Franklin Area School District.) Dan was too young to be a member of the Cub Scouts. He was, however, always at the meetings. He couldn't pronounce Cub Scouts. He called them "Scub Scouts."

Volkmar and his business partner, Pat Perry, owned not only the Perry-Megnin Cooperage Mill in Whitesburg, Pennsylvania, but also the Oldsmobile-Pontiac Car Agency in Clarion, Pennsylvania. The previous owner had retired, and Volk and Pat thought it was a good agency to own. For the next few years, we bought Oldsmobiles and Pontiacs at greatly reduced prices from their agency. Volkmar sold them to us at cost which amounted to a considerable saving for each vehicle. Our first purchase was a dark green Oldsmobile station wagon to replace our Chevrolet Malibu. The joint ownership between Volk and Pat lasted only about two years before Pat wanted to get out of the agency. Truman Mills, a resident of Clarion, bought out Pat's share and Volk and Truman renamed it, the Mills Olds-Pontiac Agency. It had been the Weaver Olds-Pontiac Agency for the previous thirty years. After a joint ownership of more than ten years, Truman bought out Volkmar's share of the agency.

Pat and Volkmar sold us two of their pickup trucks while we lived on the farm. The first one was a green Chevrolet with Perry-Megnin Cooperage Mills painted on the sides of the truck. Since I drove the station wagon back and forth to Slippery Rock, Julie ended up using the truck for her shopping trips and visits. She took Martin and some of his friends in the back of the truck to ball games or to visit back and forth. On one occasion, one of the neighbor boys fell out of the truck as she was about to drive out of his yard. He stood up just as she started driving the truck down the driveway. The boy, fortunately, fell into the grass and didn't seem to have hurt himself. Julie was concerned he might have been injured when she went to the door of his house.

"I'm sorry, Mrs. Gadsby, but your son fell out of the truck as I was starting up."

"That's okay, Mrs. Megnin. I don't think he hurt himself. I'll keep an eye on him."

Upon returning to the farm after shopping one afternoon, we noticed a series of survey stakes in the field directly behind our house. It was obvious someone had surveyed the field paralleling Route 8 which ran directly in front of our house. As soon as I could, I drove up to Franklin to the offices of the Venango County Highway Department to find out what these stakes represented.

I asked the clerk on duty, "I noticed a series of survey stakes in the field behind my house. Are you planning on putting something through my farm in Wesley?"

"We didn't do any surveying in Wesley. You better stop in the State Highway Department's Office."

He told me where it was. I went over to the state office.

The clerk asked, "Can I help you?"

"Yes. I noticed the field behind my house in Wesley has a series of survey stakes paralleling Route 8. Are you planning on doing some road construction on my farm?"

"Well, you'll have to talk with our supervisor. Let me check and see if he's busy."

"You can go in to see him."

The supervisor got up and shook hands with me as we introduced ourselves.

"I noticed a series of survey stakes in the field behind my house. Are you planning on building a new highway?" I asked.

"Actually, the State's interested in building a limited access highway to connect Franklin with Interstate 80. We're not sure yet where it's going to be located, but if you've seen some survey stakes, it could mean it's going through your farm."

"Would that mean our farm would be cut in half for this new highway?"

"It could, if it's ever completed."

"Are there any other plans for this new highway that hasn't been determined yet?"

"Here, let me show you what might happen to your farm."

He spread out a large map on his conference table of the Wesley-Barkeyville area.

"There will have to be an access route to allow cars and trucks to enter and exit Interstate 80 off this new Route 8. We're not sure yet if the current one is big enough for the volume of traffic which might occur on this new highway. We were thinking, perhaps your house and yard would be in the center of this new access and egress site, if we go ahead and build it."

"You mean you'll have to buy the house and buildings in order to construct such a route?"

"The State may have to, but at this point we really don't know if it's even going to occur. No money has been allocated for this project, so you don't have to worry about it immediately."

"But, you're telling me, if the State Highway Department decides this project is going to occur, then our yard and house will be right in the middle of a new access and egress site? Would that mean the State would have to buy our house and buildings to construct this new route?"

"As I said, the State may have to. But, at this point, we really don't know if it's even going to occur. No money has been allocated for this project, so you won't have to worry about it."

"But if the State Highway Department decides this project is going to occur, then the access and egress route would be within twelve feet of the northwest corner of our house?"

"That's what might happen. But again, we really don't know yet if it's even going to occur."

"Thanks for the information. How come no one even asked us if they could survey our farm?"

"I'm sure someone did, but if there was no one home, we had to go ahead and do the survey anyway."

We shook hands and I left. It did not seem like a very promising future to stay on the farm, I thought to myself. It reminded me of what had occurred on our farm in Upstate New York. Before Route 690 was built, the New York State Highway Department had also conducted a survey not only through Syracuse but as far east as the northern end of Route 5 at the four corners in Chittenango. The projection for the roadway was through our northern woodlot just north of our hayfields. When I walked around the farm one fall day, I discovered the survey stakes set approximately one hundred feet apart straight across our woodlot and across the Benson and Nesbitt farms as far as I could determine. No one had asked permission to conduct this survey either. Upon returning home, I asked Julie, "Guess what I've discovered about our farm?"

"What?"

"The survey stakes are the forerunners of a new highway that's going to be built connecting a new Route 8 with Interstate 80. Our house could be right in the middle of the access-egress circle with the road about twelve feet from the corner of our house!"

"It looks like we'll have to start looking for a new house again. We'd better get started before we have to move," Julie said. "I'd rather move at our own discretion than have to be out at a certain time."

"Yeah. I guess we better get started this next weekend."

We spent several weekends over the next three months looking at houses in Grove City, Slippery Rock, Franklin, and Butler. We decided we didn't want another farm. We had more than enough to do with this one and the one in New York. When Tom, Flora, Cindy, and Mike came over Christmas in 1972, we drove through Timberley Heights with them. We noticed a house with a for-sale sign in front of it. Julie copied down the number to call in case we wanted to look at it. After the Kings left that next day, Julie called and a Mrs. Pherson answered.

"We drove past your house yesterday and saw your for-sale sign in your front yard. Could we stop and take a look at your house sometime?"

"Certainly. When would you like to come?"

"Could we come tomorrow evening after supper around seven o'clock?"

"That would be okay with us," Mrs. Pherson said. "My husband may not be here. He's a doctor at the hospital, but I'd be glad to show you our house."

"Thank you. We'll be there around seven o'clock tomorrow evening."

Julie arranged to have Linda Smith come to babysit for us after supper. We drove down to Butler and wondered what the house would be like.

"We've looked at a lot of houses," Julie said. "We usually found something we didn't like. I wonder if this is going to be the same story again."

"We won't know until we've seen it, Julie. I wouldn't worry about it yet."

When we arrived, Mrs. Pherson greeted us at the door.

"Hi. We're the Megnins," I said. "This is Julie and I'm Don."

"Thank you for letting us look over your house, Mrs. Pherson," Julie added.

"Hello. I'm Ginny Pherson. Come in. You'll be the third couple that's looked at our house this week. We've only had it on the market for a little over a week. Evidently people are looking for houses here in Timberley Heights these days," she laughed. "My husband's a doctor and he wants more land out in the country. We haven't found anything yet, but we've been looking."

"That's interesting. We have a farm up near Barkeyville, but it's going to be cut up into a new highway and route access to Interstate 80 one of these days. We're also looking for some other place to live," Julie told her.

"As you can see, this is the entranceway into the house," Mrs. Pherson said as she led the way.

"Here's the coat closet." She opened the sliding doors. She then led us into the kitchen on our left. The combination living/dining room was straight ahead. She then took us down the hallway.

"Here's our linen closet." She slid the doors open. On the left was a bookshelf just before the first bedroom.

"This is our son's bedroom. He's thirteen."

We looked into the room. There was also a closet on the south wall which made the room project out into the hallway. That was the reason the bookshelf protruded into the hallway.

"This next bedroom is our daughter's. She's fifteen soon to be sixteen."

There was a walk-in closet on the northeast corner of the room with two rows of hanger space on each side of the entrance. Just across from the daughter's bedroom was another walk-in closet for the storage of larger items such as chairs, tables, lamps, etc.

"This is our master bedroom," Mrs. Pherson said. "It's not as large as we would like today, but it's served our purpose well since we built the house in 1965. John wants a bigger house. He thinks the children need more room. There's also a small semibathroom." She directed our attention to the sink and toilet just off the southwestern corner of the bedroom.

"We really should have made it into a full bathroom, but we didn't."

There was another walk-in closet similar to the one in their daughter's room.

"Let me show you the downstairs. We've finished part of it as a family room with another fireplace and bookshelves. If we were going to stay longer, we probably would have finished the rest of the downstairs. There's just an empty space there now."

Mrs. Pherson led us downstairs into the family room. The fireplace and the wood panelling on three of the walls were impressive. The northern side of the room was still an unfinished concrete block wall.

"Does the fireplace work, Mrs. Pherson?" I asked.

"It's supposed to. We've just had it finished, and since we don't have a grate for it yet, we haven't really tried it. The one upstairs works fine. We use it quite a lot in the winter."

She showed us the rest of the unfinished downstairs room, hallway, storage area under the stairs and the two-car garage.

"You certainly have a nice house, Mrs. Pherson," Julie told her. "Thank you for showing it to us. How much are you asking for it?"

"We're asking thirty-three thousand dollars. We'll be willing to carry the mortgage if the buyer can't raise the money," she concluded.

"Let us think it over," I said. "We'll let you know within a week, if that's all right with you and your husband."

"That should be all right with us. We've just started putting the house on the market. Let me have your telephone number in case something comes up if someone else is interested in buying it."

"Thank you very much, Mrs. Pherson, for showing us your house. Is there a yard that goes with it?" Julie asked.

"Yes, there is. It's too dark to see it now, but the lot is one-third of an acre and has lots of trees for shade even in the heat of the summer."

"In other words, there are a lot of leaves to rake up each fall," I laughed.

"That's true about almost everywhere in Timberley Heights. Oh, I forgot to mention. We also have a swimming area on the lake at the bottom of the ravine around which Timberley Heights is built. It's available to anyone living in Timberley, and the boys and girls love to go down there for swimming and picnics. At this time of the year, the kids go down there for ice-skating and hockey. It's a really nice place for young people here in our community."

"Thanks again, Mrs. Pherson," we both said. "We'll be in touch with you soon."

On our trip back to the farm, Julie said, "It looks like the ideal place for the boys to grow up, don't you think? It reminds me of how I felt as a little girl in Goshen. A nice community. Friendly people. Lots of things to do and a lot of other youngsters from what she was telling us. Would you be satisfied living in an upscale community like this?"

"Yes. I think I could get used to it. I've never lived in a community like this, Julie. But I can see how you'd feel right at home."

"It would be a really nice place to live. We have friends from Slippery Rock living in Butler. We shouldn't have much difficulty making the adjustment to another new house. We've already lived in three different houses plus traveling overseas. We should be able to make the adjustment once more, don't you think?" she asked, laughing.

"I'm sure we can."

VII.

Moving to Butler—Sabbatical Leave

After the school year ended in June 1974, we made our move to 127 Chippewa Drive, Timberley Heights, Butler, Pennsylvania 16001. It meant I had to resign from the Franklin Area School Board, arrange for a trucking firm from Grove City to take our furniture and other accessories to Butler, and wind down my position as the acting dean of the School of Social and Behavioral Sciences. Since I had been granted a sabbatical leave for one year, we also had to make plans for our stay in Germany for the next year. As a consequence of buying the house in Timberley, we had to find someone to rent both of our houses: in Wesley (the farmhouse) and in Timberley Heights. We advertised the farmhouse first. Three young men, who worked in Grove City, rented the farmhouse. It was the convenience of living only seven miles from work that appealed to them the most. We put another ad in the *Butler Eagle* for someone to rent our new house. We did include the proviso, however, that whoever rented it had to also look after our dog for the ensuing months. A newly hired director of PARC (Pennsylvania Association for Retarded Citizens) and his wife were willing to rent out house for the coming year from September to August of the next year.

Upon moving into our new home in Butler, one of the first things we had to do was build a doghouse for our German shepherd "Mackie." On the farm, she had stayed in the shed just behind my office. We decided to build her a doghouse in our backyard. We would then attach her, via her collar, to a suspension wire between two trees approximately fifty feet apart. This would give her an opportunity to run and also give her access to her house in inclement weather and winter whenever she wished.

Martin, Dan, and I went to the Butler lumberyard and purchased the requisite lumber, roofing, and straw for Mackie's doghouse. It only took a day to complete the job. Martin painted "Mackie" over the entranceway. The doghouse was three feet high, three feet wide, and three feet long. We put in plenty of straw so that she would be warm throughout the winter. We placed a pail of water next to the doghouse and a dog dish which we asked our new tenants to fill twice a day. Our tenants did an excellent job caring for Mackie. When they first encountered Mackie, she was very friendly and seemed to take to them right from the beginning. The running room on her chain allowed her to make her daily deposits on the extreme end of her run. By the time we returned that next year, there was very little of her daily deposits to remove. The snow and rain had largely dissipated them by the time we returned from Germany.

We had most of the summer to become accustomed to the Timberley house before we left. Julie and I occupied the master bedroom which the Phersons had used. Martin got the bedroom next to ours with the walk-in closet. Dan got the smaller bedroom just down the hallway from the living room. We had the rooms painted in the colors which the boys chose. They seemed to like the idea of each of them having his own room after sharing one on the farm. The chief attraction for them, however, was the family room in the basement. It was here that we set up the television. They spent a great deal of time watching their favorite programs (*Captain Kangaroo, The Brady Bunch,* and *Leave It to Beaver*).

By the end of August, we were ready to leave Butler for my first sabbatical leave. In all honesty, it was not a particularly "happy time" for any of us. Instead of being eager and enthusiastic about going to Germany for a year with its opportunity to visit our relatives and old friends, I looked on it as banishment from what I really wanted to do. I had not succeeded in becoming the full-time dean of the School of Social and Behavioral Sciences. Through the wise counsel of Al Watrel, president of Slippery Rock State College, and Jim Roberts, vice president for academic affairs, I was advised to apply for a sabbatical leave. "Just in case you don't get chosen to become the full-time dean" (Al Watrel). What I didn't know at the time was the search committee, which had been carefully selected by Jim Roberts and loaded with friends of mine, had decided there was so much animosity towards me; they didn't want me to have to contend with the rancor of chairmen with whom I had tangled that previous year. As Jud Hill told me years later, "You wouldn't have wanted the job, Don, if you knew how many were opposed to your selection! We felt we didn't want to put you through that kind of behavior from people who really didn't know you. That's why we voted for Tip McFadden to become the new dean. We wanted to spare you from having to work with people who didn't know you or like you like we did."

Julie didn't have the opportunity to become settled in our new home and community. Martin had to leave his neighborhood friends in Barkeyville and Franklin and had no opportunity to meet new ones yet in Butler. Dan was thrust into a completely new environment, which would have been bad enough in Butler, but in Germany he had to learn a new language virtually on his own in a German preschool where neither the teacher nor the pupils spoke English! In retrospect, I owe them an enormous apology and debt of gratitude for putting up with a despondent husband and father for their "year of exile" known as my first sabbatical leave!

Sabbatical leaves are primarily granted to faculty members to pursue travel, conduct research, establish contacts with universities overseas, and promote intellectual contacts and exchanges between the United States and other countries. The rational basis for my sabbatical was, therefore, to undertake a study of the reaction of German pupils to the concept of German reunification. Germany had been divided, at the Potsdam Conference in the summer of 1945, into four zones of occupation by the victorious Allies (the United States, the Soviet Union, Great Britain, and France). By 1949, a new West German government had been formed with the consolidation of the three western zones of occupation into the Federal Republic of West Germany. The Soviet Union retaliated by forming the German Democratic Republic in its eastern zone of occupation. The capital for West Germany was in Bonn. The capital for East Germany was in East Berlin (the prewar German capital had also been divided into four separate zones of occupation for each of these wartime Allies). The Soviet Union occupied the eastern part of Berlin and chose it for the capital of the GDR.

The subject of German reunification kept coming up at various times in my contacts not only with German family members (here and abroad) but also with our German friends. No one seemed to have much hope for such a prospect anytime in the near future. I wondered if that was the same sentiment among the wider German population. I thought by circulating questionnaires among West German pupils, I would be able to ascertain whether the German public at large believed such a prospect was possible. I, once again, turned to our old friend Walter Schaeffner to review what I had composed in my questionnaire in German to make sure it was of the standard and quality required for such an undertaking. I wanted to distribute it as widely as possible in as many West German (Laender) states as I could. Walter reviewed my questionnaire and suggested certain changes and corrections in the German text. But before we entered into any further discussion about the research project, we should understand what we had to do to get ready for a year's leave from Slippery Rock State College.

Julie, our sons, and I had to get everything ready for a year's leave living in Germany during the months of June and July 1974. We had to take enough clothes not only for the balance of the summer but for the winter as well. We wrote to Walter and Hannelore Schaeffner not only to check over my proposed questionnaire but also to ask if they would help us find an apartment for our year's sabbatical in the Radolfzell area. We had become acquainted with them through the Experiment-in-International Living program during the summer of 1962. Walter found an apartment for us at Herr and Frau Mayer's apartment house in Moeggingen, a suburb of Radolfzell. It was also within walking distance of the Shaeffners. The Mayers were longtime residents of the village. Josef Mayer was a carpenter by trade, and his wife, Rosa, was an excellent cook. They owned a two-story apartment house with five different apartments. She rented us the one on the eastern end of the second floor, adjoining a terrace. The terrace was a flat concrete roof over their garage. There were two bedrooms, a living room, kitchen, and bathroom in the apartment. The terrace was also convenient for Martin and Dan to play games outside.

Walter wrote us a letter not only with suggestions for the questionnaire but also to report on his apartment hunting in our behalf.

> Dear Donald and Julie:
>
> I've found an apartment for you and your sons not very far from where we live here in Meoggingen. The house is an apartment house owned by Herr und Frau Josef Meyer. She is willing to rent the two-bedroom apartment with a kitchen, living room, and bath for 300 German marks a month. There is also an adjoining terrace which you can use as well.
>
> I am also returning your questionnaire, Donald, on the topic of German reunification. I made a few changes, but overall it was well done. It should prove to be of interest to whomever it is distributed.
>
> Please let me know if this apartment is satisfactory so that Frau Meyer can reserve it for you and your family.
>
> With our very best wishes to you both and in anticipation of seeing you again, we remain your old friends,
>
> Walter and Hannelore Shaeffner

I wrote back and told them we would take it and were looking forward to seeing them again. I also wrote to our relatives in Vaihingen/Enz to tell them we were coming. We always stayed with Tante Luise whenever we visited Germany. She lived in the house her husband, Hermann Luipold, had built for her mother upon their return from Brazil in 1937. During the war, their home in Pirmasens had been destroyed in an Allied bombing raid. It was then that she and her three children had moved in with her mother in 1943. Following the death of her mother (my grandmother) in January of 1953, Tante Luise, together with my mother, Tante Lina, and Tante Maria, became the owners of their mother's house. Tante Luise let it be known that anytime any of her nieces or nephews wanted to come to Germany, they could always stay with her. That's what we did during the nineteen fifties, sixties, and seventies. Following Tante Luise's placement in a nursing home 1977, Liz (her youngest daughter) and her husband, Hans Grossmann, bought the house from Mom, Tante Lina, and Tante Maria. They carried on the tradition of welcoming their American relatives whenever they came to Germany during the nineteen eighties and nineties.

When we had completed all of the arrangements for the rental of our house in Butler, we packed our bags and purchased our airline tickets for Germany. We were finally ready to leave. Volkmar and Eva took us to the Pittsburgh Airport where we boarded an Allegheny Airlines plane for the JFK International Airport. Upon our arrival, there, my cousin Karl Fleckhammer met us and took us to their home in

Jamaica for dinner. Later that evening, Karl took us back to the airport to catch the KLM flight to Amsterdam. We arrived the next morning and bought train tickets for the trip to Stuttgart, Germany. Arriving late that same afternoon, we decided to spend the night in the Bahnhof Hotel. We decided to go on to Vaihingen/Enz that next morning rather than try to make connections that evening. Following breakfast in the Stuttgart Train Station, we took the train to Kleinglattbach, the nearest station to Vaihngen/Enz. I hired a taxi to take us the remaining two miles to my aunt's house. It was a joyous reunion for all of three of us (Julie, Martin, and me). Dan met his aunt and cousins for the first time. We then decided to stay over the weekend to rest and meet with all of the relatives.

On Monday morning, I walked down into town to the Bauer Car agency on Stuttgarter Strasse to see what they had available. I finally selected a blue Opel station wagon. There was enough room for our four suitcases in the back. Martin and Dan had the backseat to themselves. We spent a few days in Vaihingen/Enz and drove down to Moeggingen, a small village near Lake Constance where the Schaeffners lived and settled into the apartment Walter had secured for us. Our year's sabbatical had begun.

Walter had already talked with Dr. Bingeser, the principal of the Radolfzell Gymnasium, to alert him that an American pupil was going to enroll in his school. After settling in at the Mayers, we drove into Radolfzell to enroll Martin. As we came into the principal's office, Dr. Bingeser got up and shook hands with us.

"Sie sind Professor und Frau Megnin. Es freut mich sie koennen zo lernen. Und das ist Ihren Sohn, nicht wahr? Herr Schaeffner hat mir schon informiert das Sie vorbei kommen werden Ihren Sohn anzumelden." (You are Professor and Mrs. Megnin. I'm pleased to meet you. And this is your son, Martin, right? Mr. Schaeffner already informed me that you would be stopping by to register your son.)

In talking over what Martin had done so far in school, he suggested, "Es waer vielleicht besser wenn Martin im gleichen Klasse bleiben wuerde der schon gemacht hatte in Amerika. Es waere leichter fuer Ihm die Deutsche Sprache zu beherrschen mit die gleichen Klassen unterricht der schon gemacht hat. Er kann dann in die naechste Klasse gehen wenn er wieder in Amerika ist." (It would probably be better for Martin to stay in the same class he has just finished in America. It will be easier for him to learn German that way if he goes over the subjects he has already had. He can then go on to the next class when he returns to America.)

Dr. Bingeser went on to say the fifth-grade teacher also taught English. If Martin should have any problem understanding the subject matter in German, she could translate it for him into English. We agreed that would be best for him. I had been working with him for a few months so that he could learn German, but his grasp of it was very rudimentary.

He suggested when Martin came to school that next morning, he should check by his office. Dr. Bingeser would take him to his class and introduce him to his teacher.

"Ihren Sohn wird sehr behilflich sein in die englische unterricht. Die Schueller werden es schneller lernen wenn Sie es horen von Ihm wie Mann englische Woerter auspricht." (Your son will be very helpful in the English class. The pupils will learn how to speak it correctly more quickly when they hear him speak it.)

We thanked Dr. Bingeser for his assistance and shook hands with him before we left.

The school was more than four kilometers from where we lived. I drove him back and forth during the first two weeks. Frau Mayer suggested he could take the bus from in front of the grocery store in Moeggingen each morning and it would drop him off in front of the school. In retrospect, I'm still amazed we let him do that by himself. After another two weeks, Frau Mayer told us about a bicycle shop that had a used bicycle for sale.

"Herr Megnin, Ich glaube es waere gerade recht im groesse fuer Martin." (Mr. Megnin, I think the bicycle is just the right size for Martin.)

Julie, Martin, Danny, and I drove down to Radolfzell and found the shop she had mentioned. After talking with the owner, we agreed on the seventy-five marks price. Martin said to us, "Why don't I ride it back to Moeggingen? I can see how long it takes."

"Okay, but be careful, Martin," Julie instructed.

It was to be the first of many trips that he rode his bicycle back and forth to school, to his friends' homes, and to buy items in the local grocery store. He soon discovered the shortcut to school (going a less-traveled road) and thought he saved at least a kilometer by going on this shortcut. He made friends not only with boys in the city but also in our local village. Ralf Mayer, a boy in the seventh grade who also lived in Moeggingen, invited him to his home. Martin reciprocated in our behalf. His parents then also invited us to come to dinner at their home occasionally.

Enrolling Danny in Kindergarten was very difficult for him. Not only did none of the other pupils speak English, but his teacher, Frau Kubel, also spoke no English. While she was a very warmhearted and congenial young teacher, she was at a loss to know how to cope with this four-year-old who couldn't understand any of her directions.

"Frau Megnin, es waere gut wenn Sie bei Ihm bleiben wuerdest fuer einige Tagen bis er sich daran gewoehnt wird ohne Sie bei Ihm zu sein." (Mrs. Megnin, it would be best if you could stay with him for the first few days so that he gets familiar with our class and the boys and girls. He should be fine after that.)

It proved harder for Dan than we realized. Since he spoke no German, the boys and girls thought he was dumb when he didn't understand what they said to him. After a few days of sitting in the class with Danny, Frau Kubel told Julie, "Frau Megnin, Ich denke Sie brauchen jetzt nicht mehr jeden Tag mit Daniel im Klasse sitzen. Ich glaube er ist jetzt daran gewoent." (Mrs. Megnin, I don't think you need to sit with Daniel each day. I think he's adjusted to the routine.)

She told Julie a few days later, "Daniel sitzt an seinem Stuhl und schaut zu was die andere Kinder tun. Er nimmt nicht teil in dem was sie tun." (Daniel sits on his chair and watches what the other children are doing. He never takes part in any of their activities.)

By the end of the first month, Dan was beginning to use German words and began playing with the other children. He even preferred to walk home by himself over the hill behind the Mayers' garden. Looking out my study window, I often saw him sitting on a stump looking over the hillside and valley below before continuing his journey home.

It must have also have been a very lonely and hard time for Julie. She had left all of her friends and acquaintances behind. She had little or no contact with anyone in the community except for Frau Mayer and Hannelore Schaeffner. She walked down into the village to do her shopping for some groceries she needed. We usually did our weekly shopping in a big store in Radolfzell each Saturday. She had the job of making sure Martin kept up with his coronet playing each afternoon. She also had to settle arguments between Martin and Dan over who could play with which blocks and toys. She did write in her diary each day when she was alone. Frau Mayer's daughter, Ulrike, took the boys on outings along the Bodensee (Lake Constance), which provided her with some time alone. In contrast to my rather tolerant attitude toward the aberrations of the two boys, Julie imposed the discipline and administered the spankings when she thought they needed it. On one of our visits to the Chiemsee (Lake), she yelled at them to stop pestering each other or they were both going to get a spanking. When they did not heed her warning, she said, "Don! Stop the car!"

I did and she got in the backseat and spanked Martin on her lap.

"You'd better behave, Danny, or you're going to get the same! I don't want you constantly bothering Martin! Do you understand?"

They remained quiet the rest of the way home! I couldn't have done that. I just yelled at them when they misbehaved!

My research project entailed distributing questionnaires to German pupils in fifth, seventh, ninth, eleventh, and thirteenth grades in various Gymnasiums (university preparatory schools) to ascertain their disposition towards German reunification. I thought this subject was certainly talked about in their homes and would present an insight into the national disposition towards this national issue. As I had previously indicated, Walter Schaeffner was highly instrumental in making corrections and improvements in the questionnaire which I wanted to distribute. I contacted each of the Laender (state) education departments requesting permission to distribute the questionnaire at the convenience of the schools during the current school year. Four of the twelve West German state education departments agreed to participate. I distributed the forty-item questionnaire in the five grade levels in the states of Saarland, Rhineland-Pfalz, Baden-Wuerttemberg, and Berlin. It was only by accident that I was able to distribute the questionnaire in Berlin. Colonel Lee Hayden, his wife Sally, and children Debra and Lee Jr. had been posted to Berlin as a military officer in the American zone of occupation. In Julie's correspondence with Sally, she invited us to come to Berlin.

"Don, what would you think about taking a trip to Berlin to visit Sally and her family? It would give us an idea what the rest of Germany is like."

"That's a good idea. I could see if there would be any interest in distributing my questionnaire in Berlin."

While I had contacted each of the German state education ministries, not all of them replied. I thought a direct contact in the various ministries might be more effective. We drove to Berlin through the German Democratic Republic and noticed the conditions of the roads, houses, towns, and cities were poor. Houses were in disrepair. Tree shoots and plants were often part of the house gutters which sagged from their mountings, houses had not been painted since before the war, the factories belched smoke that discolored the communities downwind, and the smell of chemicals and other effluents were pronounced in each of the cities through which we drove. The really impressive sights were the vast fields of grain and other farm products which had been created through the farm collectivization established under the Communist regime. The farms reminded us of the vast grain fields which we had seen in our own Western states. The individual farms, which formerly had hedgerows, trees, and fences demarcating the individual farms, were now part of vast collective farms. The fences designating individual farms had been bulldozed and buried. Individual ownership had vanished. Farmers were now employees of the state with farming equipment similar to that of our largest farms in America. They were part of large-scale farming operations which none of them could have achieved by themselves.

We had been advised not to exceed the fifty-five-miles-per-hour speed limit. We noticed the Statspolizei (state police) were waiting in various roadside openings to arrest any speeders.

Arriving in Berlin, we drove to the address Sally had written to Julie. It proved to be the house of the former Nazi minister for information, Josef Goebbels. It was confiscated by the American military at the end of the war and used to house high-ranking American officers. It was a huge house on three floors in the elite section of the city which had been reserved for high-ranking Nazi party officials in the prewar days. We spent the weekend with them. While Martin and Dan rode Lee's bicycle, it gave Julie and Sally time to reconnect after several years in which they had not seen each other. I drove to the John F. Kennedy International School to talk with the principal about distributing my questionnaire in his school. He was accommodating and allowed me to leave the requisite number for each of the five classes. He also agreed to send them to me after they had been completed. The Berlin visit proved to be an enjoyable time for all of us. It was not long after our visit that we learned Sally and Lee were getting a divorce leaving Sally with the responsibility of raising Deborah and Lee Jr. on her own.

We returned to Moeggingen via the southern route through the GDR. We had entered West Berlin from Niedersaxon using the east-west Autobahn. It gave us a different view of East Germany, but the conditions, as described earlier, were much the same.

As a consequence of Martin attending the Radolfzell Gymnasium, he got acquainted with several of his classmates. They invited him to their homes. On family, in particular, was the Auer family. They also had two sons, Stephan and Daniel. Daniel became a good friend of Martin visiting back and forth. We also got acquainted with their parents and went on outings with them to different parts of the Lake Constance region. Paul was the principal of a Volksschule (lower elementary school). His cousin was a painter, and we bought an impressionistic painting of Lake Constance on one of our visits. We still have the painting hanging in our bedroom. It's a reminder of our time in this lower region of Germany across Lake Constance from Switzerland.

Another of our best friends during our stay in south Germany were Peter and Ursula Hartmann. Although German citizens, they lived in Kreuzlingen, Switzerland. He was a professor of linguistics at Konstanz University. He was also the president of the Konstanz Rotary Club during the 1974-75 year. Being a member of the Slippery Rock Rotary Club, I attended the weekly luncheons at the Konstanz Hotel. Peter invited us to come to their home for dinner and get-togethers on Sunday afternoons. They had two daughters who were students at the time, and while they were on vacation, we also met them. Dr. Hartmann had Mercedes toy cars which he let Martin and Danny play with while we were their guests. The boys were so fond of the cars he gave each one a toy car to take home with them. Professor Hartmann invited me to come to the university, not only to look over the institution, but also to meet some of his colleagues. One of the professors whom he introduced was Dr. Hans Lorenz, a political scientist who had spent a year at Dartmouth College as a Fulbright scholar a few years earlier. Subsequently, Dr. Lorenz invited us to come for Sunday dinner to meet his wife and children. They also lived in Kreuzlingen. Frau Lorenz was a Swiss citizen and an excellent cook. They had two little girls, one of whom was the same age as Danny. While the food was very good and we adults got along very well, the same could not be said about Danny and his age cohort. He kept taking her toys away from her and wouldn't let her play with them. He wanted to play with them himself. Usually, when were invited for dinner, we reciprocated. Julie decided it would not be a good idea to invite them to our apartment.

"If Danny is only going to torment the little girl by taking her toys away from her, think what he would do in our apartment!"

"Yeah, I guess you're right, Julie. There's no prospect of having them come to our place, if the kids can't get along with each other."

One of the real benefits of our contact with the Lorenzes, however, was the sabbatical leave which I had in 1982. I had written to the Political Science Department inquiring about the possibility of teaching for a semester. Hans Lorenz was the Chairman and invited me to come and teach American government for the fall semester.

"I'm sorry, but we won't be here in Konstanz ourselves during this time. I've been invited to teach for a year as a guest professor in the States myself. I've talked with my successor, and he thinks it would be an excellent idea."

One of the interesting experiences which we had was to observe the jealousy between Germans coming from different regions of the country. The old animosities of the non-Prussians disliking Prussians became paramount when we invited the Hartmanns to join us for dinner together with the Schaeffners (Peter Hartmann was from an old established Prussian family which had served in various governments under the kaisers). Walter Schaeffner, on the other hand, was from Baden (one of the southern-most German states). It proved to be a big mistake. Walter not only didn't like the Prussians, but resented anyone from the north coming into "our beautiful Lake Constance region."

It was hard enough for him to accept the Schwabens, who were also indigenous to south Germany, but anyone else should not be here!

"It's just too crowded with so many people coming into one of the most beautiful regions of Germany! Let them go somewhere else. There are simply too many people crowded into too little space!"

"So much for our attempt to have Germans from different regions of the country get to know and like each other!" Julie said after they had all gone home.

"It's just like in the States," I said. "People in Upstate New York don't like the downstaters, and the city New Yorkers don't like the upstaters!"

After spending several weeks and receiving no replies to my earlier letters to the various state education ministries, I decided to write them again. Towards the end of the year, from my letters to each of the eleven West German state education ministries, I received replies from Westphalen, Hessen, Niedersaxson, Hamburg, Bremen, Bavaria, and Schleswig-Holstein indicating they were not interested in participating. Their response was similar. "We have participated in several such questionnaires through the years. It takes time away from pupils which we feel is not warranted." Only Saarland, Rhineland Pfalz, Baden-Wuerttemberg, and Berlin indicated an interest in limited participation.

"Professor Megnin, if you will bring the questionnaires to our ministry, we will distribute them in a limited number of schools in each of the grades as you have requested."

As I have indicated, Berlin was the first state to do so in April, Saarland had completed their distribution in May, Rhineland Pfalz in June, and Baden-Wuerttemberg in July. I drove to each of these states and picked up the completed questionnaires and returned to Moeggingen. Fortunately for me, Herr Mayer constructed large wooden boxes in which I placed them for shipment back to Butler, Pennsylvania. There were over five thousand completed questionnaires which were far too many to try to take with us on the plane. For those who may be interested, the results were tabulated in a joint effort with Dr. George T. Force and was written up in an article which appeared in the *International Journal for Political Education* (1984) titled "German Youth and the Issue of Reunification: A Comparative Analysis of the Impact of the Educational System and the Family on Changing Perceptions of Reality."

One of the highlights of our stay "am Bodensee" was the visit of Mom, Volkmar, and Eva during June and July 1975. Hannelore Schaeffner had found them a place to stay in Moeggingen not far from where we were living. We not only toured the region around the lake but also took boat trips on it. We also visited all of Mom's relatives. We drove to Gerabronn to visit the Mayer family which still owned the farm Mom's grandparents had owned and which she often visited as a girl. We visited her cousin in Heilbronn, the Meyer-Koenig cousins in Stuttgart, including Werner, Anne-Marie, and their three daughters, the Otto-Meyer Koenigs in Messkirch, Frau Vogg and her daughter, Ulricke, her husband, Peter Dietrich, and their three children, Mom's sisters, Luise Luipold and Lina Bartholomae, Luise's daughter Marrianne and son Michael Roth, Luise's son Hermann and wife, Kuni, and their son Thomas Luipold and family in Muenchen, Liz and Hans Grossmann and their sons Martin and Matthias in Mom's hometown of Vaihingen/Enz. Wherever there was still someone whom she remembered, we paid them a visit.

Frau Mayer also related what it was like right after the war. She told us about the French troops that came as occupiers.

"Wir waren unter Fransaechen Besatzung kurz nach dem Krieg. Ich habe, glicklicherweise, Fransaesich in der Schule gelernt. Ich musste jeden Tag Kochen und putzen fuer zehen Officier die hier gewohnt haben. Es war nicht eine scheine Zeit fuer uns Deutsche!" (We were part of the French zone of occupation. Fortunately, I had studied French in school. I had to cook and clean up for ten officers who were living here. It was not a good time for us Germans.)

The Mayers took a real interest in Martin and Danny. Martin soon became the favorite of Frau Mayer. She invited him to come down to their apartment after school to watch television anytime he wished. Danny, on the other hand, came down occasionally. He preferred to spend his time with Herr Mayer in his workshop behind the house. Sipp (as his wife called him) and his hired man put in a new foundation for what was to become another apartment unit behind the existing one. Dan liked to walk in the wet concrete as it was being poured. On one occasion, Sipp literally had to lift him out of his boots in order to release him from the concrete. He then had to retrieve his boots.

The Mayers also had two German shepherd dogs in their kennel behind the house. They only came out when they were released by Herr or Frau Mayer. On one occasion, the dominant male forced his way past Frau Mayer and ran into the road chasing a car. Another car, going in the opposite direction, hit him, and he ended in the ditch. Rosa Mayer took him to the veterinarian to find out if he had any broken bones. He assured her he had only some bad bruises and a lacerated leg which would take some time to heal. As she put him back into the kennel yard, she spoke sorrowfully to him as if he were an ill child.

"Ja, Du armer Kerle! Haettest Du nitt in die Strasse gegangen, waerst Du jetz nitt wieder eingespert!" (You poor guy! If you hadn't run into the street, you wouldn't be locked up again!)

He must have had a more severe problem. His back didn't heal very easily. It took several more visits to the veterinarian before he could run again.

The Mayers also raised black and white Belgian rabbits in a hutch next to the dogs' kennel. Frau Mayer invited us to dinner one Sunday afternoon. After dinner, Martin complimented her on how good the chicken tasted. He had seconds; he liked it so much.

"Frau Mayer, diesen Huehner Fleisch war ausgezeichnet." (Mrs. Mayer, the chicken was outstanding!)

"Was fuer Huehner Fleisch, Martin? Du meinst diesen Hasse hat so gut geschmeckt?" (What chicken, Martin? Do you mean the rabbit tasted so good?)

I thought Martin was going to throw up! It hadn't occurred to him that the meat could be anything other than chicken! He was careful after that to ask what was being served before he ate anything at the Mayers' Sunday dinners!

By the end of July, school was over. Julie and I decided it was time for her and the boys to return to Butler. She had to enroll Martin and Dan in the Butler schools (Martin in junior high and Dan in kindergarten). She had worked with Martin all year on sixth-grade math so that he could enter junior high upon his return to Butler. The principal of the Center Township Elementary School, David Hillhouse, had told her before we left on the sabbatical, "Mrs. Megnin, be sure Martin keeps up with his sixth-grade math. He'll need that to enter junior high next year."

Since I still hadn't picked up all of my questionnaires and wouldn't be able to do so until the middle of August (the Vaihingen/Enz principal wanted to wait until the last day of class to distribute them to his classes), I drove Julie and the boys to Luxemburg to catch the Capitol Airlines flight back home. It had been a difficult year for all of us. We had had to get used to a lot of new experiences. For Martin and Dan, it was to use a new language. For all of us, we had to get used to a new community, neighbors, and making new friends almost on a daily basis initially. It was probably more difficult for Julie than it was for me. She had to adjust to an irascible husband who had a hard time getting over his disappointment in not becoming the dean of Social and Behavioral Sciences. She also had to adjust to using only German whenever she was outside of the apartment among our neighbors, family, and friends. Except for Walter Schaeffner, there was really no one else with whom we could converse in English if we had difficulty expressing ourselves in German. Peter Hartmann did have me give a speech to the Konstanz Rotary Club about my dissertation research on German economic assistance to India. I was able to give a reasonable presentation in German, it seems. The men seemed genuinely interested in finding out why the West German government had invested so much money in India.

I returned to the United States on the twentieth of August 1975, arriving in time to once again resume a full-time teaching schedule for the fall semester. Julie had registered Martin and Dan for school. They were then well on their way to becoming acquainted with our neighbors and the children down by the Timberley lake swimming area. Roy and Gerry Chuck lived next door on Chippewa Drive. They had two children: Diane, a student in high school, and Doug, one year ahead of Martin in middle school. The boys had also become acquainted with the Burtners, Borjas, Chens, and Shoemakers. Each family had one or more boys near the age of Martin and Dan and traveled on the school bus with them.

One of the first improvements we made on the house was to have a basketball backstop placed on the end of the house over the garage. Not only could our sons shoot baskets, but soon the neighbor boys joined in. The next year we had the driveway paved which made it even better to play half-court basketball in our yard.

Interestingly enough, both Mr. Hillhouse and Dr. Bingeser seemed to agree Martin should repeat the fifth grade in Germany. Learning to use German with material he's already had would be hard enough for him in the German school. With Julie's daily coaching in sixth-grade math in Germany, Martin made the transition into the Butler junior high much easier for him.

Living in Butler meant we had opportunities to participate in activities we did not have on the farm. Not only could Julie and I attend the monthly Butler Symphony Orchestra concerts from September through May, but Martin and Dan participated in baseball Little League and T-ball. Diane Chuck and Judy Wolfe were our babysitters when we attended adult functions. Roy Chuck, the manager of the Butler branch of Mellon Bank, was also an umpire for the Center Township Little League. He watched the boys play as a consequence of umpiring their games and noticed Martin was a very competent pitcher. He recommended Martin to his coach, Ken Kerner, as a good potential pitcher for his Little League team. Mr. Kerner gave him the opportunity to pitch, and he did so well. Martin continued as a pitcher not only in Little League but in the American Legion team in high school.

Dan was also a very good T-ball and Little League player. He hit home runs and was a good catcher and fielder in whatever position he played. We'll never forget the time Mr. Kerner, his coach, carried Dan into our house after having taken him to the doctor.

He rang the doorbell and Julie answered, "Hi, Mrs. Megnin. Dan had a collision with one of the posts in the outfield this afternoon. I've taken him to the doctor who says he's okay. He was just knocked out for a couple minutes."

"Come in. Is he okay or is there a danger he may have had a concussion?"

"The doctor thinks he may have had one. He said you should keep an eye on him for the rest of the day. Don't let him fall asleep, Mrs. Megnin. You should keep him awake until he goes to bed tonight."

Dan didn't seem too interested in baseball after his collision with the post. He lost interest in continuing to play the sport. He took up tennis instead and played on the varsity team during his high school career.

There was a large field directly behind our house which one of the neighbors kept mowed. Martin, Dan, and I used it for fielding practice. When the owner no longer kept it mowed, I mowed a small half-acre section just adjacent to our yard. We set up a volleyball court and horseshoes to play whenever friends or the Megnin family from Seneca came to visit us.

With so many trees in our backyard, Martin and Doug Chuck decided to build a tree house. While it was never completed, they did build a platform approximately fifteen feet off the ground. They also nailed a set of two-by-fours to the two trees to climb up to their platform. Having run out of lumber, neither Roy nor I was interested in funding any further additions to their project.

A colleague of mine, Sylvan Cohen, lived just down the street from us. Mohammad Akhtar, a psychology professor at Slippery Rock, lived on the opposite side of the valley from Chippewa Drive. Sy suggested, "Since we're all professors at Slippery Rock, why don't we alternate driving? I could drive one week, Mohammad the second week, and you could drive the third week. We could save gas that way."

"That's not a bad idea, Sy," I agreed. "Why don't you talk with Mohammad and see if he's agreeable."

We tried this alternation for a month, but I had to give it up. Since I was the advisor to CIRUNA (Council on International Relations and United Nations Affairs), I often had late-afternoon meetings with the officers to plan for upcoming events both locally and regionally. After a few late returns home, I sensed their displeasure.

"I guess there's no use in continuing the car pool, is there, Sy?"

"If you've got these late-afternoon meetings, Don, Mohammad and I better carpool alone."

I agreed. It didn't make much sense for them to wait each afternoon until I was ready to go home. Hence, Sy and Mohammad alternated driving by themselves. I didn't blame them. But I felt I had to continue with CIRUNA. It was an excellent way of not only participating in Model United Nations meetings in competition with other colleges and universities on a regional basis, but nationally as well. When Charles Hartwig (as my surrogate) accompanied our group to the National Model UN sessions at the United Nations in the spring of 1974, they won first place as the best-prepared country representative group at the conference. The weekly meetings were also an opportunity to get to know the students as individuals.

VIII.

Ventures into Politics

In early February 1976, our nephew, David Megnin, called to ask if I might be interested in running as a pledged delegate for Jimmy Carter in the upcoming primary election. David was an Armstrong County Democratic Party member at the time. He thought neighboring Butler County should also have someone running in behalf of the Democratic Georgia governor.

"Uncle Donald, how would you like to become a delegate for Jimmy Carter this year? He's a really progressive governor from Georgia, but he needs to have pledged delegates elected in the primary in his behalf. Would you be interested in running as a delegate to the Democratic National Convention supporting Jimmy Carter?"

"Wow. I've never given running for politics any thought, David. What makes you think I'd be elected to such a position?"

"We don't know, but we need delegates. A delegate simply represents one of the candidates in the primary. If you're elected as a pledged delegate for Jimmy Carter, you automatically will go to the Democratic National Convention and vote for Carter when the ballots are cast for the party's nominee. All we ask is that you stick with his candidacy for the first three ballots. If he's not elected by then, you can vote for whomever you please."

"What does it cost, David?"

"It's mostly a matter of time. It shouldn't cost you much. You'll have to make lots of appearances and speak for Jimmy Carter telling why you think he'd be the best candidate."

"Is there anyone else who's running as a delegate for Carter?"

"Yes. He's a student at Slippery Rock. His name is Jim Ross. He's the president of student government. He's a strong supporter of Carter. Maybe you can work out a combined schedule of appearances with him so that you can trade off which functions to attend. You don't have to be at each event if there are two of you supporting Carter."

"Let me think it over, David. How soon do you have to know?"

"Actually, I should know right away. Do you think you might be interested?"

"Well, I'm interested, but I want to find out something of where Carter stands on certain issues first."

"Do you mind if I put you down as a candidate? If you decide you don't want to, then I'll try and find someone else. Your name was suggested by one of your students."

"Okay. Let me think it over and talk with your aunt. If there's a problem, I'll have to back out."

"That's fine with me. If you have any questions, just give me a call."

And that's how I got my first taste of running for office. Jim Ross and I candidated together as much as possible. He had gotten some materials from the Carter Campaign Committee which he shared with me. It gave me an idea where Carter stood on some of the major issues of the day. A negotiated settlement of the Israeli-Arab Palestinian dispute, the right of choice on the part of women, support for the United Nations budget and peacekeeping efforts, a strong national defense against Soviet expansionism, removal of our warships from Southeast Asia, expansion of oil exploration in Alaska and offshore thereby lessening our dependence upon foreign oil, and keeping federal expenses under control with a line item veto by the president of all national budget items.

Jim and I spoke at least twice weekly. Usually our appearances were on weekends. We dovetailed our meetings with local candidates running for office. Renee Peritz, a fellow colleague in political science, ran as a delegate for Birch Bayh of Indiana. Our paths seldom seemed to cross. Very likely, the fact that Jim and I came out for each candidate's night helped to spread the word that Jimmy Carter had two supporters who were always on hand to pass out leaflets, bumper stickers, and buttons for Jimmy Carter. None of the other candidates had such support throughout the preprimary election period. Jim and I won over all of the other candidates. We were invited to attend the Democratic National Convention in Madison Square Garden during August 1976. I didn't see much of Jim at the convention. Our Pennsylvania delegation was headed by our Senator Wofford. I was chosen as one of his delegation whips. It was our task to make sure the delegates were seated for each of the votes on the rules, platform, order of presentation, and voting for our candidate, Jimmy Carter. It proved to be an interesting experience, but not one I want to repeat. Pete Flaherty, the Pittsburgh mayor, tried to have his name placed in nomination. It was my job to tell him the decision had already been made: the Pennsylvania Delegation was only to have Jimmy Carter's name placed in nomination for president of the United States. No local candidates' names were to be presented! He did not take too kindly to my advice. He had someone else place his name in nomination. His name was soundly rejected by the delegation chairman, Senator Wofford, and was not placed in nomination.

Needless to say, Jimmy Carter became our party's nominee. Upon our return to Butler County, it was expected that we would form local committees in support of our candidate. Jim Ross formed a local Carter Campaign Committee in Slippery Rock. I did the same in Butler. Gene Zarnick, his wife, and son Dave became three of the most loyal and supportive members of our Carter Campaign Committee. We hosted coffees, desserts, breakfasts, luncheons, and get-acquainted meetings with members of the Carter family dispatched to Pennsylvania to speak in behalf of Mr. Carter. Not only were his sons and their wives often in attendance, but Rosalynn Carter came as well! Julie and I would have hosted her as our houseguest were it not for the fact that Mom was staying with us at the time and we had no spare bedroom. Hence, the Zarnick family very graciously offered to host her overnight. As a consequence, the Zarnick family was invited to attend the inauguration of the president on January 20, 1977, in Washington, D.C.

My next attempt to enter the political arena was in 1978. Jack Arthurs, the local member of the Pennsylvania House of Representatives, chose not to stand for reelection. He wanted to retire. Members of Carter Campaign Committee said, "Don, why don't you run for this office? We need someone who listens to people to be our representative in Harrisburg."

Little did I know what I was getting into. I allowed myself the luxury of being pleased that my fellow party members thought to suggest I should be the party's candidate. What I didn't know were the names of the other candidates also seeking to win the primary in order to become the Democratic party's candidate in the fall election against the Republican candidate. Out of the six candidates running in the primary, I came in third. The winner was Joe Steightner, an old and established name in Butler. He won by a very handsome margin over the rest of us. To his credit, Joe defeated the Republican candidates for the next few years to continue as Butler's local representative in Harrisburg until he decided to retire from the House.

My last political venture was in 1990. I was asked by the local Democratic Party to run as their candidate against the incumbent Republican, Howard Fargo, for the Eighth State House District.

"If you'll be our candidate, Don, we won't run any other candidates in the primary. You'll only have to campaign for the fall election."

I accepted the party's invitation. As Julie and I discussed the prospects, she wisely said, "When the Democrats are making you their candidate against a long-term incumbent, you know what they're really saying, don't you?"

"They need a sacrificial lamb and I'm the one they've selected."

"Just so you know what you're getting into, that's all I'm saying."

Not only was it the wrong time, in the wrong place against the wrong candidate, but Julie had applied to go to China under the egis of the American Field Service Committee for two months. We had agreed if she were selected, I would go along. She was, indeed, selected and had arranged for me to accompany her to Kunming, China. With the primary a "no contest victory," I should have spent the rest of the spring and summer campaigning against my Republican opponent. As it was, from the end of June through the end of August, we had a fascinating time and experience living in a student dormitory at the Kunming Teachers College, Yunan, China. While it was a trip neither of us would have wanted to miss, it did mean we were not on hand to talk, campaign, knock on doors, and be present at the local county fairs to meet with potential voters. This is really the heart of a successful campaign. I did participate in the weekly "meet the candidates" meetings in September and October, but it was much too late to overcome the lead of my opponent. As Howard Fargo (the incumbent and my opponent) said in one of his speeches, "The difference between my opponent and me is like the story of the two men who were being chased by a bear. All I have to do is stay ahead of my opponent to keep from being eaten!" The one man thought to himself!

And *eaten* I was! I received 45 percent of the vote to the incumbent's 55 percent. The lack of time spent campaigning was an aspect I couldn't overcome. It was my last venture as a candidate for public office. I did serve on our local homeowners' association (Brae Burn) in Sugar Mill as vice president and then as president to complete my predecessor's term (he moved to Arizona). I was asked by Jane Patterson, a candidate selection committee woman to serve on the board of the Sugar Mill Country Club a year later. I asked one of the then current board members, "Don, how much time do you think you spent on the board's business each month?"

"Probably about twenty hours per week."

I declined the offer to become a candidate. He called me the next day and said, "I gave you the wrong information yesterday, Don. I meant twenty hours a month, not a week!"

IX.

Life's Changes

Mom moved from the New York farm to Seneca, Pennsylvania, in the fall of 1976. Taking care of the large house was getting to be more than she could do. She could hardly shovel the snow to the mail box in the winter, let alone shovel the snow from the driveway. Volkmar and Eva's neighbor, Ruth Schill, decided to remarry after her husband, Ray died. Since she was moving to the town from which her new husband came, she wanted to sell her house. Volk and Eva decided it would be the ideal place for Mom to stay in the winters or any other time she might chose to do so. Mom decided to take up their offer and moved to Seneca in October. It gave her her own place, but close enough to Volkmar's family to visit back and forth. She still spent a couple of weeks with us in Butler during the winter months, but it gave her a house of her own to use as long as she wished. The following spring she had the garden plowed behind the Seneca house so that she could plant her garden in the spring as she had always done on the farm. She helped with the baking and cooking in the Megnin households. She baked cookies, pies, and bread for several years on the farm even while Pop was still alive. In fact, he was her mix master (kneading the dough) from the time they gave up dairying (1953) until several months before his death in 1967.

During the winter of 1976-77, while Mom was living in Seneca, she got a call from her insurance agent, Tom Twitchell.

"Mrs. Megnin, this is Tom Twitchell. I've got some bad news for you."

"Hello, Mr. Twitchell. What is the bad news?"

"The back part of your house has fallen in from the weight of the snow. I'll send you a check for the damages, but I don't think you can use any part of the building to repair the damage. It's just broken up too much."

"Thank you very much, Mr. Twitchell. My sons will drive up this spring and see what can be done with it. Good-bye."

"Good-bye, Mrs. Megnin. If there's anything I can do in the meantime, just give me a call or have one of your sons call me."

During the Easter vacation, Volk, David, Bob, Martin, Dan, and I drove up to the farm to dismantle the caved-in structure.

"What a mess," I said as we looked over the ruins of the old house. "There's no sense trying to rebuild this section of it. The main part seems to be in good shape."

"Let's take it apart and burn what's not worth saving," Volk suggested.

"The beams may be usable," David said. "We can always set them aside in case you want to rebuild after we clean up."

We began to pile the roofing, broken boards, twisted joists, and bits and pieces of leftover debris in a huge pile in the garden behind the house. We had brought our hammers, pry bars, nail pullers, and gloves to clean up the mess.

"Hey, Dave, why don't you and Bob start the fire? It's going to take a long time to burn everything. We might better get started," Volk told his sons.

All five of us carried armload after armload out to throw on the fire. It was blazing to a height of several feet. We had to throw the broken boards and beams on the fire from a distance. It was too hot to stand next to it. While we were working on cleaning up the ruins, we heard a load crash in front of the house. We walked out to see what happened. There in the front of the driveway lay a huge dead buck. He must have been hit by a truck. He had an enormous wrack one of which had broken off.

"Let's drag him back to the fire," Volk said. "We'll burn him with the rest of the stuff. He should be gone by the time we're through."

Volk, Bob, and David dragged the deer to the burning pile. It took all five of us to lift him and throw him into the fire. By the time we had finished at 6:00 p.m., he was completely consumed along with the rest of the remains of the house. As a consequence of this cave-in and consuming fire, the original house had been reduced by seven rooms. Only the T remained running parallel with the road and was now reduced to thirteen rooms. The original structure (actually the part that had fallen in) was built in 1796. The T (the main part of the house as we knew it) was built by Ambrose Mabie in 1843. We have a lithograph of the house in its heyday made in 1873. It had been a unique and grand inn during the days of the stage coaches running on what is now Route 5 from Albany to Buffalo, New York, in the early 1800s.

Towards the end of June 1978, Mom noticed difficulty in keeping down food after eating. Eva took her to their doctor in Oil City who diagnosed it as some obstruction which seemed to be impeding digestion. He suggested he would have to operate on her stomach to find out what was causing the obstruction. He did the surgery in July. After surgery was over, the surgeon told Eva, "Mrs. Megnin, your mother-in-law has stomach cancer. It has metastasized so extensively, there's really nothing we can do to arrest the spread of the cancer. She may only have a few more months to live. The only thing we can do for her now is try to make her as comfortable as possible and try to minimize the pain. We'll keep her in the intensive care unit for a few days and see how she responds to the surgery."

"Thank you, Doctor. We were hoping it wouldn't be too serious. But it sounds as though she doesn't have long to live. We'll set up a hospital bed for her in the house and look after her when she comes home."

After a week in the intensive care unit, the ambulance took her to the Schill house next door. Eva decided it would be best for her to remain there. She would look after Mom sleeping in the bedroom next to hers. After more than a month of constant care, Inge decided she would come to help Eva during her vacation days. She and Eva traded off looking after Mom through the night. After Inge's days off were over, she called her office at the Upstate Medical Center in Syracuse to notify them she would not be coming back to work. She was going to stay and help take care of her mother.

Julie and I drove up from Butler to visit Mom almost daily. She gradually got weaker as the days dragged by. She slept most of the time. When she awoke at night, either Inge or Eva was there to provide for her needs. Her death was a long, slow, relentless struggle. They tried to give her what comfort they could knowing that Mom's time was limited. By the seventh of October 1978, having passed her seventy-ninth birthday on September 10, she died in her sleep.

Volk arranged for her body to be shipped to the Gang Funeral Home in Syracuse. We then drove up to Syracuse to pick out a coffin. She had indicated at Pop's funeral she did not wish to be cremated. I asked Alex Carmichel if he would conduct the funeral service for her. Mom had always liked Alex's sermons and had expressed the wish earlier that she would like to have him conduct her funeral. He very readily agreed. The service was held in the DeWitt Community Church sanctuary. We were all surprised how many people, both relatives and friends, attended the service. The man who rented the farm from Mom, Warner Durfee, was there. His father, Edson Durfee, had rented the farm from Pop. Now his grandson, Steven Durfee, is renting the farm from us.

When Pop died, Julie and I had bought six plots in the Woodlawn Cemetery. The first to make use of them was Pop. After his funeral, his name, date of birth, and death were carved into the granite. Of the other three plots, one was for Emilie Megnin, two for Frederick and Ingetraude Schoeck, and two for Donald F. and Julia K. Megnin. Thus far, only Mom's date of death has been added to the granite.

Julie started teaching in the Butler Area School District as a teacher of the gifted pupils in September 1978. Her assignment was to teach pupils in seven different schools throughout the district. It was an onerous task and one that kept her constantly on the move from one school to another. Dan was used to having her at home after he came home from school each day. He was now in third grade.

"Are you going to be home when I get off the bus, Mom?"

He told us he didn't feel safe coming into an empty house. He wanted to be sure there was someone at home when he got off the school bus. Julie and I talked it over.

"I don't think I can be home every day when Dan gets off the bus. It all depends on which school I'm in."

Fortunately, I was able to arrange my schedule so that I was always there when he arrived home.

Nineteen seventy-eight was also the year we bought our Mariner sailboat to use on nearby Lake Arthur. This is a three-thousand-acre lake constructed in Butler County to promote fishing, boating, swimming, and other activities for persons living in this Western Pennsylvania region. We rented a slip at the Lake Arthur Marina and went sailing on weekends as often as possible. Martin became quite proficient as the steersman. He enjoyed seeing how far he could make the boat lean without tipping it over. Needless to say, Julie and I had to remind him that we didn't want to get wet. We also didn't want to try to right an upside-down sailboat in the lake! He usually got the message, and as far as we know, he never tipped it over. When he and his cousin Mike King, however, went sailing on Lake Wawasee in Indiana one summer afternoon, they weren't so lucky. They finally got their Sunfish right side up and returned to the King dock. The only indication we had that it had turned upside down was the seaweed attached to the top of the mast! When his father asked Mike what happened, he confessed, "We let the wind control the boat, Dad. It was so strong, the boat tipped over."

We kept our boat in the barn in Wesley each winter. By the time Dan was in high school, he too became an avid sailor taking his friends along after school or on weekends.

Upon moving from Butler, years later, we had a sailboat shop sell it in our behalf. We no longer thought we would have any use for it. We've only gone sailing in California on Martin's sailboat at various times when we've been visiting him over the Christmas holidays.

In 1979, Julie and I decided it might be a good idea to buy a motor home. We thought it would be a good way to travel with the boys to different parts of the United States. We bought a twenty-eight-foot Coachman from a dealer in Meridian just west of Butler. It had room to sleep six persons, two up in the front over the driver and passenger seats, two bunks toward the rear, and two by folding down the dinner table into a double bed. It proved to be a very comfortable investment and provided us with transportation that summer on a three-week trip to the Midwest, the northern plains, the Rocky mountain states, the West Coast and the return to Butler. One of the highlights for me was to be able to drive to the top of the mountain where I was on lookout in the summer of 1952 (Camel's Hump). When I first went there, we could only reach it by foot or by horseback. There was now a fairly comfortable road which allowed vehicles to drive to the top.

We stayed at KOA campgrounds usually. These facilities offered all of the needed amenities: bathroom hookups, water, and electricity. We had, literally, all of the comforts of home plus places to play catch or the use of club houses for various games. In our travels with the Coachman, we visited the Kings at Lake Wawasee, Indiana; Phoebe Honnold on her farm in Paris, Illinois; the Badlands; cousins of Julie's, Mary Jane and Gene Baker in Woodland, California; and Annette Jensen in San Francisco, Death Valley; Bryce Canyon, the Grand Canyon; Donna and Karl Conley in Missouri. After these weeks underway, Martin and Dan were eager to return to Butler. After our last night in a KOA near St. Louis, Missouri, we made the rest of the trip home in one day.

X.

Our Involvement with Rotary International

In the fall of 1969, Joe Marks, the registrar at Slippery Rock State College, asked if I would be interested in joining the Slippery Rock Rotary Club. Since I had never been a member of an eleemosynary organization, I asked him what was included.

"You have to pay a yearly membership fee, plus pay for your weekly luncheon on Tuesdays, Don. There are other types of requests for funds throughout the year, but it's money well spent on worthwhile causes. You shouldn't have any problem moneywise other than what you prefer to spend. There is the Rotary Foundation which raises money to eliminate polio around the world that you can contribute to, but these types of expenses are tax-free contributions."

"Where do you meet?"

"We meet in the basement of Mellon Bank. Gary McDougal, the owner of the Camelot [restaurant] brings the food over each Tuesday noon. There are tables and chairs set up for our use. Why don't you come to our next meeting and see how you like it?"

"Okay, Joe. I'll be there on Tuesday."

And thus began our involvement with Rotary International on a very local Rotary Club visit. I knew most of the people in the club. They were either from the local community or from the college. The majority lived in Slippery Rock. Each Tuesday at noon, the president called the meeting to order. Everyone stood up, faced the flag, and recited the pledge of allegiance. The president then asked one of the members to give the blessing followed by everyone sitting down and having lunch served by Gary and one or two members of his staff. Around one o'clock, the president introduced the speaker of the day who spoke for twenty or thirty minutes followed by a question-and-answer period.

Upon joining, we had to choose which of the four areas of service we wished to support. Since I was the director of international education at the college, I chose International Service. The main thrust of this area was foreign exchanges, both student and adult. In 1973, Slippery Rock was one of six clubs in our district which participated in a young business and professional men's group exchange. As a consequence, Julie and I hosted Luipold von Klencke, the son of minor royalty from the German town of Hameln (home of the Pied Piper of Hamelin fame). Luipold owned a castle in Hamelin. Julie and I visited him and his wife, Elizabeth, and family during our trip to Germany in 1976. Since then, Luipold went on to complete his legal studies and has become a judge in Lower Saxony. His castle is an eighty-room edifice which now houses not only his family but several apartments, a museum of ancient and medieval arms, torture paraphernalia, and other weapons from earlier periods of warfare.

In 1976, under the leadership of Bill Blank, a past district governor of Rotary, Julie and I were asked to join a planning committee to recruit high school students from the district (then, 728, now 7280) to go to Germany for two months as chaperones. The following year a similar group of German students and chaperones would come to our district to live and interact with the family members of those who had taken part that previous year. The intent was to enrich cultural exchanges through living, traveling, and interacting with each other on a daily basis for two months. As members of the planning committee, it was taken for granted we would become part of the adult team to accompany the American students. Four other members of the committee were also expected to participate (which each of us did). With two young sons at home, we had to arrange for their care and supervision in our absence. We were very fortunate in having Anna Marie Bottachi, a high school senior living two houses from us, come and stay with Martin and Dan in our absence. If there was a problem Anna Marie couldn't handle, her mother was always available for counsel and assistance. We felt reassured the boys would be well cared for during our chaperoning of American students in Germany.

Since the exchange was with a sister district in northeast Germany, Julie and I stayed with Elsie and Hans Kosmieder in Bremen. They had a beautiful apartment on the top floor of a high-rise with a balcony overlooking the adjoining street and park. Hans was the vice president of the local Bundesbank. His wife, Elsie, was the official host for us and one of the cochairmen of the German exchange committee. She not only showed us around Bremen but also arranged for a bus trip for all of her students and guests to visit the West and East German border. It proved to be a sobering highlight for all of us. One of the West German Border Patrol officers explained the reason for the division of Germany into the Federal Republic of West Germany and the German Democratic Republic in the East. He explained the consequence of this division has resulted in an electrified fence, watchtowers, and armed guards patrolling the fence on the east side of the border. He pointed out the towers which we saw every three hundred feet along the border on the eastern side. Armed guards were watching us through their binoculars during the entire time we were on the border.

"This fence is part of the entire 845 miles which separates the two parts of our country. If you went the entire distance, you would find the exact same conditions. The East German regime does not want to lose any of its citizens. That's why the fence has been put up. Not so much to keep us from the West out, but to keep their East German residents in The GDR!"

"We really wonder how we'll ever get back together again," Elsie said. "We certainly don't want to ever become Communist! We just hope you Americans continue to be interested in our long-term security!"

The officer in charge of the tour nodded his head in agreement. We also saw American tanks and troops not far from the border which seemed to reassure Elsie of our determination to protect the West Germans from the eastern Communists.

One year later, Elsie was one of German chaperones escorting the German students coming to spend two months in our district in Western Pennsylvania. The highlight of the German students' visit was going to Washington, D.C. We toured not only the Congress, but the monuments, the White House, and the Smithsonian from front to back.

"It was one of the best trips we've ever had," several of the German students told us. We were pleased the excursion had gone so well. We kept in contact with Elsie for several years until her death in the early nineties.

During the 1979-80 Rotary year, Paul Rizza was president of the Slippery Rock Rotary Club. I was elected as vice president. Both Paul and I were members of the Slippery Rock faculty. He was the chairman of the Geography Department. It was also the first time one of our past presidents, Bradley Keith, was elected District 728's governor for the year. It meant our club had to act as the host for all of the member clubs in the annual district conference. Brad decided he wanted to hold his annual conference in West Middlesex, Pennsylvania. It was almost at the outer limits of our district not far from the Ohio state line. Surprisingly, the meetings went better than some of us expected. One of the major issues was whether or not to recruit women for membership in Rotary Clubs. Our district governor, Brad, was opposed to the idea.

"There are no women members in any Rotary Clubs around the world," he told our conference. "Rotary is essentially an organization for men in every country of the world."

Several of us members from the Slippery Rock Club were opposed to our governor's views. When the vote was taken to change the conference's bylaws to allow women to become members, it was overwhelmingly defeated. It was more than ten years before this anachronism was finally removed and women were allowed to become members of Rotary International. I had to admit, however, for all of my years of travel overseas, I had never met any women Rotarians.

In 1981, I was asked by the district governor if I would be willing to head a team of young business and professional men to participate in an exchange between our district and the Hyderabad District in Andra Pradesh, India. Since I had spent some time in India, Bill Blank, the chairman of our District Student Exchange Committee, had suggested I might be the person to head such a team.

The members were recruited by the various Rotary Clubs throughout the district. After a month's recruitment, six young men (under thirty-six) had been found who were willing and able to go to India for the eight-week exchange. We held weekly meetings during the fall of 1981 in different locations throughout the district to familiarize them with the history, customs, culture, and expectations of ambassadors of goodwill between our two Rotary districts. We were our district's counterpart to the group of young Indian business and professional men who had come to our district in the spring. As part of the exchange, we were to host and be hosted by the families of the same men who had been part of the Indian team. The member of the Indian team whom we hosted was a banker from Hyderabad. Different Clubs hosted these young men and had them give speeches, participate in club activities, and become part of the family where they were housed. We would then have the same experiences in India as our guests had had in our district.

Shortly after Christmas 1981, we met at the Pittsburgh Airport to catch the Allegheny Airlines plane from Pittsburgh to the JFK International Airport in New York. We then boarded a Swiss Air flight to Zurich, Switzerland, for our first overnight. We had a short bus trip around the city before continuing on to Athens, Greece. We again took a local tour bus to the acropolis, some ancient Greek outdoor theaters, the Parthenon, and the national museum before continuing on to Tel Aviv, Israel. Once again we hired a bus to take us to Jerusalem and to visit the historical sites en route. It was a very brief visit. We had to catch the next day's flight to New Delhi, India, on our way to Hyderabad. For those who had never been abroad or seen or experienced the nuances of life in third world countries, I shall never forget the words of Steve Hall, a young attorney from Sharon, Pennsylvania, who, upon landing at the New Delhi international Airport, asked

"Dr. Megnin, what's that smell?"

"As you can see, Steve," I said, "there are animals all over the airport. But it's not only the animals that make their contributions, human beings do too. If the workers have to relieve themselves, they do so wherever they can find a hidden spot."

"I don't know if I can get used to it. It almost makes me sick!"

"Well, Steve, I've got news for you. You'd better get used to it because wherever we go in India, you're going to find the same smells more or less. If you can't take it here at this international airport, then your only choice is to get back on the plane and return to the States! It's not likely to get any better!"

He didn't say anything. To his credit, he didn't allow himself to get sick to his stomach from the stench.

We boarded an Air India flight for the continuation to Hyderabad where we were met by our host families. These families were the same ones whose sons had lived in our district during their spring visit. Only the menfolk met us at the airport. We didn't meet the women of the households until after our arrival in their homes. The host families were middle-aged or older, I thought. There were no younger families who served as hosts for this exchange (in contrast to our district). Our hosts were the parents of the young men who had spent time with us in District 728. As guests of the clubs throughout the Hyderabad District, we were expected to give speeches on our line of work, where we came from, our hometowns and our families. Each of the officers of the host clubs introduced themselves. By the time we had given our presentations after dinner, it was late in the evening. Our hosts took us back to their homes, and the next day, we moved on to another club in the district. We were often placed in cars normally for five passengers. We gradually became accustomed to having as many as seven or eight crowding in. The roads were sometimes rather improvised or more like fields over which we bounced. Invariably, however, we were met by interesting and accommodating Rotary members. Whatever it took to make us feel at home was done in our behalf. Some of the homes where we stayed were lavishly built and adorned with expensive furniture, silverware, china, and refrigerators (usually placed in the living room to provide cold drinks). The toilets, however, were built for the squat method. It was a bit of an adaptation for most of our members to adjust to this unusual position! They had never done this before! Since I had often used the barn gutters for such purposes years ago, I had no difficulty making this adjustment. One house in which I stayed was indicative of the sanitation needs of most of the homes in the region. The interior of the house was of the latest design with flush toilets and running water throughout. As soon as we stepped out of the house, however, we were confronted with the wastes and water flowing by in the open ditches. Since more than forty-seven years have passed since that time, these problems have no doubt been rectified with modern sewage and water systems in the homes and cities of modern day-Indian Rotarians.

    In retrospect, as a member of this international organization, wherever I went, I attended Rotary meetings. It was an excellent way to meet local people in a variety of countries. Whenever we went overseas, we met men who had extensive contacts with government and business executives. For a professor conducting research in a variety of countries, such contacts were invaluable. Doors were opened which otherwise would have remained closed. Rotary, as an organization, has contributed enormously to the elimination of polio and malaria around the world through its fund-raising activities. It is now open to women, and many clubs have voted them into the presidency and boards of their clubs.

XI.

Highlights of the Eighties

In June 1981, Martin graduated from Butler High School. In the fall of the previous year, we had visited RIT (Rochester Institute of Technology) and Penn State University with him since he was trying to decide where he would like to go to college. Once he saw Penn State, he didn't wish to explore anymore. He made up his mind to enroll in the School of Agriculture as an agricultural engineer. He had thought of attending Penn State in the fall, but when he was offered early admission starting at the end of June, he enrolled. Two of Martin's good friends from high school also enrolled at that time. Butch Rittleman, Martin Rice, and Martin were not only classmates in high school but in college, and have remained friends ever since. We helped him move into a high-rise dormitory for that first year. He roomed with both boys during his career at Penn State.

Julie and I decided to give Martin our blue Toyota Celica for his transportation back and forth from Penn State to Butler. We bought a maroon Oldsmobile Starfire, which I used. Julie continued to use the Oldsmobile station wagon to haul her books and supplies from school to school as an itinerant teacher of the Butler Elementary gifted pupils.

During the summer of 1981, Martin Grossmann, the son of my cousin Liz and her husband, Hans, in Vaihingen/Enz came to spend a few weeks with us. While he was only seventeen, because of his height, he was often mistaken as an adult. One of his favorite avocations was singing and playing his guitar.

We drove our motor home to Arrowhead Campground in Myrtle Beach, South Carolina, and spent a month swimming, riding air mattresses on the surf, playing cards, and volleyball. It was a very enjoyable time for all of us even though Dan resented the fact that Martin got by as an adult to do adult things such as smoke and drink beer. Dan was only eleven and wasn't allowed into any of the bars.

In September 1982, I had another sabbatical leave to teach American government at Konstanz University. It was the result of the letter I had written to the dean of the School of Social Sciences earlier in the year requesting information of whether or not there would be any interest in such an arrangement. I received an immediate reply from Dr. Hans Lorenz, whom we had met during the 1974-75 sabbatical leave. He responded immediately and said he would make the local arrangements at the university for the fall semester. However, he apologized for not being on hand when we arrived in September.

"I shall be going on a Fulbright leave from Konstanz with my family to teach in America for the academic year 1982-83. I have completed my three years as dean, which all of the faculty members do on a rotational basis. My successor is pleased that we will have you as a faculty member of a semester. We try to obtain faculty from universities abroad as often as possible. We have your class in American government listed for the fall semester. We shall also rent an apartment for you within walking distance of the university at number 6 Werner Sombart Strasse so that you will not have to search for one upon your arrival."

Towards the end of August, I left for Germany to spend a few days in Vahingen/Enz with the Grossmann family and Marianne and Michael Roth. We visited Tante Luise in the nursing home where she had been living since 1977. It was to be the last time we saw her. She died within a week after Michael, Marianne, and I visited her. She did not seem to recognize any of us and even had a hard time accepting the food Michael was giving her during lunch in the nursing home. Julie and Dan arrived in time to attend her funeral on the fifteenth of September.

In preparation for the funeral, Liz arranged with Herr Bauer, the minister of the Vaihingen/Enz Evangelische Kirche, to conduct the service. When he called upon her at her home, she introduced me to him and invited me to the participate in the discussion of what should be included in the service.

"What particular scriptures would you like to have me read, Frau Grossmann?" he asked.

"The Twenty-third Psalm, selections from the book of John, and other psalms."

She then turned to me and asked, "Donald, what additional scriptures do you think would be good to use, since you were a minister too?"

She then turned to Herr Bauer and said, "Mein Vetter war auch Pfarrer ehe er Professor wurde. Er ist viel weiter gegangen als Sie, Herr Bauer!" (My cousin was also a minister before he became a professor. He went on much farther than you did, Herr Bauer!)

Herr Bauer laughed. Liz apologized. "What I meant was, he studied much longer than you did, Herr Bauer!"

Each time I saw Herr Bauer thereafter, he said, "Ah yes, you're the one who has gone on much farther than I," and we both laughed.

The service was conducted in the Vaihingen/Enz Friedhof Chapel followed by the burial in the plots which the Grossmanns had purchased. Among the relatives in attendance were Tante Lina, Marianne and Michael Roth, Hermann and Kuni, Thomas and Ursula Luipold, Renate and Dieter Kuckenberg, Eberhard Kuckenburg and his wife, the Luipold aunts and cousins, Liz, Hans, Martin, and Matthias Grossmann, Frau Fink and Giesela (Kuni's mother and sister) from Illingen, and the three of us from America. A few of Tante Luise's neighbors were also in attendance. It had been a hard life for Tante Luise. Not only had she gone to Brazil with her husband and brother-in-law (Friedrich Megnin) at a young age, but she also lost two infants while in Brazil, their home had been bombed and destroyed in Pirmasens during World War II, and her husband, Hermann Luipold, was killed during the German retreat from Leningrad in January 1945. She had struggled to make a living after the war sewing gloves for the local factory in Vaihingen/Enz plus having a small pension following the death of her husband.

We left shortly after dinner for Konstanz. Our Toyota station wagon, which we had purchased in Stuttgart with Michael's help, served us well during our stay. After our first overnight at number 6 Werner Sombart Strasse, Julie, Dan, and I drove over to the Wollmatingen Gesamtschule (comprehensive school) to enroll Dan in the seventh grade. His German was so good no one could tell he was an American. He had learned the language the "hard way" in the Moeggingen Kindergarten in 1974-75 when he was the only pupil who spoke no German!

The principal was very helpful. He placed him in the same class he would have been in at home. The Gesamtschule was an integrated school comprised of pupils who would go on to the university upon graduation, complete their high school diploma, and enter the work force or go on to a trade school. Whatever they could qualify for was open to them. Most of the schools in Germany were either college preparatory or trade schools. The Wollmatingen school was one of the newest types trying to integrate all three aspects of a public school system as we know it in the United States. Dan made the adjustment relatively quickly. He was also chosen to play on his class's basketball team which helped him gain acceptance and approval from the other pupils relatively quickly. We bought him a bicycle which he rode back and forth to school. There was only one day in which he had a bit of a scare. Someone had loosened his handlebars. Fortunately, he noticed it before he set out for home. He walked his bicycle back to our apartment where we tightened the handlebars up again. He didn't have any problems after that one incident.

Our apartment had two bedrooms: one upstairs and one downstairs. There was also a long counter in Dan's room which I used as a work area to prepare my lectures in German. I taught three days a week. I relied heavily on my German-English dictionary to translate some of the more difficult concepts into workable German. Even though all fifteen of the German students had studied English throughout their elementary, secondary, and college careers, it proved to be a trying experience for all of us. Especially for the professor. One of the students was a Turkish girl who had grown up in Germany. She seemed to grasp some of the concepts and ideas I was trying to convey more easily than her classmates. She often clarified what I was trying to say in better German than I was using! My Schwaebischen dialect often came through unintentionally, which the north German students didn't understand. Overall, I was very impressed with my students. There was only one student who received a B—for the course. The rest of the students had Bs or better for the semester.

Living so close to the university, I often walked back and forth along a path through the woods surrounding the campus. It rarely took more than fifteen minutes one way. I only drove when it rained or snowed. There was a huge three-story garage in which to put our cars in the inclement weather. It was still necessary to carry an umbrella for the walk from the garage to the classroom buildings.

On one of our first weekends in Konstanz, we decided to take a drive around the Bodensee (Lake Constance). As we came to the Swiss border, the German border police noticed I did not have a Konstanz sticker on my car license.

"What happened to your license sticker indicating you are now living in Konstanz?"

"What license sticker? I was just at the license bureau last week getting my new license!"

I knew when we moved from Vaihingen/Enz to Konstanz, we were obliged to get a new local plate and sticker indicating we were now local residents.

"Park your car over there by the office. We've got to check you out. You're not legally a resident without the Konstanz sticker on your license."

Needless to say, we were all upset with this interruption in our travel plans.

"What are we supposed to do in the meantime?" Julie asked the policeman.

"You can either stay in the car or go over there and do some shopping, but you can't go into Switzerland without the license sticker. The Swiss border guards won't let you in."

I followed the officer into the customs headquarters and was told to sit down. The policeman then explained to his commander we were trying to enter Switzerland when we weren't legally residents here in Konstanz!

"What I can't understand," he explained to his superior, "how he could have gotten by so long without anyone noticing it?"

The commander then asked me, "Where did you get your new license plate? It's no longer from Ludwigsburg, where you say you bought the car. You would have gotten it from here."

I explained I had gone to the local licensing bureau in Singen the same day we arrived in Konstanz. I then received the new Konstanz license plate which was on the car.

"But why didn't you get the sticker from the bureau at that time to put on your license plate?"

"I don't know. No one told me I needed another sticker on my plate after I bought it!"

"You do understand that you are not legally here in Konstanz without that sticker?"

"I didn't even know I didn't have one!" I said as indignantly as I could.

"Well, you're going to have to wait here until I get information about you from the State Police Authority in Stuttgart. I can't release you until we get to the bottom of this investigation."

I spent the next four hours in the border police office waiting to hear what my disposition was going to be for illegally having driven around with an invalid license plate! Fortunately, I got into an interesting conversation with one of the police officers who told me about his experiences in Russia during the war. I had just recently read an autobiography of an ex-German prisoner of war who spent ten years in Soviet captivity and was familiar with much of what he related. The conversation was not only interesting but seemed to parallel some of the experiences he had which were similar to that of the ex-prisoner of war. We also talked about what life was like after the war.

"The United States was an enormous help to us here in Germany. If it weren't for what you did for us, I don't think we'd be a democratic country at all!"

The border police commander returned and said, "Herr Megnin, evidently the license bureau didn't give you the right information. You were supposed to come back the next day to get a sticker. They were out of them when you were there. I'm sorry for the delay, but there's nothing more we can do about it now. You can't go through the Swiss border station without a valid car license. So you'll have to turn around and go back home. We're not going to arrest you because it was our mistake and not yours!"

It was a total of four hours during which time Julie, Dan, and I were separated. They had gone shopping, eaten lunch, had ice cream, and returned to the car just as I came out of the police station.

"Well, what happened?" Julie asked.

"It turns out I was supposed to come back to the license bureau the next day to get the sticker that's missing from our license plate. Since I don't recall having been told to do this, I didn't. We've been driving around illegally for the past week. I'll have to go back to the license bureau first thing Monday morning to get the sticker. The German border policeman says we can't enter Switzerland without it. The Swiss would turn us back as illegal aliens!"

I drove back to the license bureau Monday morning and got the required sticker. When I told the official what had happened at the border between Konstanz and Kreuzlingen, he said, "You should have known the sticker was required."

"Even though no one told me to come back because there weren't any?"

"I'm sure the official told you. You just don't remember."

During the fall vacation, we drove through Germany, Denmark, Sweden, and Norway. The weather was a bit cool, but sunny. We visited the homes of Hans Christian Anderson in Odense, Denmark, and that of Pier Gyient in Norway. The boat trip from Denmark to Sweden was relatively short. We continued via road and train across the Danish islands to the Swedish mainland. The trains and cars simply rolled on the ferry to connect with the Swedish railroad and roadway systems by crossing the narrow waterways among the islands separating the two countries. There were restaurants on board as well as small shops for the passengers who preferred to stay awake rather than sleep through the trip.

Upon our arrival in Sweden, we were as impressed with the beautiful farms in Sweden as we had been in Denmark. The farms reminded me of how similar they seemed to be with the types of family farms we had in the United States for their size and productivity.

The days were generally bright and sunny. The evenings came early. By four o'clock in the late afternoon, dusk was already falling. By five o'clock, it was dark and the streetlights were already on. We bought some beautiful Norwegian sweaters in our walks around the Norwegian capital. We thought a trip through the fjords would be one we should someday undertake.

Since we were on a limited-time basis (Dan had to return to school and I to teaching), we only had a week for a trip which should have been longer to really explore these delightful countries. We decided to take the overnight ferry from Oslo, Norway, to Frederikshavn, Denmark, rather than retrace the roads we had already covered. It's not a trip I would ever recommend to anyone who cannot take rough weather and even rougher seas! It was by far the worst boat trip we had ever taken! I had failed to take any Dramamine or seasickness pills with me. As soon as we hit the open water in the Skagerrak, I started vomiting. We had a cabin in the front of the ship with four bunks. Fortunately, there was also a washbasin, toilet, and water in the compartment. With the up-and-own motion of the ship, I couldn't stop vomiting. Dan soon followed, and even Julie, who had never gotten seasick on a boat before, began vomiting as well. We literally took turns at the toilet bowl! The ferry seemed to hit bottom each time it dipped following the passage of a huge wave in front of it. It literally felt as if we had struck rocks with each passing wave! We eventually arrived in Denmark that next morning. We could hardly wait for breakfast. We went into the first hotel we saw. It was a smorgasbord breakfast which allowed us to return several times to try something new in buffet style.

We then continued on to Konstanz arriving late Sunday afternoon. The next day, school and the university were again in session. We didn't have time to visit the relatives in Vaihingen/Enz.

Martin came to join us over the Christmas holidays. He was in his second year of a bachelor's degree in agricultural engineering. We spent Christmas with the Grossmann family in Vaihingen. Dan and Martin Grossmann played their trumpets as a duo. Dan was taking trumpet lessons in Konstanz just as Martin had done in 1974-75. We then followed up the Vaihingen trip with one to visit Henry and Linda Lenz's group skiing in the Obertauern Mountains of Austria. It was by far the best skiing we had ever experienced! The slopes were well above the tree line, so there was no danger of any collisions with a tree. The sun was bright and sunny from morning until late afternoon. Martin and Dan traversed most of the mountain trails in the area. Julie and I stayed closer to the lodge. Our bodies became tired much more quickly than those of Martin and Dan! While we had gone on family skiing trips to Peek'n Peak, the Laurel Mountains, Wing Hollow, Mt. Pleasant, and Seven Springs in Pennsylvania, we had also gone skiing on Gore Mountain in the New York Adirondacks. These were all fine ski areas, but none of them could match the mountain skiing we did in the Austrian Alps.

On January 15, 1983, Julie and Dan left Konstanz to return to Butler. I took them to the Frankfurt International Airport. I couldn't return until the semester was completed at the end of January. With the oncoming German elections in early March, I thought I would stay until the results were known. In the meantime, my cousin Bill Megnin, the son of Karl and Anne Megnin, called Volkmar to ask if he could borrow ten thousand dollars to help him over the loss of his disability payments until he found a new job. He had been told these payments were to end on the thirty-first of January 1983.

"I'll pay you back, Volk, in monthly payments as soon as I get another job."

"I'd be glad to do so, Billy, but I can't. We don't have any surplus that I can draw on. Maybe this spring when we start getting in more logs, I might be able to help you. But I really can't do it right now. I'm sorry, Billy."

"Okay. I just thought I'd ask."

Shortly thereafter, he loaded his father's army rifle which Pop had brought over with him from Germany in 1927. Billy had asked him, shortly before Pop died, if he could have his father's rifle since he used it as a German soldier in World War I. Pop gave it to Billy shortly before he died in 1967. Billy, evidently when no one was at home, went into the bathroom and pulled the trigger with the barrel just under his chin. He died instantly. Carol found him but could do nothing more for him. Julie called to tell me, "Don, your cousin Billy committed suicide. His funeral is this coming Monday. I can't leave on such short notice having just returned to teaching."

"I can't leave either, Julie. I have two more weeks of classes and then the final exam to give."

Volkmar and Eva attended Billy's funeral. While it was a tragedy for Billy's family, we decided we couldn't do more than send our profound regrets and sorrow at his death. He lies buried next to his parents in the White Chapel cemetery on Kinne Road in DeWitt.

With the final exam in American government completed at the end of January, I completed my stay at Konstanz University. I returned to Vaihingen/Enz to await the outcome of the German elections. The results in early March indicated the Green Party had gained enough votes to become a member of the German Bundestag (House) for the first time. The Christian Democrats, Social

Democrats, and Free Democrats continued to be elected. The Greens would not be strong enough to join a coalition government for another ten years. But at least this election had demonstrated what the future might hold for future German governments. The Greens were beginning to become recognized as responsible members of the parliament with whom to form coalition governments.

In the summer of 1983, it was the turn of Matthias Grossmann to come to the United States and spend a month with us. We did a repeat of the same motor home trip to the Lake Arrowhead Campground in Myrtle Beach, South Carolina. Our stay and beachside activities were the same we had done each summer. The difference this year was that Martin wanted to go with us. He drove the station wagon while Julie and I drove down in our motor home. Dan and Matthias rode with Martin. Once they reached our camping area, Dan and Matthias slept in the bunk beds while Martin put down the dinner table each evening to convert it into a bed. The motor home had all of the conveniences of home. We had a toilet, shower, refrigerator, stove, television, and air-conditioning. All we had to do was plug in our electric cord to the outlet on a post next to the motor home in the camp area which we rented. In the evenings, we played Monopoly or cards after the boys came back from the outdoor fun of surfing on our air mattresses, swimming, pitching horseshoes, or playing volleyball. Dan and Matthias were just two years apart in age. They got along much better together than Dan did with Matthias's older brother, Martin, two years earlier. We also played golf with Matthias. Martin and Dan had played it many times. It was a new experience for Matthias.

Martin finished his bachelor's degree and decided to stay on for a master's degree in agricultural engineering. He had been dating Jan Miller, a year behind him, at Penn State. She lived on a farm in central Pennsylvania. Her brother, Cory, was Martin's roommate and had introduced them. Martin and Jan traded visits between her family and ours for two years. When Martin graduated, we held a special dinner for Jan's family inviting Volkmar and Eva to join us at Penn State. When Jan came to Bob's farm on one occasion, we discovered she could throw hay bales around as well as Martin. When Jan graduated that next year, he helped her move into an apartment of her own. By then, however, the relationship was beginning to cool between them.

The Rotary Youth Exchanges between our District 728 and West Germany continued throughout the eighties. Brad and Donna Keith were the leaders of the high school pupils from our district who were going to the Bremen region in 1984. Dan went with the group. Brad was especially impressed that Dan could speak German. If he needed a translator, he felt he had one in his group. The following year, the German students came to the States. The family with whom Dan stayed was the Tontrop family. They had a son just one year older than Dan. Hence, the following year, 1985, Christoff was also our guest when it was Liz Grossmann's turn to visit us that summer. They accompanied us to Myrtle Beach. Dan called him Khrushchev because his name sounded so similar to that of the former Soviet premier. Christoff took it good-naturedly. Liz arrived in early July and stayed with us until the later part of August. One of her first local visits in Pennsylvania was with Volkmar, Eva, David, Cindy, and Emily, Bob, Judy and Matthew, Mary and Steve, Stevie, Christine, Catherine Forgenie, Elizabeth Megnin, and Kitty Smith with her son, Zachary. Inge Schoeck had driven down from Syracuse to meet Liz and to participate in the family picnic which Mary had arranged at Presque Isle State Park on Lake Erie. It was an excellent time for Liz to become acquainted or reacquainted with her American relatives.

After a weekend in Butler, we drove to Syracuse to visit Inge's family and to see the farm. En route, we stopped in Wesley to show her our Pennsylvania farm and where we used to live. She thought it was an ideal place to raise a family.

Since I had sold the New York farmhouse to Jeff Finch earlier that year, we rented a parking spot for our motor home in the Green Lake State Park Camping area. We drove out to the farm a few times. She wanted to see as much of it as possible. We took Liz for long walks down to the woods, the creek, the sawmill site, and to the top of the hill behind the old farmhouse. I shall never forget her amazement when she saw the New York farm spread out before her as she looked down from the top of the hill. As I pointed out the borders of the farm, she exclaimed, "Was? Diesen grossen Hof ist Deins?" (What? This large farm is yours?)

As we walked around some of the fields, she noticed many rocks had bits and pieces of fossils, seashell, calcified prehistoric quartz, and smaller stones of various shapes and sizes. She wondered why we didn't chisel these items out of the rocks since they were so unique.

"Aber Liss, es gibt thousande solche steiner ueber all auf diesem Hof. Es taet mehr Zeit versaemmen als es waere wert!" (But, Liz, there are thousands of such stones all over this farm. It would take more time than it's worth!)

She didn't say anything more. After some thought, she said, "Ich hab nur solche sachen in einen Museum gesehen, aber niemals aufs Land!" (I've only seen such things in a museum but never just out in an open field!)

On our trip to Myrtle Beach, I told her about the letters her mother had written to me and my parents after my abortive engagement to Hannelore Kuehner.

"Your mother suggested I should marry you. You would be of an age to marry and would be a very good wife for me. She wrote you knew how to cook, sew, and take care of a family. She wrote you had really been impressed with me when I was in Germany during the summer of 1956. I should be glad Fraeulein Kuehner had changed her mind!"

Liz was sitting in the back of our new Pontiac STE. Martin was driving the motor home with Dan and his friend from Germany, Christoff Tontrop. I couldn't gauge her body language or facial expressions. But she did seem to be genuinely amazed at what her mother had written.

"So that's why your father and mother came to Vaihingen in 1958! Your father was probably looking me over to see if I could become your wife!"

We all laughed.

"Your mother never told you she had written to me and my parents in 1957?"

"No. She never did. You would have made a good husband, Donald, but we are first cousins after all. I don't think that would have been a good idea. You wouldn't have gotten to know Julie if we had gotten married." We all laughed again.

"Well, I just thought you might be interested in what your mother proposed when you were still a teenager."

"Thanks for telling me, Donald. After my mother's fall down the cellar steps in 1977, I was never again able to talk with her about anything very long. She became so forgetful so quickly. Tante Lina never said anything to me either. So this is all new to me."

"At least you now know what your mother proposed in your behalf. I wrote her that I didn't think it was a good idea for two first cousins to get married. I never did hear from my parents what they found out from their trip to your home that year. The subject just sort of stopped being talked about any longer, as I recall. Your mother didn't answer my last letter, so I guess she must have gotten the message that I wasn't interested."

During the spring semester of 1986, I applied for a summer's Fulbright grant to Marburg University to study the current situation between East and West Germany. I was accepted and spent from the middle of June to the middle of August in Marburg. We lived in one of the dormitories about ten minutes from the classroom where the lectures were conducted by the German faculty. We also attended movies, held discussions, had field trips in and around Marburg, and an extensive bus trip into East Germany. Not only did we visit the major sites of interest in Berlin but in Weimar, Erfurt, and Thuringen. We visited the castle room in which Martin Luther wrote his ninety-five theses of objections to the claims of the indulgences of the Roman Catholic Church. The spot on the wall of his study was also shone to us. The guide claimed Luther had thrown his ink bottle against the devil who was tempting him. (The ink spot was supposedly still on the wall.)

One of the most interesting aspects of the seminar was getting acquainted with other participants. Professor John Nagle, from the Maxwell School at Syracuse University, was also in the group. My cousin Liz's husband, Hans Grossmann, had given me their car to use during my stay in Marburg. It allowed me not only to visit Vaihingen on a couple of weekends but also to drive to Frankfurt International Airport with John to pick up his wife, Ann. She came to spend a week with him. We ate breakfast and lunch together almost daily in the mensa. The evening meal had to be eaten "off campus." In other words, in the local restaurants scattered around the Marburg area.

As a consequence of going out with the Nagles and getting to know them better, I shall never forget the compliment Ann gave me. After telling them my life's story, she said, "Don, you can leave your slippers under my bed anytime!"

One of the most interesting sites we visited in East Berlin was the old Jewish cemetery. The gravestones of the 1800s and early 1900s had long been destroyed in the Nazi era. A few of the more ancient ones, hardly legible, were still visible along the outer wall of the cemetery. It was in process of being restored and used again by the local Jewish community. As our guide from Marburg pointed out, among the remains were men who were among the most highly decorated units in the German Imperial Army from World War I. These graves had been desecrated by the Nazis.

"The Balfour Declaration of 1917 was directly an attempt to influence the ten million Jews of the German and Austrian empires. The British government thought a promise to establish a Jewish homeland in the Middle East would influence Jewish soldiers serving in the armed forces of the German and Austro-Hungarian empires to be more favorable to an Allied victory than to a Central Powers victory. It didn't produce the desired effect. The Jews fought as gallantly for Germany and Austria as any other citizen of these empires."

The seminar gave me additional information useful for teaching my Elements of World Politics course. The integration of theory into practice has always been one of my major goals as a professor of international politics.

In the summer of 1987, I taught the Elements of World Politics course under Slippery Rock University's study abroad program at the Kando University in Budapest, Hungary. Since this was the first time a course had been taught in a Communist country, the requirement of ten class members was overlooked. Not only was Julie a member of the class, but other family members: Martin, Dan, Inge and Eva, were in the class. Roy MacPherson, from Pittsburgh, was the only nonfamily member. It proved to be an interesting summer's class. We stayed in a dormitory which also housed members of the Elder Hostel program organized by Professor Susie Kneierem, from the Physical Education Department at Slippery Rock. Each morning, Susie organized some physical exercises held on the rear porch and steps of the dormitory. The exercises were a series of stretching and conditioning feats such as standing first on one leg and then the other, deep knee bends, reaching for the sky, and running in place. We then ate breakfast together in the cafeteria. The food offered included oatmeal and bran flakes, red and green pepper slices, an occasional fruit (apple or plum), coffee, milk, and toast. We rarely had eggs or bacon. As Dan characterized the Elder Hostel Program because of the daily criticism voiced by the members, "the Hostel Elders," which did seem to express the outlook of many of the participants.

We had to take the city bus back and forth to the classroom building several blocks from our dormitory each morning and noon. Eva and Inge sometimes skipped the class, preferring to sleep in. Martin and Dan went out in the evenings and got back late. Martin was able to stay awake, but Dan slept through many of the classes. Surprisingly, he did well on his weekly exams.

Each evening, we went to Buda (the plateau half of Budapest) to eat at a different restaurant. The food was excellent, and there was usually a gypsy band playing at the same time. The spicy goulash was one of our favorites together with noodles, rice, or potatoes. The view from the parapet overlooking the Danube River and the Pest side, with its magnificent parliament building, was always impressive at night.

Budapest also had been one of the Roman frontier posts for a few hundred years. The ruins were well worth seeing both above ground and below. There were also Roman baths still being used by the local population. Our rides into the local countryside were also worthwhile. The enormous fields of sunflowers in full bloom on the collective farms were not only beautiful to see but also impressive for their size. Our local guide used a van to transport us around on these daily outings. He also took us to Lake Balaton, not far from Budapest. He arranged for whoever wished to sail could board a large yacht for a two-hour ride. Martin, Dan, Inge, and Eva decided to take advantage of the offer. Upon coming back to the beachfront where Julie and I were swimming, the passengers were expected to jump over the side and swim to shore. The four of them jumped over the side, but the water was deeper than Inge thought. She struggled to stay afloat. In order for her to reach the shore, Martin swam beside her and noticed she was having trouble swimming. He assisted her for about twenty feet until she could walk into the shore. Eva and Dan had no trouble since both of them were good swimmers. We spent the rest of the afternoon on the beach taking turns lying in the sun and swimming. Following the end of the course, we boarded a hydrofoil passenger boat for the trip to Vienna. The cruise was the first we had ever had on such a ship. The scenery was exceptional, and the opportunity to go up to the viewing deck added to the pleasure of viewing the towns and cities plus the countryside along the Hungarian and Austrian Danube borders. While Inge, Eva, Julie, and I visited the relatives in Munich (Hermann and Kuni) and Vahingen/Enz, Martin and Dan rented a car and drove to Zurich, Switzerland, to visit Dan's tennis team star at Butler High School, Ralf Kuenstler. After a short visit and tour of Zurich, they drove to the Vaihingen/Enz for a short stay before we all returned to Munich for the flight home to Pittsburgh.

In 1987 I was elected chairman of the Political Science Department. It was a matter of changing offices. I moved from one side of the large office space to the other. The room had originally been a classroom on the second floor of the World Culture building. When it was discovered there were too few faculty offices, classrooms were refitted to accommodate the need. In the case of political science, the classroom was divided into the chairman's office, a faculty member's office, and an office for the department secretary. I was the faculty member who now switched offices with the previous chairman, Rich Martin. One of the benefits of being so close for each of us was we only had to carry our books, files, and records a short distance.

As chairman, I taught two classes and had a half-time designation for administrative duties. Normally, the assignment for faculty was twelve hours of teaching each semester. I taught my Elements of World Politics in the World Culture auditorium and a seminar in international politics. Fortunately, I had a graduate assistant to keep track of the three hundred students in the auditorium. My lectures were on Tuesday and Thursday mornings. My assistant helped in passing out the exams and collecting them during the semester and keeping track of attendance. Of necessity, I had to use computer-designed and graded tests. I much preferred to give essay exams which I did in my other class. The essay exams were not only a good indicator of the student's grasp of the concepts and ideas of the subject, but also gave them an opportunity to work on their writing skills. I discovered some interesting anomalies among my students. Some of my best classroom discussants who also did well on their objective-type tests were often unable to formulate coherent sentences in their essay exams. I strongly encouraged one of my best students to take a writing workshop class in order to graduate with the grades he deserved rather than what he would have received had he not had his writing skills improved.

In our weekly departmental meetings, which Dean Charles Zuzack held in his office, no one was designated to take notes. I took it upon myself to keep the notes of the weekly meetings and distributed them to my colleagues the following day. I only learned much later the dean really didn't want any notes taken during the meetings. Why he never told me not to take them, I never did find out. I took it for granted notes were to be taken by someone. When I worked as an assistant vice president for academic affairs in our weekly staff meetings, the vice president always asked someone to take notes. They were then distributed among the participants. I couldn't imagine not taking notes in such an administrative environment! It was only after my term was up that my predecessor, Rich Martin, told me the dean didn't want any notes taken during the meeting. It was a way for some information to be discussed which the dean thought shouldn't be made public.

Dan attended Butler High School as did Martin earlier. His interest in sports turned to tennis. In junior high we took him to the Lakeview Racket Club (south of Butler) for tennis lessons. He not only liked the sport but became quite proficient in it. He was recruited for the Butler High School Tennis Team and played weekly during the season. One of the stars of the team, as I mentioned earlier, was Ralf Kuenstler, from Zurich, Switzerland.

As a junior in high school, Dan wanted to visit various universities before sending out his applications for admission. Since Julie and I had both attended Boston University, we thought he should visit there as well as Tufts, which was one of the preferred schools Dan wanted to consider. Following the visit to Boston University, we thought we would introduce Dan to Professor Harrell Beck, the Old

Testament scholar in the School of Theology. Professor Beck was very gracious and said Dan could come and visit him and his wife as often as he wished when he entered the university.

Our visit at Tufts was for an orientation session for potential students. We were not only shown around the campus but also attended a briefing from the enrollment staff of what courses students were expected to take, where they would live, and what types of majors were available. Dan seemed so suitably impressed with both universities he decided to apply for admission. We had also taken him to Syracuse University after the New England visitations in case his choice of either of the other two failed to materialize. As it turned out, he was put on the wait list by both Boston and Tufts universities. Hence, he was not only accepted by Syracuse University, but we helped him move into Watson dormitory on University Place in late August 1988. He decided to choose a dual major of international relations and German. To my pleasant surprise, Dr. John Nagle, in the Maxwell School, whom I had first met in Marburg, Germany, became his advisor.

After Martin completed his master's degree in 1988, he began to look for employment using his agricultural engineering as the means to apply to farm implement companies. In each case he was told, check with us later. At present we have enough staff. He applied to other companies and was hired, beginning on August 1, 1988, by the Texaco Research Laboratory in Beacon, New York. One of his fellow engineers was from Delaware University. Her field was chemical engineering. The Pennsylvania romance with Jan faded as he became better acquainted with Lynne Boyle. He brought her to Butler on various weekends and gave us an opportunity to become acquainted with her. He also introduced her to his uncle Volkmar, aunt Eva, and his cousins and their families. We also took a trip to New York City during the Easter recess with them in 1989 to take in a Broadway show. It was clear to us Martin was interested in more than an acquaintanceship with Lynne Boyle.

During the summer of 1989, I was selected by the international education director, Stan Kendjiorski, to teach for a third time in the Salzburg Summer Studies program. My course was again the same one I had taught in Budapest, Hungary, Elements of World Politics. For the first time, Volkmar and Eva signed up to participate along with their grandson, Stevie Forgenie. We also had Julie as a student along with her cousin's wife, Phoebe Honnold, and her friend from Madison, Wisconsin. It was the first time Volkmar participated. Eva's enthusiasm from her Hungarian experience must have convinced him to take part in our next overseas class. It also gave them an opportunity to help their fifteen-year-old grandson make the trip and become part of the Salzburg experience which his mother, Mary Forgenie, had enjoyed in the 1969 Salzburg class. Our classroom discussions ranged far and wide but at least opened the door to considering some of the key issues which nation-states encounter in different parts of the world. I ended up teaching a noncredit course. The answers on the tests were interesting but did not meet the standard for receiving credit for a course successfully completed.

We all stayed at the same hotel, Gold Fasan, Henry and Linda Lenz used for their Cultural Studies Academy. It was approximately twenty blocks from the school where the classes were held. We enjoyed the daily breakfasts of simmel (hard rolls), butter, jelly, and coffee. The rolls were outstanding, and we sometimes took a couple from the bread basket of a neighboring table. We also had our daily dinner there, but we were left to our own devices for the evening meal. There were many different restaurants in the area from which to choose.

Henry arranged for bus trips to the local sites including the salt mines, lakeside villages, and ancient burial sites. One of the most interesting was to visit the caves in which the dried bones of persons who had died hundreds of years ago were kept. Skulls, arms and legs, rib cages, plus a miscellany of odds and ends which had become detached from the original skeleton to which they had once been connected. On one of our afternoon outings, a woman and her-five-year-old son were sitting in the second seats on the bus. The woman asked the driver to stop so that her son could get off and throw up. Volkmar helped the little boy clean up after vomiting and suggested to the mother, "Why don't you and your son sit in the front seat and my wife and I will sit behind you? He's not as likely to get motion sickness if he can see directly out the front window of the bus."

"Thank you very much. I'm sure it'll help him to look directly out of the window."

Volkmar and Eva gave up their front seats, and the little boy had no further difficulty from getting motion sickness.

After the classes ended, we rented a car and drove to Munich to visit Hermann and Kuni. We then went on to visit Mom's cousin Frau Vogg and her daughter, Ulricke, and her husband, Peter Dietrich, and their three children in Heidelberg. After dinner at the Dietrichs, Ulrike took us on a tour of the Heidelberg Castle and community before we drove on to Vaihingen/Enz to stay with our cousin Liz and her family. Volkmar, Eva, and Stevie stayed in the Post Hotel, just about three blocks from the Grossmanns. Julie and I stayed in the little upstairs bedroom which we had used ever since our first visit at Tante Luise's in 1962. As Liz told us, "Das kleine Stieble ist immer bereit fuer Euch. Wenn Ihr nach Vaihingen kommen, wissen Ihr wo Ihr wohnen koennen." (The little room is always available for your use. Whenever you come to Vaihingen, you know where you can live.)

It was the first time Volkmar had been to Vaihingen since the end of World War II. Liz was just four years old when he saw her for the first time. As Volk told her, "Wir sind ein bissen elder gewoten seit dem." (We've gotten a little older since then.) We all laughed. We had all gotten older. Liz had had three boys the oldest of whom had died at age three. Volkmar and Eva had five children. Julie and I had two boys. Indeed, time had intervened. The destruction and scope of the war of 1939-45 had been overcome. Germany was soon to be reunited and the Soviet Union was coming to a rapid end.

XII.

Highlights of the Early Nineties

In the course of my teaching career, I often came across students who were having financial difficulties. One student from West Africa was short on funds. A geography professor, Bill Martin, asked me, "Don, one of my African students is having problems registering. He's having financial difficulties. Could you pay his tuition this semester?"

"I'd like to meet him, Bill. I've heard his name, but I've not met him."

"Okay. I'll go down to my office and get him."

Bill walked downstairs to his office on the first floor of the World Culture building. He came up shortly thereafter and introduced him to me.

"Dr. Megnin, this is Winston Smith. He's the student I asked if you could help with his tuition this semester."

"Hello, Winston. Where are you from?"

"I'm from Sierra Leone. My major is geography. I'm having difficulty with the transfer of funds from my family. I don't know what the trouble is, but as soon as I graduate and get a job, Dr. Megnin, I'll pay you back."

"What semester are you in, Winston?"

"This is my first semester of my senior year. I should graduate next May."

"I'll pay your tuition, Winston. You can pay me back whenever you can."

"Thank you, Dr. Megnin."

Another student who graduated from Slippery Rock who had been active in Ciruna was David Musila. He was an excellent student from Kenya. Upon graduation, he told me he had been accepted into the graduate program at the University of New Mexico.

"Why do you want to go to New Mexico, David? There are plenty of graduate schools here in the East."

"I'm being given a scholarship, Dr. Megnin. Could you help pay for my expenses in driving out to Albuquerque until I receive money from my family? My uncle hasn't sent me any money yet for this next year and I'm really short of money for gas and hotels."

"I really don't think you're going to like it out there, David. Why don't you apply for a graduate school here in the East. It would be a lot cheaper just in transportation to say nothing about getting used to an entirely different environment."

"I haven't received any offers of assistance anywhere else, Dr. Megnin. The University of New Mexico has agreed to give me a tuition, room, and board scholarship for the year. I've not had any similar offers from any schools here on the East Coast."

I reluctantly wrote a check for two hundred dollars for him to cash.

"I hope, for your sake, you're not disappointed in this decision, David."

At the end of his first semester, David returned. I was surprised to see him as he came into my office.

"What are you doing here, David? Aren't you staying for the whole year in Albuquerque?"

I didn't feel comfortable there. I felt uneasy most of the time. Neither the students nor the faculty were very friendly. It's not at all like here at Slippery Rock! I did well this past semester, but I didn't want to stay there any longer."

"What do you propose to do?" I asked.

"I was accepted at Indiana University of Pennsylvania. I thought maybe I could go there for the master's program in international relations."

"You say you were accepted?"

"Yes. But there was no money available for scholarships when I applied. That's why I went to New Mexico."

"Let me call a friend of mine at Indiana. I'll see what's available for this next semester."

I called Bob Morris, my counterpart in international education and asked the status of David's application this past semester.

"He can come, Don. He's been accepted in our program, but there's no more money available for a scholarship. If he had come this past semester and demonstrated he could do the work, we might have been able to help him this semester. But since he didn't accept our admission, his application was set aside."

I asked Bob what the tuition cost would be. I decided I would write David another check to take with him to Indiana for the spring semester. It took him two more semesters (with another grant from me) in addition to his one semester at New Mexico before he completed his master's degree. By the time I retired from Slippery Rock, he was interested in going to Howard University for a doctorate.

"Dr. Megnin, could you help me with money to go to Howard University?"

"David, at this point in my life, I don't think I can make any further commitments. Why don't you go to Howard and make some contacts with their faculty? They may be in a position to help you. I don't think I can afford to pay for your doctoral program."

Martin and Lynne had gotten very well acquainted following their chance meeting at the Texaco Research Laboratory. She was a chemical engineer and he was an engineer testing the performance of the oils used in different types of engines. As time went on, the romance blossomed into a full-fledged pledge of marriage. During the 1989 and 1990 vacation periods, either we visited them in Poughkeepsie or they came to Butler. By the spring of 1990, Martin and Lynne had decided to get married. They came to visit us at Easter time and announced their engagement.

"Mom and Dad, Lynne and I have an announcement to make. We've decided to get married this fall!"

Both Julie and I were overjoyed by the prospect of a wedding. We hugged and kissed them.

"Have you set the date?" Julie asked.

"Yes, we have, Mom. You don't mind my calling you Mom, do you?" Lynne asked Julie.

"Not at all. I've never had a daughter. I'd be pleased if you called me Mom."

"We've set the date for September 29. I've already checked with our priest and the church will be available in Newark, Delaware. That's my hometown. I was wondering if you could give me your address list for all of your relatives and friends who might want to come to our wedding."

It was at this point that I made a very poorly phrased comment to Lynne. "Lynne, Julie doesn't want to lose her list of addresses for her relatives and friends. Just be sure that you send the address book back to her when you've finished."

She didn't say anything. She took the list from Julie, sat down at the kitchen table, and for the next hour copied the names and addresses of all of our friends and relatives!

"Lynne, I didn't mean you had to copy them all down now! I just wanted to be sure the list was returned to her!"

"That's all right, Dad. I don't want you to lose the list. I'll copy them down right now."

It was not my intent to have her do it then and there! I was only trying to emphasize how important these names and addresses were and that we didn't want them to be lost! It was an example of my subconscious fear intruding into what I thought was part of our conversation!

In 1989, we concluded a contract with the Adobe Coal Company to strip-mine our farm in Wesley. The company was marketing its coal in Cleveland, and since we were just off Interstate 80, the company was trying to engage as many local acres as possible. We were amazed how deep the strip-mining operation went. The trucks were switchbacking more than seventy-five feet to the bottom where the shovel filled their bins for shipment to Cleveland. The company sent us a monthly accounting of the tonnage and subsequent check for the royalties at two dollars twenty-five cents a ton. It was a very beneficial account which we used in paying our numerous bills and gratuities. The farm now has a large pond of a few acres in size behind where the barn had been before it was destroyed in a fire. There is also another pond on the northern end of the hill down which we used to toboggan. There is still a large quantity of coal in the ground which was not strip-mined. The Adobe Coal Company quit its operations in Wesley because of the high sulphur content in the coal. The Cleveland Power Company no longer wanted to use it because of the environmental damage resulting from burning such coal.

During the spring of 1990, Julie had applied through the American Field Service to join a group of thirty educators to travel to China for a six-week exchange in order to learn something of the Chinese language, customs, and culture in Kunming, China. While her way was paid, I had to pay my own way. We joined the group headed by an educator from Washington, D.C., for a brief orientation prior to boarding the plane for China. At our brief stopover in Hong Kong, the director asked, "Who would mind going on ahead to Kunming to make sure everything is ready for our group's arrival?"

Since I had been in Hong Kong on a couple of occasions and had seen the sights, Julie and I volunteered. Upon arrival in Kunming, we were taken to the hostel (formerly a hotel) for students of the Kunming University's School of Education. It was about two blocks from the college where our classes would be held. Our group was to be distributed on the top two floors of the hostel. Each room had a dresser, bed, bathroom, and view out to the street. There was also a large dining room set aside for all of the students. Our group had a small alcove with just enough room for all of us to have our meals served. Our meals were termed "Western" and were different from the fare eaten by the Chinese students. Our breakfasts were usually eggs and toast, fruit and coffee. The dinners were soup, some kind of fruit, rice, or noodles with a variety of meat products accompanied by hot tea. The suppers were a variety of sandwiches, tea, and some kind of dessert. We couldn't help but notice our meals seemed of much better quality than that eaten by the students. Their meals were buffet style, not served as ours was. We had the main dishes placed on the tables so that we could help ourselves to second helpings. The Chinese students did not.

The classes were interesting and the lectures were well done by the Chinese staff. We even learned a few Chinese phrases and words which we still use today in a Chinese setting. We walked back and forth between the college and the hostel. There was a small shop on the main floor of the hostel just inside the door where persons could buy sodas, peanuts, candy bars, etc. The mode of transportation into the downtown areas of Kunming were by city bus. These were usually very crowded. Members of our group rented bicycles from the hostel to pedal back and forth to the downtown area.

The building construction was remarkable. Huge hotels and office buildings were being constructed using bamboo scaffolding from the ground to the top of fifteen to twenty stories above the street. We were really amazed how the Chinese construction workers could negotiate these narrow bamboo rails and not fall. It was my assumption that the death rate among the workers would be rather high although I had never seen any statistics among construction workers anywhere, let alone China.

One of the most interesting side trips upon which our Chinese instructors took us was a bus trip over the old Burma Road from the World War II era. It connected China with India as the only overland means of shipping supplies to Chinese forces fighting the Japanese invaders. We stopped occasionally to look down the steep mountainsides to see the wrecks of trucks that had slid off the narrow road during one of the monsoon rainstorms. As our hosts told us, "There were probably as many trucks that didn't make it to China as there were those that did! It wasn't only the narrow roadway and the storms, but the trucks were also subjected to attacks by Japanese fighter planes. Once they were hit and burned, they could only be pushed over the side to get them out of the way for the next trucks coming through."

It was an interesting comment from the followers of Mao Zedong who lamented the losses incurred by the Chinese nationalists in their fight against the Japanese aggressors. Nationality seemed to override political identity.

Another of the spectacular outings that we had was to visit an ancient shrine on top of a mountainside. If we did not hug the cliffside of the trail leading to the top of the mountain, there was a drop-off more than one thousand feet! Needless to say, whenever we met someone coming down the mountain, we kept close to the inside of the trail and waited for them to pass! The scenery was breathtaking. The fields below were visible for miles in which we saw nothing more than rice growing and here and there and the farmers' huts.

There was also one other sight which was one of the most unique we had ever seen. It was called "the Stone Forest." It is an immense outcropping of limestone rocks with pointed shapes giving the impression of trees and animals from a distance. It was only when we were actually on the site that we saw them not as living trees but as rocks and stone columns giving the appearance of millions of trees and animals. It was necessary for our group to stay close together lest a person get lost in the myriad channels, twists, and turns of the alleyways coursing through the rocks!

One other unique feature of our stay in Kunming was to be hosted by faculty members of the teachers' college. The woman of the family where we were hosted was the assistant dean of the college. She, her husband, and their two sons lived in a two-bedroom apartment near the Yunnan University. Madame Fang prepared a sumptuous dinner of *joasa* dumplings, egg *fu yung*, a vegetable salad, and tea. It was an excellent meal! We then played bridge with her and her husband (also a faculty member). I'm sure he was disappointed he had to play with such bridge novices! Bridge is not our favorite card game!

We did notice, however, that both the toilet and bathing facilities were just down the hall from their apartment. These facilities had to be shared with other residents on the same floor. There was a faucet in the kitchen for cold water and a gas stove heated the water as needed for cooking. If a member of the family wished to take a bath in the apartment, it was necessary to turn on the gas burner to heat the water prior to using the zinc tub. I couldn't help but remember we had similar facilities on our farm during the nineteen twenties, thirties, and early forties! The only difference was our bathroom facilities were an outhouse, water pumped at the well, carried in a pail, and then dumped into a zinc tub. Instead of gas in those days, we had a woodstove to heat the water! But that was more than sixty years ago.

Mrs. Fang was a very gracious hostess and had cooked an excellent meal. We couldn't help but feel sorry for her and her family having to live in these conditions! Needless to say, Julie and I were enthralled by our first visit to China. We planned to return at some future date.

Martin and Lynne made all of the plans for their wedding that spring and summer. The invitations were sent out. Following the rehearsal and subsequent dinner on the Friday night before the wedding, the ceremony took place at Lynne's church at 2:00 p.m., September 29, 1990. I was asked by the priest at the rehearsal, "Professor Megnin, would you like to give the homily at Lynne and Martin's service tomorrow?"

"Yes. I think I would like to do that."

Subsequently, following the rehearsal dinner on the twenty-eighth, I wrote the homily that evening and next morning.

Dan was Martin's best man. Lynne's sister, Barbie, was maid of honor. It was a very joyous occasion and conducted in the Catholic tradition. Following the dinner/dance reception and toasts proposed by Dan and Barbie, Martin and Lynne spent the night in the Christiana Resort prior to their honeymoon trip to St. Thomas and St. Croix islands in the Caribbean for a week. Upon their return, they moved into an apartment in Poughkeepsie. We all felt the marriage was off to a great start.

Over the next three years, we traded visitations back and forth. Lynne and Martin had joined the Texaco softball league early in their joint employment, playing ball each spring and summer. Julie and I enjoyed watching them play when we visited them. We even saw Martin hit a home run at one of the games and made some spectacular outfield catches.

The High Commission of the European Union advertised its Educational Program for Scholars interested in understanding the structure and work of the union as it was expanding its membership across Europe. The course of study would be for three weeks at the University of Maastricht, the Netherlands, from December 27, 1991, to January 10, 1992. Since my professional interest had always been studying and observing the growth and development of the European Union, I talked with Rich Martin, the political science chairman, about participating in the program.

"Don, why don't you talk to Chuck Zuzack to see if there would be funds available for you to go? I think it's an excellent idea, especially since you want to develop a course to teach on the European Union in the next couple of semesters."

"Thanks, Rich. Since you're in support of my interest, I'll talk to Chuck about it."

I went over to the dean's office, and after giving him a brief resume of what I proposed to do, he said, "That's an excellent idea, Don. I'll make some funds available for you to participate. I think Chuck Foust might even kick in some funds [Dr. Foust was the vice president for academic affairs). I'll see him tomorrow and let you know what he might be able to do."

The next day Dean Zuzack called and told me, "Don, you're all set. Chuck and I will cover all of your costs for the study program in Maastricht. He agrees it's an outstanding opportunity for anyone interested in learning more about the European Union."

During the rest of the year, I read as much as possible about the growth and development of the union. After Christmas, I left for the Netherlands and became a participant in the seminar. We stayed in one of the dormitories on campus and had not only our lectures, but our meals there as well. The professors were from the Netherlands, Belgium, and Germany. The lectures filled in the details of why, how, and what the future held for the expansion of the European Union not only in its growth but in its daily operations as a viable political community. As one of the speakers said, "It will be generations away from the coordination of governing functions such as that of a nation-state, but it does hold the promise to become the most integrated series of states that we have ever seen. We are setting the example of integrating different customs, cultures, and peoples into a community of which they feel themselves a vital part even though they may speak different languages and have had a different set of historical experiences which have differentiated them from their European neighbors."

Part of the experience we had also included visits to the European Commission Headquarters, the European Parliament, and the European Court of Justice. It was most helpful in preparing me to teach the growth and development of this new political example of how the world community may one day become more integrated and responsive to the needs of peoples around the world.

With the collapse of the Berlin wall and the German Democratic Republic in 1989, Liz Grossmann suggested in a telephone call, "Donald, why don't you and Julie come over this summer [1991] when we're not teaching, and we'll visit Hans's family in East Germany? You haven't been there, and it would be the perfect time to see what life is like over there."

"Let us talk it over, Liz, and we'll let you know."

Julie and I talked it over, and we both agreed it would be an excellent idea. Dan was again working for the second summer for the Pennsylvania Department of Highways trying to earn some money for his college expenses. We left him in charge not only for his dog but also for mowing the grass and keeping track of what was going on in Butler.

We left towards the end of June. After arriving in Vaihingen/Enz, we stayed with the Grossmanns and used the little upstairs bedroom (Stieble) for a few days before setting out with Liz for Leipzig. Our first stop was to visit Georg and Baerbel Grossmann. Georg was Hans's next oldest brother (there were four). Georg had been a physical education professor at the University of Leipzig for over twenty years and accompanied the East German ski teams to the winter Olympics for several years. As a Communist Party member, he had lost his position with the demise of the Communist regime. Party members were not permitted to continue in their previous positions as government employees. Subsequently, he worked at a resort owned by a friend near the Czech border. His wife continued to teach since she was not a party member. We also visited Hans's other brothers, Eberhard and Walter, and his aunt. The contrast with West Germany was dramatic! Buildings, other than those built and used by the East Germany Government, were old and dilapidated and badly in need of repair. The same applied to the roads throughout the countryside. The same huge collective farms that we had seen earlier in 1962 and 1975 were the mode of organization and use. The hedgerows, so prominent in West Germany separating individual farms, were no longer there. The fields were vast and similar to our ranches in the western part of the United States. Collectivization was complete, and the reclaiming of individual farms had not yet taken place.

Georg showed us around Leipzig. Not only did we visit the university, but the downtown areas in which demonstrations against the Communist regime had been held prior to the collapse of the regime. Amazingly, no one was killed in these massive nightly demonstrations over the several weeks that they were held. Georg gave an accounting of those events at considerable length as he showed us around the city.

"There were hundreds of East German police outfitted in riot gear. Some of the leaders of the protests were Lutheran ministers of the major churches in the city. Their aim was to get the Communist regime to work more closely with the West German Federal Republic in easing travel restrictions from East to West so that family members wouldn't have such a difficult time making connections with their relatives in West Germany. Liz, Hans, Martin, and Matthias came to visit us each summer, but the East German regime wouldn't allow any of us to visit them in West Germany. Only our father was allowed a yearly visit to Vaihingen/Enz. He wasn't allowed to take any gifts with him to the West. Liz and Hans always brought a considerable amount of food to us in each of their trips over here, but we couldn't reciprocate. Even my father had to wear a smaller-sized shoe so that he could bring Hans a gift for his birthday! He couldn't take them with him as a gift!"

It was quite a resume of some of the hardships which the East Germans had to endure under the Communist regime. It also helped to explain why the Berlin wall was so willingly and ardently breached on November 9, 1989!

Georg and Baerbel took us to Dresden and gave us a tour of the old royal palace and museum along the Elbe River. We also toured the Meissen China factory. It was still producing, even under the Communists, some of the finest china in the world! They also took us to the mountain resort where Georg was now working south of Chemnitz. They wanted to show us the Soviet uranium mines which were now off-limits. Not only were there signs everywhere Danger Radiation Exposure, but Georg told us to stay off the old trails which used to course through the region.

"Before the Soviets came, people used to hike all through this region. It's too dangerous now. That's why the signs are everywhere."

It reminded me of what I had read about other areas of East Germany. Wherever Soviet forces had been stationed in East Germany, almost 25 percent of the landscape had been ruined by indiscriminate dumping of radioactive wastes, oil, and the junking of old unwanted military equipment.

Needless to say, the trip was well worth taking. It will take years until the environmental damage has been corrected. Nuclear contamination, however, may never be corrected. It will be a matter of having to live with it while the radioactivity danger continues from generation to generation. I couldn't help but wonder what will become of the people who live near these dumping sites and are exposed daily to the wind blowing across these wastelands?

Our next trip was to the Soviet Union after its collapse in 1991. My third sabbatical leave was to take place for the spring semester 1992. Julie had read an announcement in the teachers' information sheet about a Penn State history professor who was leading a group of teachers to the Soviet Union in February and early March. Since Julie had not been there, she very much wanted to take part in the visit. We applied and were accepted as part of the twenty-member group. Julie had been granted a leave of absence from the Butler Area School District for the spring semester to accompany me to Germany. I was going to conduct research on the Green Party's likelihood of one day becoming a member of a ruling coalition government in Germany. We still had an unresolved problem, however. What were we going to do with Dan's dog, Tyler? Since he could not be housed in the Syracuse University rental unit which Dan shared with four other students, he had remained with us in Timberley Heights. Julie and I decided it would be too expensive to place him in a kennel. The last time we had done that, Tyler had literally torn apart one of the doors of the kennel in which he had been placed.

"I had to place him in a metal cage. He tore through any other type of pen I tried to put him in," she told us.

We had to pay for the doors he had destroyed. There was only one other alternative. We tried to give him away. When the families came to get acquainted with him, he intimidated the children who came with their parents to see him. There was only one avenue left. We had to take him back to the Butler SPCA where Dan had originally gotten him.

The group going to Russia had a brief orientation at Penn State. The leader was not only fluent in Russian, but she had been there several times under the Soviet regime.

"The old staid, safe Soviet Union no longer exists. It's a society in flux. You want to be careful with whom you interact," she counseled. "Keep your valuables with you at all times. Don't let your passport out of your sight. Keep your money with you wherever you go."

We weren't quite sure what she meant by this comment. But whenever Julie and I went anywhere, we took our passport, money, and camera with us. We learned the hard way. Even with these items, we thought, securely in our possession, we still encountered a theft which I didn't think possible. Julie and I were walking down one of the major boulevards in St. Petersburg, Nevsky Prospect. We were approached by three young men interested, we thought, in selling us fur hats. One of them took my hat off and placed a fur hat on my head holding my rain hat where I could see it. A second man placed a beautiful scarf over my camera case which I had hanging around my neck. The third man suggested I could buy these items very cheaply.

"No thanks. We're just walking down the street to our hotel," I told him as I took off the fur cap. I handed it back to the first man and he gave me back my hat. I then did the same with the scarf. All three seemed to be very disappointed. As Julie and I walked down the boulevard, I noticed my camera case seemed lighter than usual. I opened it and found my camera was gone! While the young man placed the scarf over my camera, he must have opened it and taken out my camera! When we looked back to where we had been, the three young men were gone. The visit to the Hermitage Museum, the two grade schools, and the shops we had visited and photographed as slides were gone. I was not able to record the details and sights of this trip to Russia as I had done in the Soviet Union in 1958. I did buy a Russian camera shortly thereafter, but it was nowhere near as good or expensive as the one I had lost!

Our tour guide (the Penn State professor) arranged for us to take the train from St. Petersburg to Moscow. The compartments were comfortable. Two women train attendants brought us hot tea in a huge samovar and sandwiches for the overnight trip. We each had our own bunk in the six-passenger compartments. In Moscow we were housed in a recently decommissioned Communist Party hotel (now open to foreign guests). We were shown the sights of the city, touring not only the Kremlin but also the burial site of Lenin, the Bolshoi Theater topped off with a visit in Gum (the former huge government mall) to shop. We walked down the huge square around the Kremlin where Soviet armed forces had paraded. We also visited Moscow University and were told by one of the deans, "These towers [forty stories and higher] were actually built by German prisoners of war after World War II."

The buildings reminded me of the Tower of Learning in Pittsburgh, except instead of one tower, there are several. Each of them had a spire top similar to what is usually found on a cathedral. The very impressive series of buildings had more than fifty thousand students at that time.

For the conclusion of our stay in Russia, our guide had arranged for us to take the train northwest of Moscow approximately five hours distant. Since this was winter, there was plenty of snow and ice wherever we went. We stayed in the Yaroslavl hotel. Our guide had, however, arranged for us to be hosted for dinner in what she called family visits. The purpose was to have us meet a Russian family with whom we could interact on a personal basis. Julie and I were hosted by a husband and wife, their two sons and the wife's mother. The mother-in-law did most of the talking since she spoke German and understood a bit of English much better than her daughter. She had been an electrical engineer and was well schooled in her field. She had only recently retired. We had long conversations with them about what life was like under the Stalinist era and during World War II.

"We suffered greatly during the war," the grandmother told us. "We were constantly short of food. We had to learn to survive on very little. No one was overweight. I'm really looking forward to this new era," she told us. "I just hope the transition doesn't take too long so that people don't get discouraged and wish the old days would return! One of our major problems currently is that these apartment buildings in which we live are no longer being cared for by the State. Each person is responsible for his own apartment, but no one has any interest in taking care of the whole apartment complex. We've got to learn how to work together to keep this apartment in the same shape as our individual units. Otherwise our hallways, stairs, and exterior will continue to deteriorate. No one seems to know how to work together without someone directing them in what they should do!"

We noticed the dirty hallways and stairwells as we came up the stairs to their apartment. What she was telling us was certainly going to become even more obvious as the building aged!

We thanked our hosts for an enjoyable and illuminating evening shaking hands with everyone.

"Thank you very much for the excellent dinner," Julie said. "We hope your country continues to become more prosperous and democratic as time goes on," I stated. "Your country is much different from what I remember it was like in 1958."

"Yes," the grandmother concurred. "We all had jobs. We all had a good education. We all had enough to eat. The only thing we didn't have was the right to do what we really wanted to do. We had to go where we were assigned by the party until we retired!"

We returned to Moscow from Yaroslavl by train in order to catch our flight to Helsinki, Finland. While the rest of the group left for their return trip home, Julie and I booked an overnight trip on the Finnish ship (*Da Silva*) for Stockholm, Sweden. We took a cab from the airport to the harbor. The ship proved to be one of the nicest we had ever been on. It was an overnight cruise from the Baltic Sea up through the Bothnian Gulf to Stockholm. We spent another three days touring Stockholm before boarding the train for the long ride back to Stuttgart, Germany. We were scheduled to pick up our new Mercedes in Sindelfingen on the twenty-fifth of March.

The trip to Russia had been an add-on. The sabbatical to undertake the research on the Green Party was the main focus for the spring semester. We were glad to have had the opportunity to include the Russian trip. Julie had not been there before. It had been more than thirty-four years since my previous excursion to the then Soviet Union. The contrast between then and 1992 could not have been greater. The streets were safe during the Soviet era. There were scarcities of many items to buy in the stores at that time, but the visitor didn't have to feel uncertain or insecure about his/her safety. On this trip, while we were walking across the Kremlin Square, for example, with a small group of our fellow Americans, two of our younger women carried their purses over their shoulders. We were set upon by a large group of young gypsies. They tried to rip the purses off the shoulders of our group members. The rest of us crowed around the two women and succeeded in driving them off. When we reported this incident to the police, the officer in charge of the detail told us, "These gypsy youngsters have been known to beat up older people before taking their purses from them! It was fortunate you were all together!"

As our guide told us after the event, "This would never have happened in the Communist era! Control over the population was the most important feature of the Soviet system!"

After a long day and evening on the train through Sweden, Denmark, and Germany, we arrived in Stuttgart on the morning of the twenty-fifth of March. We took a cab (most of which are Mercedes) to the Mercedes-Benz factory in Sindelfingen to pick up our car. We were given a tour of the factory, a dinner, a three-night stay in a five-star hotel, two weeks of automobile insurance, plus Julie's airfare from the United States to pick up our car! Following our stay in Stuttgart, we drove to Vaihingen/Enz and spent the weekend with Hans, Liz, Martin, and Matthias Grossmann. We were glad to be among our relatives again in a warmer climate than the snow and cold of Russia and Sweden. March is the time of the year when Southern Germany begins to bloom in a panoply of fruit blossoms and new leaves heralding spring. We took walks with Liz and Hans to Schloss Kaltenstein where we could look out over the landscape from the ramparts of the old walls surrounding the castle down into the Enz River valley far below. On the following Monday, we took our leave and drove to Bonn to find a place to live during our semester's leave.

We arrived in Bonn in the early afternoon and began the process of making inquiries of where we might stay. There was nothing available near the Bundestag (parliament). When we inquired in the older part of the city, we found the Hotel Aigner still had a room to rent. It was on the second floor and looked out over the street and shops across from the hotel. We had breakfast in the dining room each morning, and the rest of our meals we ate at various restaurants nearby. The car couldn't be parked on the street overnight without being ticketed. The hotel had a parking lot about one block up the street from the hotel's entrance. It was a safe place to park because the gate was locked each evening at 10:00 p.m. If a patron didn't arrive in time, he had to try and talk the night desk clerk to give him the key in order to gain access to the lot.

I had drawn up a series of questions of what I wanted to ask the Green Parliamentarians prior to leaving the United States. I had then sent them to our English teacher friend, Walter Schaeffner, to look them over and make improvements on the German as he had done with each previous sets of questionnaires I had used in Germany. He made his suggestions, and I made the corrections prior to our departure. The real difficulty in this research project was trying to arrange an hour's time for each member of the Green Party to be interviewed. I had written to Ms. Heide Riele, the chairwoman of the Green Party, while still in Butler to request interviews for my research. She gladly obliged herself, but told me when I paid her a visit in Bonn, "Dr. Megnin, das muessen Sie selber tun. Ich werde mit unsere Mitglieder Ihren Angebot besprechen, aber eine festen Termin kann ich leider nicht setzen." (Dr. Megnin, you will have to request the interviews yourself. I will tell my colleagues to expect you to contact them and ask them to participate, but you will have to approach them yourself. I can't set up the interviews for you.)

After my interview with Fraeulein Riele, I sensed she seemed to appreciate what I was trying to do. She said she would put in a good word for me with her colleagues. She also invited me to come to the Green Party's National Convention in Berlin during their June meeting "to see for yourself what the party stands for and why it would be highly appropriate to join in a coalition government at some point in the future."

I was successful in interviewing each of the Green Parliamentarians and attended their national convention. The results of the interviews with the ten Green Party members may be found in "German Politics and Society," Issue 29, Summer 1993, in the *Journal for German and European Studies*, University of California, Berkeley.

The Greens were getting ready to become a coalition partner with one of the major German political parties. In a few short years, their expectation became a reality when they joined the Social Democrats in their first coalition government.

While Julie and I were in Germany in May 1992, Dan graduated from Syracuse University. His uncle Volkmar, aunts Eva and Inge, attended together with some of his Syracuse cousins. Uncle Volkmar and Aunt Eva treated him and his girlfriend, Katie Feiman, to a graduation dinner together with Aunt Inge, cousins Pauline DeMartino and Irene Woolsen. We had met Katie for the first time in January of 1991 during our visit with Dan before the spring semester began. He had been dating her for more than a year. She got her first introduction to some of the wider Megnin family while attending Dan's graduation.

By the summer of 1992, Lynne was pregnant. Needless to say, her ball-playing days were over. Martin and Lynne had bought a house in the suburbs and had done considerable work on it getting ready for the birth of their first child. On May 7, 1993, Corinne Lynne Megnin was born. We visited them as often as we could during the holidays. It was a joy to hold our first grandchild. I have a picture which Julie took of me holding Corinne on my desk. It's amazing how people change the older they get. Corinne has become a very pretty high school teenager. Her grandfather on her father's side has become quite an old and rapidly aging octogenarian over the years. As youth grows and matures, the aging becomes the aged and less capable to conduct the affairs of the world! But such is life.

Julie had decided to retire at age sixty-two in June 1993. She really wanted to spend more time with our first grandchild.

"Don, I think it's best if I retire while I'm still of an age to help with our grandchildren. The older I get, the less able I'll be to help."

In February of 1994, Martin was offered a job with the new Texaco-Chevron merger in Dallas, Texas. After flying down for an interview and visit, he and Lynne decided it would be a real advancement in his career. Martin accepted the position.

Julie and I drove to Poughkeepsie to pick up Corinne and brought her back to Butler to spend the weekend with us while Martin and Lynne house hunted in Dallas. It was the first time we had a baby in our house since Dan was a baby. She was a very good baby. She didn't cry and seemed to enjoy her time and interaction with us. Julie did a good job making sure she was fed on time and slept when she was tired. After reconnoitering the Dallas area, Martin and Lynne decided on a house in Flower Mound, a Dallas suburb. We drove back with Corinne to Poughkeepsie after her parents' return from Dallas. The next step for them was to arrange for the shipment of their household furnishings and goods to their new home. Martin even came to Butler in order to drive his GTO from the barn in Wesley where he had been keeping it, to Butler, to make sure it was also shipped to Texas. We kept it in our garage until the shipping company's truck stopped to pick it up.

Since Julie had retired from teaching in June of 1993, she suggested I ought to give retirement some thought as well.

"If we want to do any traveling together, Don, maybe you ought to consider retiring. It would be better to do so now, while we can, rather than later, when we're too old and unable to do so."

"You're right. We're in good health now, and we don't know for how long. I'll talk with the business office and find out what the procedure is."

Allan McClymonds (Slippery Rock's business manager) suggested, "Why don't you talk with the Pennsylvania retirement representative when he comes for his yearly visit in June? He'll know exactly what to do and give you an idea of what you can expect to earn each month. In the meantime, I'll alert the administration that you will probably retire after this semester."

When Stan Kendjiorski, my successor as director of international education, heard I was thinking of retiring, he called me, "Don, I hear you're going to retire after this semester, is that true?"

"It probably is, Stan. I'll know more after I talk with the retirement specialist from the State's Department of Education in early June."

"Why don't you apply to teach a course in Salzburg this summer and then retire? It'll boost your retirement pay considerably, and we need someone to teach a course there in your field."

"That's not a bad idea, Stan. I could use the materials I gathered in the workshop last year in Maastricht for a course on the European Union. Okay, I'll submit my application and tell Rich Martin [Political Science Department chairperson] this will be my last class at Slippery Rock."

I talked with Rich that same day. He said he'd talk with Dean Zuzack about getting a replacement for my position.

"We need someone who's a specialist in international politics, Don, if you're leaving. Right now, Rene Peritz is the only one who comes closest, but he's really more into comparative politics. I think Stan's suggestion about teaching a course this summer in Salzburg sounds like a good idea. You've been there before and know your way around. It shouldn't be a problem for you to recruit students for your course."

Rich talked with the dean. The dean then talked with Dr. Charles Foust, the vice president for academic affairs, about hiring a replacement for me. As soon as he got the okay, Chuck called Rich and told him, "You can go ahead and hire a replacement for Don Megnin. He really should be the chair of the committee to hire his replacement in your department. Why don't you talk to him and get started as soon as possible? You'll need someone by next fall to teach the course in international politics. If you start now, you should have someone on board by the end of this semester."

Rich called me into his office.

"Since you're the specialist in international politics, why don't you head the search committee for your replacement? The dean thinks you would be the best person to head the committee in the department. I'll recruit a couple of your colleagues to assist you, but you'd be the expert in this field."

"Okay. I'll do that. Let me know when you've recruited my committee and we'll get started."

Rich talked with Walt Powell, our constitutional law professor, and Alice Kaiser-Drobney, an assistant professor and department community specialist, to complete the search committee.

Our first meeting was to prepare an ad in the *Chronicle of Higher Education* advertising the position as an assistant professor for international and comparative politics. The response was quick and extensive. We had more than fifty applicants interested in the position including the husband of one of our colleagues (Sharon Sykora). This raised the issue of nepotism. We asked Rich to clarify the university's position with Dean Zuzack. Rich reported back to us, "The dean says we can't hire anyone who is related to a current member of our department. It's contrary to the guidelines issued by the State Education Commissioner's Office."

"Well, that precludes his becoming a viable candidate for this position," I told Walt and Alice. "He does have a strong file, but we can't consider him for the position."

We had such good candidates; it really wasn't a problem finding a replacement. We interviewed three candidates and found Daniel MacIntosh to be the best candidate to fill the position. He is still with the department and teaches international politics, comparative politics, foreign policy, international organizations, and occasionally, American government.

Between Stan Kendjiorski's efforts and my own, we recruited students to take my final course in Salzburg during July 1994. I had four "built-in" recruits: my wife, Julie; a grandniece, Christine Forgenie; a grandnephew, Matthew Megnin; and our son, Dan. As soon as Mary Megnin Forgenie heard this was going to be my last time teaching in Salzburg, she wanted her daughter, Christine, to do what she did in 1969: be a student of mine in Salzburg. Christine had just finished high school and had been told she could have the course credited as an elective at John Carroll University where she was scheduled to enroll in September. Matthew was also in college (the University of Pittsburgh), and he found out he could also use the course as an elective. Dan had been with us in Hungary in 1987 for the course, Elements of World Politics. He was now in the graduate school at the University of Denver for a master's degree in international relations. He took the course as a free elective. Altogether there were nine students in the class, while the number was one less than the required, the university approved the course. The final exam was given on July 31. My retirement took effect on August 1, 1994. Dan, Matthew, and Christine took the train from Salzburg to Spain for a brief vacation prior to our return to the States. Christine had studied both Spanish and French and became the translator for the three of them. They returned via France. We held one final reunion in Vaihingen/Enz before saying good-bye to all of our relatives. It proved to be the last time that I taught a course in Salzburg, Austria. It has always remained one of Julie's and my favorite places for both professional and personal reasons. Julie and I shall never forget Salzburg, especially Groedig!

XIII.

Beginning Retirement

Our retirement parties had already taken place: Julie in June 1993 and mine in June 1994. The Political Science Department hosted a retirement dinner at the School House Restaurant in Slippery Rock. George Force, my last office mate, presented me with a clock set in wood on a stand holding two pens on each side. My name, Slippery Rock University, and the years of service were set in a gold plate, which I've had on my desk ever since. Except for the change of a battery every few years, it has run well.

The university also held a retirement party at the University Club hosted by Dr. Charles Foust, vice president for academic affairs honoring all of us retirees. Dr. Foust presented each of us with a certificate of thanks, followed by a brief word of thanks, a handshake, and a final word of farewell. Later that fall, I received notice that the university's Board of Trustees had awarded me with the designation "professor emeritus for international politics." Our years, first, at Slippery Rock State College, and then, at Slippery Rock University, had come to an end. It seemed the culmination of a career of administration, teaching, and the counseling of students which had been far more of a career than I had ever expected as a boy growing up on a farm!

With the removal of the stress of preparing lectures, attending meetings, and commuting back and forth to the university, Julie raised the question, "When are we going to visit Martin, Lynne, and Corinne in their new home?"

Julie retired a year earlier from teaching elementary gifted pupils. She felt a real liberation and also no longer had to prepare for her daily classes. She wanted me to join with her in using our time to travel, visit our families, and enjoy the years we still had ahead of us. We decided first to drive to Texas to visit Martin, Lynne, and Corinne. We had an enjoyable time with them. After a two-week visit using one of their five bedrooms, Julie suggested, "Since we're so close to Colorado, why don't we drive out to visit Dan in Denver?"

"That's a good idea."

We drove out to Denver and found Dan's apartment on Arapahoe Drive. We stayed at a nearby motel and spent a few days visiting Dan. He took us around the university, the Iliff Theological Seminary, and to visit Katie's parents: Marie and Ed Feiman in Parker, Colorado. After spending a few days with Dan, we decided to return to Dallas before heading back to Butler, Pennsylvania. Since we had been there, Lynne invited us to come again for Christmas. Her parents were also going to come.

"We should have a good time together, Mom and Dad. It'll give you a chance to get better acquainted with my folks. We'll invite Dan too. It should be a good time for all of us."

We took up her offer and returned to Flower Mound in time to spend Christmas with Dan, Martin, Lynne, Corinne, Marylou, and Neil Boyle. They flew in from Delaware. It was a pleasant time for all of us. We played pinochle with Marylou and Neil quite often. They were as pleased to be around their first granddaughter as Julie and I were. Following Christmas and New Year, the Boyles returned to Newark, Delaware. Julie and I looked for an apartment somewhere near Martin and Lynne. We thought within fifteen or twenty minutes would be about right. After checking out the listings in the newspaper, we found a second-floor apartment in Irving, Texas. We had a bedroom, living room, kitchen, and bathroom plus a place to park our car under an outdoor shelter. It gave us a place by ourselves, yet was close enough for us to drop in at Flower Mound whenever we wanted. On Sunday mornings we attended the Treitsch Memorial Methodist Church with them. In the afternoons, we visited for a few hours in order to spend time with granddaughter Corinne. Lynne was pregnant with their second child. It was to be Colin, born on the fourteenth of June 1995. In retrospect, we were probably visiting too often. We enjoyed the afternoon walks around Flower Mound with Lynne and Corinne. What finally made itself clear about being there "too often" was the failure of Lynne to give us a key to their house when she and Martin were involved in a church meeting following a Sunday-morning service. They couldn't leave until two hours after the service. Instead of driving back to Irving, we drove to Lewis Lake and watched the boats and landscape for two hours! We would have appreciated having the key to their house. Since it was not offered, we felt we were a burden to them.

It was not an enjoyable experience. It did help, however, in making our plans permanent about returning to Upstate New York for the summers, once we sold our Butler home. Living that close and noting the pressure our visits seemed to impose on Lynne, we certainly didn't think we should live nearby permanently. She gave us the impression she didn't care whether we stayed or left. The only time Lynne really seemed to appreciate having us with them in Flower Mound was when a squirrel had chewed through one of the cornices on their house and had fallen into their attic. He kept running around and made a constant noise trying to find a way out of his imprisonment. I got Martin's ladder out from the garage and placed it against the back of the house where I had seen the chewed-through hole. I nailed it shut with a small board. Hence, since the squirrel couldn't get out, he became even more rattled and raced around the attic. I climbed into the attic and saw the squirrel. He stayed as far away from me as possible. There was no way I could coax him out. After a few days, we did not hear him anymore. A week later, the stench of his decay began to become noticeable. I don't think anyone ever found the corpse even though the stench was around for several weeks. I suggested to Lynne, "Keep the windows open. At least the smell won't be so bad! Once the corpse has dried out, you won't even know he was up there."

On the first of March, Julie and I left Irving, Texas, having said good-bye to Martin, Lynne, and Corinne the previous day. We decided we would visit Tom and Flora in North Fort Myers, Florida, before returning to Butler. Looking over the map, we thought the drive along the southern coast of the United States would be interesting. We decided to stop whenever there was something of interest en route on Interstate 10 and see the local sights. We drove along the northern edge of New Orleans but decided to continue without stopping. When we got to Mississippi, we drove along the shore and saw the beautiful homes and boats along the gulf. In Alabama, we stopped at the Bellinggrath Gardens and spent some time walking through them. The number of flowers and the beautiful park were impressive.

Continuing along the Florida panhandle, we decided, since we were driving down the West Coast, we would stop in Sun City Center and visit Iona Bishop. Dr. Bishop had died the year before. He had been one of my chief advisors and supporters in my graduate studies in the Maxwell School at Syracuse University. Julie and I had gotten very well acquainted with Iona when I sponsored Dr. Bishop to come to Slippery Rock for three years after his retirement from Syracuse University to teach. We often did things together and had visited them in the early seventies when we took Martin and Dan to Disneyland. If it were not for Dr. Bishop, I probably wouldn't have had the Shell Foundation Dissertation Research Grant, which allowed me to study German economic assistance to India.

Iona was glad to see us. She wanted us to spend the night in her home, which we did. We not only had dinner with her, but she showed us around the club house at Sun City Center.

"This is a nice place to live. You ought to consider moving down here, Don and Julie. Since you both play golf, there are nice golf courses here in Sun City. There's no snow and the winters are never cold. If you're looking for a place to live in retirement, this is a great place in which to do it!"

"Thanks, Iona. We'll keep your advice in mind, but right now we're going to visit Julie's brother and his wife in North Fort Myers. We'd like to see as much of the state as possible before we return to Butler," Julie reminded her.

Our next stop was North Fort Myers where Tom and Flora lived. They had often suggested we should come and visit them, but we had never done so. We arrived at Lake Fairways and found their manufactured home which they had been renting for several years. It was a pleasant community with more than twelve hundred units. Each one had a kitchen, dinning room, living room, a lanai, two bedrooms and a covered shelter for the car alongside the unit. There was also a small lawn around each unit and usually some flowers planted in the front and driveway. Perhaps an orange and/or grapefruit tree grew in the yard. We stayed with them for a couple of days before continuing our trip southward to Naples. I wanted to visit Jud Hill, the sociologist from Slippery Rock who was now living there with his wife. Julie and I stayed in one of the downtown hotels and invited Jud and his wife to join us for dinner. She couldn't make it, but Jud did. It was an interesting evening, and he filled us in again on the dean of Social and Behavioral Sciences Search Committee's decision in 1975 to hire someone from outside the university as the new dean.

"The committee was in complete agreement, Don, you shouldn't become the dean. The animosity of some of the chairmen against you was more than we thought you should have to take. We knew you better than they, but we had to make the decision. We felt you didn't deserve to have to work with these unscrupulous chairmen who had nothing at all good to say in your behalf! We thought we did you a big favor by not subjecting you to having to try to work with these men!"

"That's what's I've heard from some of the other members of the committee, Jud. I really wanted the job, but that's water over the dam now. I'm slowly getting over the disappointment, especially since all of you committee members were such good friends of mine. I had a hard time trying to accept your decision. The sabbatical helped, but it proved harder for the family probably than it did for me. Spending the year in Germany was difficult for Julie and our sons. They all had to get used to living in a foreign environment and trying to adjust to making new friends, attending new schools, and living apart from the way of life they had been used to in the States."

"It was no doubt hard for all of you. Jim Roberts suggested the sabbatical leave. He thought it would be a good alternative to take you away from Slippery Rock for a year. He knew you would be greatly disappointed."

The next day, Julie and I played a round of golf. There were several in the area. We played the one nearest our hotel. I called Bob Ford and invited him and his wife for dinner that evening. His wife was not feeling well and couldn't come. His mother, Jessie Ford, was visiting, and he brought her. It proved to be an enjoyable evening. We reminisced about growing up in Mycenae. He has been one of my friends whom I've known the longest from grade school through high school. Jessie had lived in Mycenae ever since she married Wallace Ford in 1927. The family had lived at the head of the T where the Green Lake Road came directly into Route 5 in the center of the village. Bob had worked for the Florida Highway Department as a toll collector prior to his retirement. He was glad he no longer had to worry about the winter cold and snow anymore.

"Florida's a good place to live, Meg. You don't have to worry about your pipes freezing in the winters, and you don't have to have snow tires on your car."

Jessie invited us to visit her in Chittenango.

"Fritz and Julie, don't forget to come and visit me when you come up to central New York next summer. I'd like to have you see my new apartment just as you come into Chittenango. I'm glad I sold my house in Mycenae. It was just getting to be too much for me."

We promised her we would.

Julie and I looked over a couple of condominiums next to the golf course where we had played the day before. The realtor wanted to sell us one. I told him, "We'll have to think it over first. It's a nice place, but it's on the second floor. We'd rather have one on the ground floor. We'll get back to you if we're interested."

"Don't wait too long. These condos go very quickly."

We continued our drive across Alligator Alley to Boca Raton. We spent the night in Boca, an upscale community where the hotels were among the most expensive we encountered anywhere in Florida. The next town to the north was Highland Beach. We had Alex and Betty Carmichel's address and looked them up. They owned a beautiful condominium on the top floor of the building overlooking the Atlantic Ocean beachfront.

"What a surprise to find you here, Don and Julie. How long can you stay?"

"We're just passing through, Alex. Since we had your address, we thought we'd look you up. You've got a beautiful place here," Julie said.

"How long have you lived here, Alex?"

"We bought it a couple of years before I retired. We didn't want to stay up north during the winters anymore. Sandy, Karan (his wife), and daughter live about two hours north of here. We thought this was the perfect place to retire."

"You've picked out an ideal location!" Julie emphasized.

Following lunch, we dropped them off and continued our journey northward. We knew that Walt and Nancy Powell had recently built a house in a place called New Smyrna Beach. We checked into the Holiday Inn also on the beachfront. After breakfast the next morning, I called Walt.

"Hi, Walt. This is Don Megnin. How about you and Nancy joining us for lunch today?"

"I'd like to do that, Don, but I'm talking with a group of lawyers today. How about getting together for dinner tonight at one of our local restaurants? We've got a lot of good ones here in New Smyrna Beach."

"Okay. We'll stay an extra day and see you and Nancy this evening."

"We'll pick you and Julie up at six o'clock."

Julie and I talked it over. "What should we do today? Should we play some golf?"

"Why don't you go down to the front desk and ask if there are any golf courses nearby?" Julie suggested. "We've got all day."

I went down to the front desk and asked, "Are there any golf courses nearby that we might be able to play today, since we're going to stay an extra day?"

"Certainly. Here's a list of them with the addresses and phone numbers."

At the top of the list was Sugar Mill Country Club. I called the pro shop and Don Hicks answered, "Would it be possible for my wife and me to play your course today? We're passing through and visiting some friends this evening before continuing on to Pennsylvania."

"Yes. In fact, if you and your wife can get here within the next half hour, you can get right on."

"Okay. We'll be there."

It was the start of an adventure which changed our lives as never before. The drive to Sugar Mill took about fifteen minutes up Route 44 to Sugar Mill Drive (the clerk had given me directions).

"Just before you come to Interstate 95, you'll see the road sign saying Sugar Mill Drive. Turn right on this road and follow it straight through to the gate entrance. They can tell you where to go from there."

The directions were very clear, and we had no difficulty finding the Sugar Mill Country Club. After telling the officer at the gate what we wanted to do, he issued us a pass and told us to proceed to the sign directing us to the parking lot. I did so, and as a person was driving by in a golf car, I asked, "Where's the pro shop?"

"Go up the hill and the building just beyond the club house is the pro shop. You can't miss it."

We walked up the hill and saw the long low building adjacent to the driving range down in the valley. We had no trouble finding the pro shop.

As we approached the counter, I introduced us.

"We're the Megnins. I'm Don and this is my wife, Julie. We talked with you a short time ago about playing a round of golf."

"Oh yes. I'm Don Hicks. You called and asked if you and your wife could play. Once you give me your credit card, you'll be all set to play the white and red courses. The cart is just down the driveway by the cart barn. You shouldn't have any trouble finding it."

We carried our clubs down to the cart and drove up to the white course. We were both impressed with this golf course. We had only played a country club course once before. It was the Grove City Country Club as guests of Henry and Linda Lenz. That course could not compare with this one! As we played the last three holes of the white course, Jim Wilson and Ralph Ely caught up with us. I invited them to join us, which they did. They told us about the development of Sugar Mill from its earliest days to the present. They were both members and had been coming to Sugar Mill for a few years. It was an interesting tale and gave us insight into the development of the club. Since they had already played nine holes, they left us after the ninth green of the white course.

"If you ever decide to retire in Florida, you really ought to consider joining this club. You won't find a better one for the price you have to pay for membership," Ralph told us.

"We've looked over a number of them in Texas," I said. "We haven't decided where we'll spend our winters yet," Julie offered.

We played the red nine next and found it to be even more challenging than the white course. As we drove through the woods between the seventh and eighth holes, a mother armadillo and five little ones crossed the path in front of us.

"Just like Texas!" Julie exclaimed.

We had seen a few of them along the roadsides and on the edges of some of the golf courses near Dallas.

After completing the red course, we drove the cart back to our car, unloaded our bags, and changed our shoes.

"Why don't we stop at that real estate office that we saw driving up the hill from Club House Boulevard?" Julie suggested. "I'd like to see what houses are available here."

I stopped in the parking lot adjacent to the reality office of "Mille Martin Reality." We entered and were greeted by an elderly lady who was one of the realtors.

"Can I help you?" she asked.

"Yes. I'm Don Megnin and this is my wife, Julie. We just played a round of golf and would like to know if you have any homes for sale?"

"We'd be interested in condos too," Julie added.

"We have several of each at the moment. Let me show you a few in different sections of Sugar Mill. Have you ever been here before?"

"No. This is the first time we've ever been in New Smryna Beach," Julie said. "We were impressed with your golf courses and noticed homes along the edges of the fairways and wondered if any might be for sale."

"Oh yes. We have several at present. Let's start with the condos since they're right here at the entrance to Sugar Mill."

She drove us to the Pine Valley Condos and showed us the first two. One was a one-bedroom unit and the other a two-bedroom. We noticed each of them was furnished.

"Any unit you buy in Sugar Mill is furnished. Most of the owners have used them as their second home and have simply bought what furniture they needed if there was something lacking in their unit. It makes it convenient for the buyer not having to ship their furniture especially as most of the members of the club are snowbirds. They have their permanent homes up north and only come down here for the winter months."

"Are there any owners from Syracuse?" I asked.

"Oh yes. In fact, Millie Martin, the owner of this agency and her husband are from Syracuse."

She took us to the Brae Burn units next. We looked at some that were not on the golf course that seemed reasonable enough in price. She evidently got the correct impression we wanted to look at a unit along one of the golf fairways.

She showed us 322 Gleneagles Drive and said, "This unit may not be on sale yet, but will very likely become available. The owner has had some health problems and his wife really wants to sell it. Even though it's not technically for sale, we are starting to show it. Millie will probably know whether or not it's for sale by this next week."

After looking at six different units in the A, B, and C size category, I said, "Well, you've certainly showed us what we wanted to see!"

"It gives us an idea of what to look for if we should want to move to Florida for the winters," Julie exclaimed.

The agent drove us back to the office. "Millie's here," she said. "Why don't you come in with me and I'll introduce you to her? She's the owner of the agency. Since you're also from Syracuse, you may know some of the same people she knows."

"Okay. We don't have to rush off yet," Julie said.

She opened the door and looked in Millie's office. "Millie? There's a couple out here from Syracuse. They've been looking at some of the homes we have listed."

We followed her into Millie's office.

"This is Don and Julie Megnin."

"Hi."

She extended her hand, and Julie and I shook it.

"You're from Syracuse?"

"Originally. I was a Methodist minister there and did my graduate work at Syracuse."

"We live in Butler, Pennsylvania now," Julie clarified.

"Where did you live in Syracuse?"

"My husband was the minister of the First Ward United Methodist Church on the north side of Syracuse when we moved there from Boston," Julie said. "It was on Bear Street."

"I know where that is. It's in the oldest part of the city."

"Where are you from?" I asked.

"We lived in Manlius. My husband had a business in Syracuse."

"How long are you going to be in New Smyrna Beach?"

"Only until tomorrow. We're meeting a colleague of mine from Slippery Rock for dinner tonight."

"You've just played golf here, haven't you?"

"Yes. We played the white and red courses."

"Why don't you stay another day and be my guests to play the blue course?"

"That's a possibility. Then we would have played all three courses. What do you think, Julie? Should we stay an extra day?"

"It's okay with me. We don't have to be in Butler on any particular date."

We extended our stay for another day. We met Walt and Nancy in the lobby of the Holiday Inn. They took us to Blackbeard's restaurant for supper. Walt filled us in on what was going on in the department and the university.

"Your replacement, Dan MacIntosh, is doing well teaching your international politics courses. Some of your students still ask about you and want to know what you're doing."

After dinner, Walt and Nancy took us back to their new house. It's on Fairmount Street, past the New Smyrna Beach airport. Because Walt was an air force veteran, he wanted to be close to the airport to help restore some of the old aircraft from World War II. He and his fellow airmen wanted to use them for air shows around the country.

The next morning, we drove out to Sugar Mill again. With Millie having arranged with the pro shop to have us play the blue-white courses combination, we had an even better picture of the entire golf layout of the country club. Upon completing the white course, we stopped in Millie's office again. She was there.

"How did you like the blue course? Isn't it a beauty?"

"It's even more impressive for its beauty than the white course," Julie stated. "We are really impressed with Sugar Mill, Millie."

"Millie, would you mind taking us to the unit we looked at on Gleneagles Drive?" I asked.

"Not at all. I'll take you over there."

We got into her car, and she drove to the Brae Burn III section of Sugar Mill. She opened the door to the villa, and Julie and I walked in. We looked around the living room briefly, and I sat down on the couch and looked out the patio windows. The pond was clearly visible, as were the ladies' tee, and the fairway leading to the eighth green.

"How much did you say the owner wants for this unit with the certificate of membership?"

"The unit itself is $94,000. The certificate only applies if you are approved for membership by the Sugar Mill Membership Committee."

"We'll take it at that price, Millie." I said. "When could we find out if we quality for membership?"

"Well, I'll have to call the McMichels first and find out if this price is acceptable. Let's go back to the office and I'll give them a call up in Canada. That's where they live."

Before we got back in the car, I noticed the water pipe in the garage seemed to be leaking. The wall was wet where the outlet to the faucet came out of the garage.

"Millie, I think there's a leak in the pipe in the garage. The wall's all wet."

"Ill have my repairman look at it. If it needs to be fixed, I'll see that it's fixed."

She called him on her cell phone and he came immediately. While we were looking the house over one more time, he had arrived. I watched as he put a new faucet on the pipe and tightened it so that no more water leaked from it.

"That should do it. You won't have any problem with it now," he told me.

"Don't you have to put in a new pipe?" I asked.

"No. All it needed was to be tightened."

"Thanks, Frank," Millie said.

Frank drove off and we got into Millie's car to return to her office.

"I'll call the McMichels and make sure they'll accept your offer."

Millie called but was unable to reach them. She left a message for them to return her call.

"I'll keep calling to find out if the offer is acceptable to the McMichels, Don and Julie. Once I have an answer, I'll call you in Butler and let you know. You're leaving tomorrow for Pennsylvania?"

"Yes. If we buy this place, we'll have to get our place ready to sell."

"Why don't you let me put you in touch with a friend of mine who works for the Sun Trust mortgage department? I'm sure she'll be able to work out an arrangement for you to buy this place."

"That's a good idea, Millie," Julie said.

Millie's friend came immediately. Julie and I talked with her as she filled out the forms for the loan to buy the Brae Burn unit.

"It shouldn't take more than a month for approval. I'll have you both sign this mortgage application and you should know by the middle of April whether or not your loan has been approved."

We thanked her for her help. She took us back to Millie's office.

"What's your telephone number in Pennsylvania? I'll keep calling the McMichels. Once I have an answer, I'll give you a call. Is that okay with you?"

"That's fine," Julie answered. "Why don't we set a date for the closing around the middle of May provided everything is approved by then."

"That would be just about right," Millie said. "You would know about getting a loan, and I should certainly know by then the McMichels' answer. Let's set the date tentatively for the fifteenth of May."

"Okay. Unless we hear otherwise from you, Millie, we'll be here on the fifteenth of May for the closing," Julie confirmed.

With that sudden change in our lives, we took our leave. We had already checked out of the hotel after breakfast. We headed north on Interstate 95 reaching Butler on the afternoon of the second day after leaving New Smyrna Beach, March 24, 1995.

With this decision to buy in Sugar Mill, our next step was to put our house up for sale. We interviewed three different Butler realtors and decided to go with ReMax. The agent suggested we should have the boys' rooms and hallway painted.

"The room colors and the hallway should really be a more neutral color," she told us. "A buyer will respond much more favorably to a neutral tone than to a bright one. You don't want to give the impression that the owner is extreme in any way. That's why you ought to have these rooms painted. The rest of the house is in color tones which reflect a subdued atmosphere in this shaded neighborhood. It will really appeal to prospective buyers."

We followed her advice and had the rooms and hallway painted. It took the painters only two days to complete this transformation. We had had our bathrooms redone just a few years previously. Our master bedroom did not have a full bath when we bought it. With the renovation of our large bathroom, we had the plumber also put in a shower adjacent to our half bath. The agent assured us we had made a very good decision.

"All of the houses in this neighborhood have at least two bathrooms. If you hadn't done it, you would have had to reduce your price by at least twenty thousand dollars."

Julie and I decided to go through our things from top to bottom and sort out what we wanted to keep and what we were willing to discard. With our prospective new home in Florida completely furnished, we only had to look for a condominium in Syracuse where we could ship our furniture. We decided to take a trip towards the end of April to Syracuse in order to see what we might be able to buy from the Oot Bros., Inc., in Erie Village. We had talked with Judy Miller, an agent for the Oot Bros., earlier and told her what we wanted. She showed us several units already completed. When we returned to the office, Judy introduced us to Tim Oot, the sales manager and vice president of Oot Bros., Inc.

"Tim, the Megnins want a unit near the golf course. Do we have any available?"

We shook hands with Tim. He showed us different types of units they were building.

"We've got one that we're in process of building on Summerhaven Drive North. It's an end unit and just across the street from the golf course. Why don't we look at it, and if you're interested, you can tell us what types of items you want us to include as we're building it."

"That sounds good," Julie and I agreed. "Let's take a look at it."

We got in Tim's SUV and he drove us to the construction site.

"As you can see, we're going to finish building in Erie Village within the next three to four years. There are over one hundred units finished so far. We've got room for another fifty or so, and then Erie Village will be completed."

He pointed out the areas where they were still going to build. He turned down Summerhaven Drive North to the end of the block. The units on the north side of the street were just being built. The south side was still an open field. The golf course (the Links of Erie Village) was just beyond the row of completed condominiums to the east. There was only one unit still vacant which he showed us. It was too small for all of the furniture which we wanted to bring with us.

"Here's the one I was telling you about in the office. As you can see, the frame is up and the roof is just being put on. Let me show you the interior so that you can get some idea about the layout."

Tim took us inside and pointed out the rooms. The hallway led directly into the combination living/dining room similar to what we had in Butler. Just inside the front door to the left was the kitchen with a small dining area towards the front of the unit looking out into the yard and street. A gas fireplace was at the far end of the living room. An archway in the center of the living/dining room led to another hallway connecting a bedroom on the right, a bathroom directly adjacent, a closet and laundry room next to the bathroom, a large master bed room at the northern end of the hallway, and another large bathroom connected to the bedroom. There was also a porch with sliding glass doors leading from the master bedroom and another set from the living room. It was a plank deck with a fence and no steps or exit except through the living room or bedroom.

Just off the hallway from the front door, a stairway led to the basement. It had a concrete floor and walls with small windows on the north end of the basement.

"This would be just the place for me to do my writing, Julie. Do you think you could put in a separate room for me on this north side for my study, Tim?"

"Yes, we can do that. We'll put in another set of windows on the north side and a set on the east side. That'll give you more light. Do you want a door and wall between this room and the basement?"

"That would be perfect. I could put some of my bookcases along the wall, and my desk would fit perfectly into this space."

"It's a good thing you're looking over the unit now, Don. What about the upstairs? Are there any changes you'd like to have us make? I assume you'll want fans in each of the rooms. Most of our buyers have requested fans to turn on in the summer rather than use the air conditioners all of the time."

"Yes, that would be a good idea," Julie added. "How much would this unit cost, Tim?"

"It depends on what you want us to put in it. Usually, it sells for one hundred twenty-five thousand as the basic cost. Depending on what you want us to put in it, it could go up to one hundred thirty or forty thousand. If you're interested in this unit, Mrs. Megnin, the basic price is one hundred twenty-five thousand dollars. The cost of the carpet, tiles, fans in all of the rooms, and anything else you may want us to add would be an additional amount."

"You understand, don't you, Tim, we have to sell our house in Pennsylvania first before we can buy the condo. We're just in process of buying a house in Florida at the same time."

"This unit won't be finished before this summer. We'll hold it for you in the meantime. Let us know when you've sold your house. You probably should pick out your carpeting."

"Where do we do that?" Julie asked.

"At the tile and carpeting store in Fairmount. That's the supplier we've used for all of our units. It's on Genesee Street just west of the first streetlight in Fairmount."

"You might want to pick our your own refrigerator too, while you're shopping. We've had too many people complain with our choice in the past, so we let our buyers pick out their own. Obviously, you'll have your own washer and dryer to put in the unit. There's just one other item that's left up to you, and that's putting in a sliding door on the shower off the master bedroom. I can give the name of the plumber if you don't already know of one. But you'll have time to have that done after you've bought the unit."

After a bit more chitchatting, we took our leave. We were most impressed with the layout of the village. There were several lakes both in the village and on the golf course. We both felt it would be an ideal place to spend our summers!

Upon our return to Butler, we arranged for two Saturday garage sales in June. We thought we would have completed going through our things by then. Our agent wanted us to leave things pretty much as they were in the house.

"It's always easier to sell a house that's lived in than one that's empty. A buyer wants to get an idea of what it looks like with furniture in it. It gives them a picture of where their own furniture might best fit."

"That's fine with us. We've still got to go through our things to find out what we're going to keep and what we're going to sell," Julie explained. "We've done this before. We just have a lot more to go through than the last time we did this."

"How much are you asking for your house?"

"We thought around one hundred twenty-eight thousand, "I answered.

"That's pretty high compared with what the other houses have sold for in this neighborhood. I'd say one hundred twenty-five thousand would be a good price."

"Okay. You're the expert. If we get less than what we'd like to ask, then you're also going to get less commission," I laughed.

"I'm just suggesting what the price should be compared with other sales that I've had recently, Dr. Megnin. If you want to ask more, then that's your privilege. I'm just telling you what I think you can get for it."

She set the price at the amount she suggested. While Julie and I were going through our things in the attic and basement, she brought a few potential buyers to look over the house. It was a slow process. Most of the potential buyers seemed to like what they saw. A few of them said, "We like the house, but we just can't afford to pay that much for it."

After two months of having buyers look over the house, the agent told us, "If you really want to sell your house before the summer is over, I'd suggest you lower the price to one hundred twenty-two thousand. I've had a few couples willing to go that high, but not at one hundred twenty-eight thousand."

"Well, I guess we can live with that," Julie said. "But the buyer has to be willing to wait until the end of August before moving in. Our place in Syracuse won't be finished before the middle of August. Is that going to be a problem?"

"I don't think so. I'll tell the buyer the timeline for the availability of the house. I don't think that'll be a problem."

In the meantime, I arranged for a dumpster to be set up at the upper end of our driveway nearest the garage. We deposited all of the items we no longer wanted and couldn't sell into it. By the time the two garage sales were finished, the dumpster was more than fifteen feet above the top rail! All of our notebooks, term papers, letters, broken furniture, and files had been deposited. The attic was cleaned out for the first time since we had moved into it in 1974!

Fred and Marian Curran and Sally Hayden helped us price each of the items on display in the garage that were on sale. We were amazed how many people came to look over our things and usually left with at least one item which they felt was of value and purchased it. By the second weekend, I made sure everyone left with something even if they hadn't bought anything. I simply gave them an item by way of saying "Thanks for coming!"

For the few items which remained, we had a man from Good Will stop by to take them with him. His car was loaded, and he promised the items would be well used by people who had little or nothing. Needless to say, Julie and I were relieved. We had gotten rid of those things which we simply had failed to weed out years ago!

XIV.

Purchase of Sugar Mill Home

On May 13, 1995, Julie and I headed for New Smyrna Beach. The fifteenth was the closing date on our villa in Sugar Mill. The McMichels had accepted our offer and our loan had been approved by Sun Trust Bank. Millie had arranged for us to meet in the office of the lawyer representing the McMichels near the inland waterway. After the signing, we asked Millie about the steps we should take to apply for membership in the Sugar Mill Country Club.

"I've arranged for you to meet with Andy Walsh and his membership committee this morning in the Sugar Mill Administration Building. You had said you wanted to join the club. Since the committee was available this morning, I thought you could do both the signing and the application. If you'll follow me out to Sugar Mill, I'll introduce you to the committee. You might find out before you leave if your membership application is approved."

"That sounds like a good idea, Millie. We're going to spend a week or so at any rate in our new home," Julie responded.

"Before I forget it, here's your key."

We followed Millie out to Sugar Mill and parked just outside the administration building. She escorted us into the meeting room next to the office. Andy and his committee were concluding their meeting.

"Andy, here are Julie and Don Megnin. They're interested in joining our club."

We shook hands with Andy. "Come in. Our committee has just been meeting. I'd like to introduce you to them."

"I'll leave you in the hands of Andy, Don and Julie. Good-bye."

Andy introduced each member. He then asked us various questions about where we were from, what kinds of occupations we had held, if we had been members of a country club before, and what our intentions were about moving into the Sugar Mill community.

"Are you both golfers?" Bernice Woodson asked.

"That's why we're here," I answered. "We were most impressed with your golf course. That's why Julie said we should see what houses might be available after we played that first day while we were visiting in New Smyrna Beach back in March."

"It's about the nicest one I've ever seen," Julie added. "We're used to playing public courses, but none of them can compare with what you have here!"

Needless to say, after a few more questions about where we were from and why we wanted to join Sugar Mill, Andy said, "Thank you both for coming. We'll let Millie know our decision about your membership application. She's your official sponsor. Are there any other questions anyone has?"

There were no further questions. We shook hands with Andy and his committee and left. The next day Millie stopped by and said, "Congratulations! The committee is going to recommend to the board that you both be accepted as members of the Sugar Mill Country Club as golf members!"

After our week's stay to become familiar with the community and New Smyrna Beach, we returned to Butler. We had to continue with our plans to conduct our garage sales. With all of the items marked, Fred and Marion Curran came to join us on the first Saturday. We opened the garage doors at nine o'clock. We had put up signs at the entrance to Timberley Heights and in front of our house advertising our garage sale. The cars were soon streaming into Cherokee Drive (our renamed street) and parked along the roadside. The piano was one of the first items to sell. It had been my mother's. We had it shipped from her home in New York to our farm in Wesley. We then had it shipped to Butler after buying our house. It hadn't been used very much. It had sat in the garage most of the time. We had boxes of books stacked on a storage rack in the rear of the garage. I had packed them from my office in Slippery Rock and from my study on our Wesley farm. Some of these books sold for fifteen or twenty cents. Towards the end of the sale, I gave them away. Fred and Marion took a few which they hadn't read.

By the end of our second garage sale, our house was sold. Our ReMax agent told us, "The couple that's buying your house will wait until after the twenty-fifth of August to take possession."

"Excellent! That's the date we've set for our furniture to be shipped to our new town house in Erie Village near Syracuse."

We had arranged with Tim Oot to buy the town house. He promised it would be completed by the first of August. We had our closing for the town house on the fifteenth of August. We made a hurried trip back to Butler to prepare for the Mayflower Movers to pack our things for the trip north to Erie Village.

XV.

Moving to Erie Village

On the twenty-fifth of August, 1995, the movers arrived at 322 Summerhaven Drive North (the number was the same as our new home in Florida) to unload what they had packed in Butler. It took the two men a little over two hours to complete the job of placing the furniture where we wanted it. There were no units completed across the road from us. The only units that were completed nearby were to the east of us along the seventh fairway of the Links Golf Course.

We arranged for a plumber to come the next day to install a sliding glass door on our shower stall. The workman completed the job in a little less than two hours. The summer move was now complete. We could settle in for the rest of the season before heading south to Florida. By the middle of October, we closed the condo, made arrangements with Frank and Margaret Van Nortwyke to take our key and look over the unit once a month until we returned in the spring. As new members of the Erie Village community, we joined the Links Golf Course even though it was not completed. Since it was still under construction, we could only play the front nine. The back nine was not completed until a year later.

Before we left New Smyrna Beach after the closing in May, we had a local builder, Richard Spangler, convert our back porch into an additional room. By the time we returned to 322 Gleneagles Drive, the project was completed. We placed a sofa bed for two in the room. Julie and I used the front bedroom. Guests could use the second bathroom by going through the living/dining room and passing through the accordion doors separating that room from the rest of the house. It was fortunate we had made these changes before we returned from Erie Village. My cousin, Liz Grossmann, wrote to ask if her daughter-in-law (Regina) and her future daughter-in-law (Simi) might come to visit us in December.

I wrote back and invited them to come in early December. I should have also suggested that they come through Daytona Beach. We got word from Liz they were arriving from Stuttgart at Miami International Airport. It meant a difference of five hours drive from New Smyrna Beach, rather than forty-five minutes just to the north of us. Julie and I met the girls at the Miami Airport after having them paged. We then met them at the gate, gathered their bags, and drove north. We stopped en route home for dinner and had a chance to catch up on what was happening in Vaihingen/Enz. It was a very enjoyable two weeks that they stayed with us. We toured most of the sights on the East Coast of Florida from Cape Canaveral to St. Augustine and inland to DeLand with visits to the horse farms in Central Florida.

Nineteen ninety-six was the fiftieth year that our 1946 class graduated from Fayetteville High School. The local committee composed of Ned Mann, Betsy (Volles) Fairbanks, Bill Dupree, and Dorothy Roberts arranged for our class members to gather at the Links Golf Course Club house in late August for a reunion reception and dinner. It was the first time some of us had seen each other since graduation. I was asked to say a few words in behalf of those who had died. As each name was cited, Ned banged the chimes commemorating their passing. It was an excellent opportunity to get together with old friends. The reunion was followed up by a picnic at Martha (Trinder) and Neal Coust's home on Oneida Lake. A few of our classmates joined in the weekly golf outing at the Links for the balance of the year. There weren't too many takers. Most of our classmates who were golfers felt the course was too hard to play. There was no room for errancy in a chip shot. The abundance of water and woods were simply too formidable for most of the amateur golfers in our class of '46! Unfortunately, we did not have a follow-up reunion on the sixtieth year. Our classmates are getting older. The yearly Fayetteville High School reunion has pretty much taken over the task of encouraging all graduates from the old high school (now the Wellwood Middle School) to attend as they see fit. These reunions have been under the direction of Pat and Louise Jerome, Bill and Ann DuPree, and Bob and Faith Hall.

On September 28, 1996, our third grandchild, Christine Julia, was born in Dallas, Texas, to Lynne and Martin. We went to visit them again at Christmas. We had a very nice time together. We were pleased to see how the children were growing and becoming more and more the focus of attention for Lynne and Martin.

Dan and Katie had been dating since their college days at Syracuse University in 1991. Dan had moved out to Denver expressly to begin his graduate studies in international relations. In actual fact, we think it was to be closer to Katie. While in graduate school, he had decided to join the air force ROTC program. Upon graduation he was to be sworn in as a candidate and sent to a training camp. The commanding officer told the recruits, "If after three weeks you do not think this is the kind of life you want to lead, then you may resign with no questions asked."

Dan did, indeed, resign. Neither he nor Katie was at all enamored with the prospect of being separated for long periods of time. After Dan originally enlisted, Katie called and was crying profusely. Through her tears she said, "Do you know what your son did? He enlisted in the air force! I don't want the government sending him wherever they please! I don't want to be a service widow! I want to be with him! Can't you talk him out of this decision? I can't get through to him! I don't want him to join the air force!"

"I'll talk to him, Katie. But if that's his decision, then that's what he'll want to do. Thanks for calling. I didn't know you were so strongly opposed to his decision."

I called Dan and told him about how upset Katie was over his future.

"I'm giving it some thought, Dad. I know she's totally against it. I've got three weeks to make up my mind."

Dan did, indeed, make up his mind. He resigned from the air force's officer's training program to Katie's great relief! Dan went to work for Chrysler in Dearborn, Michigan. He used our 4Runner to haul his things in a trailer from Denver to Rochester Hills. We met him there and helped him carry his furniture into his second-floor apartment. I thought I was going to collapse helping him carry his huge-screen television set up the stairs to the first landing and then farther up the stairs to his apartment! We did finally make it, but I told him, "I'll never do that again, Dan! If you move somewhere else, you'll have to get someone else to help you. I'm not as strong as I was on the farm anymore!"

The absence of each from the other prompted them to get married. They selected November 22, 1997, as the date of their wedding. Since Katie had been baptized in the DeWitt Community Church, they wondered if Alex Carmichel might be willing to conduct the service in the Vail, Colorado Chapel. With Julie and me having returned to the Syracuse area and living in Erie Village over the summers, we had frequent contact with Alex and Betty. They lived in Lyndon just off Maple Drive on Knollwood Drive. After Betty died in June of 1996, Alex continued to live by himself for the next two years. We took him out to dinner frequently. I asked him, "Alex, how would you like to go to Vail, Colorado, as our guest and conduct the wedding ceremony for our son Dan and his finance, Katie Feiman? They tell us you baptized her in the DeWitt Community Church some twenty-five years ago."

"I'd be delighted to go!"

"Excellent! We'll make all of the arrangements to leave Hancock Field on the twentieth of November and check into the Alpen Hof Hotel in Vail. It's just a couple of blocks from the chapel."

Julie made the arrangements for the flight, and I made them for the hotel. We picked up Alex and drove to the airport, where I checked the car. By the time we arrived in Denver, it was cold but with very little snow on the ground. When we had driven to Vail, there was snow and ice everywhere. The mountains had already experienced the onset of winter.

Martin, Lynne, Corinne, Colin, and Christine had arrived earlier. Martin was Dan's best man and came in time for the wedding rehearsal and dinner. The rehearsal went very well. Alex had performed so many weddings; he didn't need any notes to remind him of who was to stand where or who was to say what at the right time. After the rehearsal in the chapel, we held a dinner at a German restaurant about two blocks from the hotel. By breakfast the next morning,

Volkmar and Eva, Bob, Judy and family, Steve, Mary and family, Liz, Tom Neil and family, and Kitty had arrived for the wedding. By two o'clock in the afternoon, it was a cold but sunny day on November 22. Alex conducted the ceremony without notes. Colin had a tendency to want to roam around the Chapel. He wanted to be with his dad. Bob took him outside and then into the backseats of the chapel for the ceremony. Dan and Katie had decided to take a carriage ride around the center of Vail in an open horse-drawn carriage following the wedding. Neither of them had a sweater or coat for this freezing temperature. By the time they returned to the chapel, Dan had given Katie his tuxedo jacket to place around her shoulders. Fortunately, neither of them caught cold. They left shortly after the evening's dinner for a trip to Paris for their week's honeymoon followed by a trip to Vaihingen/Enz so that Dan could introduce Katie to his German relatives. They very much enjoyed their travels and the opportunity to be alone together for a while.

Upon their return to Rochester Hills, Dan called to tell us, "Dad and Mom, Liz has colon cancer. If you can, you ought to pay her a visit. It may be the last time you'll ever see her. Her prognosis is not very encouraging. She should have gone to the doctor in the spring but waited until after Mattz and Simi's wedding to be checked. By then, as the doctor told her, 'Frau Grossmann, Sie haetten sollen letzten Fruejahr zu uns kommen fuer eine Untersuchung. Es ist jetzt fasst zu Spaet!' [Mrs. Grossmann, you should have come to us last spring for an examination. It's almost too late now!]"

Julie and I flew over to Stuttgart and visited Liz in the middle of January. She was already in the hospital and had had chemotherapy. She was now receiving radiation treatments. We stayed at Hans and Liz's home in Vaihingen and drove to the hospital in Stuttgart each day to visit her. We also helped her celebrate her fifty-seventh birthday with her family and grandchildren on the twenty-third of January. Martin, who was returning from a South African business trip, came by way of Vaihingen in order to visit Liz for the last time. While he was there, he listened as I read parts of my first novel, *The Security of Silence*, for Liz to hear. Even though it was in English, she thought she understood enough English to understand what had been written. She seemed to like what she heard even though I didn't finish it before we had to return to Florida. I skipped certain sections when her grandchildren were there. Liz lived until November of 1998. She is buried next to her mother and sister in the Vaihingen/Enz cemetery.

As a Slippery Rock Rotarian, I continued attending Rotary Club meetings in both Florida and Fayetteville. The weekly meetings of the Fayetteville-Manlius club were held at the Cavalry Club near Manlius. The meetings were interesting, and the food was excellent. A good friend and classmate from high school, Ned Mann, was the district governor for the 1994-95 Rotary year in Central New York. He decided to hold his annual Rotary conference in Ottawa, Canada. As attendees at the Fayetteville-Manlius Rotary Club, Julie and I decided to attend the conference as affiliates of this club. While staying at the Westin Hotel in downtown Ottawa, we thought we ought to try to make connections with the people from whom we bought our Florida residence. We knew the McMichels lived in Ottawa. I looked up their phone number and called. Margaret answered. After telling her who I was, she suggested, "Why don't you and your wife come over for coffee and cake this morning?" (The conference had just ended.)

"Fine, we'll be there shortly, Mrs. McMichel."

We had no difficulty finding their high-rise. It was along the Ottawa River just a few blocks from the hotel. They lived on the tenth floor. Gordon was a barrister and had been on the legal staff of the Canadian government for many years. He had represented Canada at the Nuremberg Nazi War Crimes trials in 1947-48. He was ninety years old but still in remarkable shape. Over coffee and cake, Margaret related how Mille Martin had called after we had decided to purchase their villa in Florida.

"Millie called and said you were interested in buying our villa. I said just a minute, Millie, let me talk to Gordon. He was walking down the hall to the elevator. I called down the hall to him 'Gordon! It's Millie!' He waved his hand towards me to signal he wasn't interested in talking to Millie! He had a client in Ottawa by the name of Millie whom he couldn't stand. I came back to the phone and told Mille, I think that's a fair price you were going to pay for our villa. And that's how we sold it. Gordon had a hard time getting used to it. But he had a chance to object. Because he didn't come back to talk with Millie on the telephone, we now no longer own the place on Gleneagles."

"So that's how it happened?" Julie asked. "Millie Martin told us you had agreed on the price when she called you. I'm sure she didn't know your husband was against the idea."

"I liked to play golf," Gordon said. "My wife never did. She had been after me to sell it for several years."

"Gordon was seriously ill last year. We had to fly him home and put him in the hospital. We were concerned he wouldn't make it. I didn't want to have to deal with selling the house myself," Margaret explained. "I'm glad you bought it. When Gordon came back later, I told him what I had done. He was very upset. He didn't think it would go so quickly."

"We're certainly glad you said yes, Margaret," Julie laughed.

"I'm glad we bought it. We have a very fine location on the eighth fairway of the red course, Gordon. I'll think of you every time I play it!" I joined in the laughter. Margaret thought it was funny too.

"I suppose it was the right decision," Gordon acknowledged. "I just wasn't prepared for how fast it was sold. You've got a nice place. We've enjoyed it ever since we had it built in 1980. We also had a nice place in Jamaica which Margaret talked me into selling. She said it was too dangerous for her to be all alone every time I went out to play golf."

"Yes, Gordon loved to play golf. I didn't. He was the golfer. I couldn't care less. I enjoyed meeting the ladies at Sugar Mill to play bridge and bingo."

By our second summer in Erie Village, the units across from us were completed. Judy and Ron Robinson moved directly across from us. As we got to know them, we would play pitch on a weekend evening. They knew some of the same friends from DeWitt whom Julie and I knew.

I tried to organize a group of Erie Village golfers to play each week. It worked out for the first few years, but the interest dropped. I no longer wanted to call the members each week to find out if they were interested in playing.

For Thanksgiving in 1998, Martin, Lynne, Corinne, Colin, and Christine came to Sugar Mill for their second visit with us in Florida. Uncle Tom and Aunt Flora came to join us together with friends from Sugar Mill: Jim and Dianne Wilson, and Ralph and Nancy Ely. With my seventieth birthday only days away, Lynne and Christine, baked a cake for the occasion. It was an excellent topping off the meal which Julie prepared of roast pork, German potato salad, spaetzle with gravy, and iceberg lettuce on the Saturday before they left to return to Flower Mound, Texas. It was the last time Martin, Lynne, Corinne, Colin, and Christine came as a family over Thanksgiving.

Dan and Katie came in a surprise to visit us over my eightieth birthday. Julie, again, made an excellent dinner of roast beef, German potato salad, spaetzle with gravy, and iceberg lettuce followed by cake and ice cream. It has also always been a pleasure when Dan and Katie have come to visit us. In more recent years, they have come with their two sons, Heath and Seth, for weekends of sightseeing and swimming. The only time we all spend together in recent years with Martin, Corinne, Colin, and Christine, and Dan, Katie, Heath, and Seth is over the Christmas holidays. We alternate between California and Colorado from one year to the next. It gives us all an opportunity to see each other and enjoy each other's company.

XVI.

Overseas Travel

During May of 1999, Donna Barron, a fellow member of the Coronado United Methodist Church of New Smyrna Beach, asked if anyone was interested in joining her for a trip to China. She had spent three years there as a teacher of English in Jaiozoa and had been asked by the vice president of the Jaiozoa Teachers' College to come to teach for a six-week summer session. The vice president had also written to her to invite any other American teachers to come with her to teach as well.

We had gotten to know Donna through our membership in the Coronado United Methodist Church where Julie and Donna were both choir members. As they became acquainted, Donna mentioned her plan to return that summer to Jaiozoa to teach English for three weeks. She had talked with several other members of the church who had indicated an interest. She knew we had been to China in 1990, and when she mentioned it to Julie, she asked, "Why don't you and Don join the group I'm putting together to go to China this summer, Julie? There'll be time for personal travel at the end of our stay. I think Gail and Mike Pregman are interested. I've got an excellent Chinese student who will be our translator. He's Tony Lee, and his English is about the best I've ever heard in China. The Chinese students at the teachers' college are all teachers of English in Chinese schools. They desperately need to hear and practice English as it's spoken by native speakers. You know what it's like."

"Let me talk it over with Don. We don't have anything else planned for the summer. If he's agreeable, we'll go with your group."

On our way home from church, Julie said, "Guess what. Donna Barron wants us to go with her to Jaiozoa Teachers' College in Chengdu, China, for three weeks to teach English."

"What's that?"

"She wants us to go with her and some other church members to China to teach English for three weeks!"

"Where did you say she's planning to go?"

"It's a place called Jaiozoa in Chengdu province. It's in south central China in a region near Yunnan where we were in 1990. She says she has a few others interested. She'd like to have us join them. What do you think about it?"

"I guess it has possibilities. What's it going to cost?"

"Just the price of the air tickets and any internal travel we want to do in China. I don't think it'll be too expensive."

"If we're interested, she wants us to attend a meeting at the Shaffers this next Saturday evening after dinner."

"I guess it wouldn't hurt to hear her out."

Julie and I joined a group of about eight persons who had expressed an interest in participating. Donna told us what she had done in China and how eager the Chinese were to learn English.

"It's a nice town, and we would stay in a nearby hotel not far from the teachers' college. We will have no expenses in Jaiozoa other than what we want to do and see on or own. The room and board is all covered by the college. After the three weeks, you can travel anywhere you like."

By the time the decision had to be made of who and how many persons were going, the group was down to six of us: Donna, Gail, Mike, Julie, me, and one other person, Doris Mates, who joined just as the plans were being made for the tickets. Since Mike Pregman had traveled extensively in Asia, he suggested he knew of a travel agent who could get us a special deal if we went through his travel agency. Donna thought that was a good idea, and Mike's friend made the travel arrangements. Doris Mates, Julie, and I flew out of Syracuse Hancock International Airport in business class. It was one of the most comfortable trips we have ever taken. Each of us had his/her own television console in seats that were not crowded and three meals served with snacks and drinks during the times in between. We had a brief stopover in Japan. When we arrived at Jaiozoa, Tony and Donna were there to greet us. They took us to our hotel and were shown to our rooms.

"Get some rest," Donna suggested. "It's been a long flight. The college is starting this coming Monday. We'll eat breakfast, lunch, and dinner together. I'd like to have us meet at seven o'clock each morning for a Bible reading and a brief prayer before we go to breakfast. We'll rotate the readings and prayers so that everyone gets a chance to contribute."

We spent the rest of the day sleeping between meals and getting familiar with the bathroom facilities. We were on the top floor of the five-story hotel. Each morning at six o'clock sharp the chimes on the city's clock played followed by the hour being struck at the conclusion of the chimes. It was an automatic wake-up routine which did not vary even on weekends.

Tony was indispensable as a translator. If we didn't like some of the food being served, he would ask for something else. Fried eggs, toast, and bacon became almost a daily breakfast start for us. Our dinners were soup, rice, some meat, and vegetables with bread followed by fruit. The suppers were usually more soup, bread and fruit, ice cream, or cake for dessert.

The college supplied the taxis to take us back and forth between the hotel and college. Needless to say, these shuttle trips were by far the most dangerous we had ever traveled. The drivers thought nothing at all about driving down the extreme left lane (heading towards oncoming traffic) if they were passing a heavily loaded truck or ox cart. They seemed to take their obligation more seriously than we did. They wanted to make sure we got to the classroom on time, even if it was extremely dangerous!

There were about forty students in each of the classes. The object was to give them as much experience learning and speaking English as possible. Theoretically, they had all studied English, but their use of speaking it was limited at best and the written at least understandable. Julie was the teacher and I was her assistant. She made up the lesson plans, and when she wanted me to read certain sentences of stories, I would do so. The intent was to have the students repeat what I read. It reminded me of my experience in Thailand trying to get the students to use English as much as possible. Aside from the lectures, speaking drills, and writing practice, neither of us could quite get used to the clearing of throats and the spitting on the classroom floor! Not all of the teachers did this, but enough to make us careful where we stepped as we walked around the room. Our speaking drills usually meant we had to have the individual teachers repeat after us what we had said or what they were reading.

At the conclusion of our stay in Jaiozoa, the vice president of the teachers' college held a special dinner in our honor at our hotel. There were a variety of Chinese soups, vegetables, meats, rolls, plus a special serving of baby turtles still in their shells. From our previous trip to China, Julie and I recognized we could confront all kinds of rare and, for us, almost uneatable dishes placed before us as guests of honor. I did sample a small piece of one, but couldn't continue. It was simply too unappetizing for me in its appearance, to say nothing of its taste! I'm not sure whether or not I offended our hostess, but I simply couldn't eat any more than a taste of the turtle!

After our stay in Jaiozoa, Julie and I traveled to Beijing and visited the ancient royal palace, the summer residence and gardens. The Great Wall of China was indeed impressive. It has lookout towers every five hundred feet built over the path on the wall. The wall itself is wide enough to have three horse-drawn chariots riding abreast its entire length. We also visited the excavated sights of some of the ancient emperors in Xian who were buried with not only horse-drawn chariots but also armed soldiers to escort the monarch to the next life. The clay figures were actually made from models of real men, horses, and chariots after having been modeled by live men and horses. Little wonder the wall can be seen from outer space! It did not serve the purpose for which it was constructed. The Mongols of Ghengkis Khan simply went around the end of it and overwhelmed the Chinese defenders.

On our return to the States, Julie and I stopped in Japan for two days of sightseeing in and around Tokyo and the Narita Airport area. Japan has become a very highly modernized society. The shops, stores, and exhibits were as similar as those we would see in any American city.

In January of 2001, Julie and I took a trip to the Republic of South Africa. Martin, Lynne, Corinne, Colin, and Christine had been posted to Cape Town. Martin's job was to oversee the marketing interests of the company which had established a series of Caltex gas stations throughout the South African provinces in the late nineties. They lived in a house rented by the company from a Swiss couple in Hout Bay, Cape Town. The view of the south Atlantic Ocean was spectacular. The owners weren't sure they were coming back to South Africa. There were safety locks on the outside gates which could only be opened from inside the house for anyone to gain access to the compound. There was also what Lynne called "a rape prevention gate" between the living room and the bedroom. It was made of steel bars and had a lock on the inside. If someone tried to enter, it would be impossible for him to go any farther than the gate. The yard was a large one. Martin and I pitched horseshoes while the children played in their sandbox. There was also a large yard extending down the hillside to the fence just above the yard of their neighbor. The fence, however, was not as formidable as the one off the main road in front of the house. When Lynne's folks visited in November and December of 2000, they had traveled extensively with them in South Africa. Lynne encouraged us to see as much of the country as possible. We arranged a trip through the eastern part of Cape Town and the southeastern provinces with a local travel agency. The agency supplied us with a driver and a van for the duration of the trip. The driver was, in effect, also our guide. He had grown up in this region and had traveled through it many times. One of the first places he took us to was a huge ostrich farm. We not only had ostrich steak for dinner, but we also had an opportunity to ride one. A large flock of them was driven from one farm to another along the highway over which we traveled. The countryside was both beautiful and formidable in appearance. Much of it seemed desolate and relatively unoccupied. The few farms we saw were like huge plantations with a central homesite surrounded by smaller homes in which the farmworkers lived.

One of our first overnight stops was at the Addo Elephant Park. It is a huge preserve featuring elephants, zebras, gazelles, impala, and rhinoceros. Our cabins were at the entrance to the park. We could only gain access to see the elephants and the other animals aboard a sightseeing truck especially built to transport the passengers in rows of seats in the back of the truck body. It was, indeed, impressive how close we could come to the elephants and watch them as these grazed on grass, bushes, and tree limbs. In contrast to the next park that we visited, these animals seemed to take us visitors in stride. They continued whatever they were doing without seeming at all concerned with us a visitors riding in our sightseers truck.

Our next stop was at the Shamwari Game farm founded by the older brother of Gary Player, the great South African golfer of the forties, fifties, and sixties. We spent two days touring the vast park. We, again, rode in the back of an open truck which had seats for twelve passengers behind the driver. The park guide drove us to see a huge herd of elephants.

"Keep very quiet," he told us. "Don't make any loud noises or quick movements."

He drove the sightseeing truck to within fifty yards of the herd. As we approached the herd again grazing on grass, twigs, tree limbs, and bushes, one of the large female elephants looked at us very intently.

The guide spoke to us almost in a whisper. "Stay in your seats and be very quiet. She's used to the truck. She's seen us many times. So long as you don't make any movement or sound, she'll continue to graze. She'll think you're part of the truck and won't charge."

The elephant kept looking in our direction for some minutes until she moved on followed by the rest of her herd.

"The females are especially alert when there are small calves around. But as you can see, there are only a few, and they're in the midst of the herd for protection."

We watched for some time before backing away some fifty yards to continue our observations. The waste deposits were prodigious in size and reflected the fact of their very large appetites! Having grown up around cows, I was amazed how one elephant could produce the equivalent feces of four cows at one time!

The guide continued to drive us around different parts of the preserve. We also encountered large herds of impala, zebra, monkeys, gaur, gazelle, ostriches, wildebeests, meerkats, and a variety of deer. We also saw a hippopotamus in one of the rivers and a rhinoceros grazing with her young calf. We didn't see any lions, leopards, cheetahs, or hyenas.

"Where are the big game cats?" One of our visitors asked.

"We don't have any yet. This park has only recently been opened. These large predators won't be brought in until next year. We've got to keep the game under control ourselves at present. You're right though. The best way to do that is by natural selection. The hunters select which animals they can catch and eat."

The trip to the east coast was a long one with relatively little traffic on the highway. We did stop at a huge cave which was another tourist attraction. Actually, it was a series of caves with lights throughout. As all of us tourists were led though the caves, the guide told us as we reached the final assembly room, "I'm going to turn out the lights. I'll give you five minutes in which to try to find your way out of here in the dark. If you haven't made it by then, I'll turn on the lights again so you can see the door leading to the exit."

By the time Julie and I had reached the door, the guide had turned on the lights. No one had made it out on his/her own.

Once we arrived at Knysna, our driver-guide told us we should take the local train to Port Elizabeth and back.

"It'll give you access to local travel which is the only way you can view the dense forests, slum dwellings around the edges of the towns and villages, the beautiful beaches, and catch a glimpse of where the Atlantic and Indian oceans meet."

We also saw the hotel and beachfront in Elizabethtown where Sue and Leon Pullen (Sugar Mill neighbors) had stayed during one of their trips to South Africa.

As we returned to Knysna, our driver-guide asked, "Wasn't that the best way to see some of the country which you can see in no other way?"

"It was worth it," we both agreed.

He then took us to the Knysna hotel situated on top of a hill overlooking the valley and beaches below. It was owned and run by an Afrikaner family. The neighboring houses, surrounded by iron bars and gates, were also owned by white South Africans. We caught a glimpse of what life must have been like during the days of apartheid. It was an era that had passed, but remnants of it still remained in isolated pockets as the domain of the former rulers of this country.

Upon our return, Martin, Lynne, and their children took us on a tour of tabletop mountain in Cape Town. We took the cable car to the top and walked around viewing a grand vista in almost every direction. It reminded us of some of the mountaintops we had visited in Germany and Austria. The only difference was the lack of snow and ice, but just as beautiful scenery in every direction!

As we stood near the edge of the southern perimeter, Martin pointed out Robben Island. "That's where Nelson Mandela was imprisoned for twenty-seven years. It would be worth a trip to take the ferry over to see it."

We were glad he pointed it out. "When can we go to visit it?" we asked.

"I'll take a day off and take you over there," Martin said.

That next Wednesday morning after breakfast, Martin said, "How about going to Robben Island today? I've made arrangements for my assistant to take charge of the office today. Lynne won't be able to go. She has to be here when the kids come home from school."

Corinne, Colin, and Christine were all attending what was called "the British School" in Cape Town. The bus dropped them off each day at three o'clock in front of the house. Lynne would be waiting for them at the gate to let them in.

Martin's driver took us to the ferry where we bought our tickets for the twenty-minute boat ride to the island. The prison location was purposefully placed on the island so that if someone tried to escape, it would be a long swim back to the mainland. Very few, if any, prisoners would be able to make it. We were a large group of visitors. Hence, our guide met us as we got off the ferry and took us in tow to lead us through the compound, the prison cells, and the work areas where the prisoners broke rocks with hammers day after day.

"What was done with the broken rocks?" a tourist asked.

"They were used for road building," the guide explained. "The prisoners sat in the heat of the sun day after day, breaking rocks under the watchful eyes of the guards. No one was allowed to leave without permission of the guard commander."

"Were they given water to drink?" I asked.

"Every two hours, the prisoners were allowed a drink and a five-minute bathroom break if they needed one. Otherwise, they were not allowed to leave their positions. Nelson Mandela had to break rocks just like everyone else. He preferred to work with the other prisoners instead of being kept in solitary confinement. He was often put in solitary confinement whenever he tried to speak to the other prisoners. They were supposed to remain silent for the entire day."

The guide also showed us the cells into which the men were placed each evening. There was a barred window at the top of the outside wall of the cell. There was a bunk with a blanket, a sink with cold water, and a primitive toilet and an iron door with a slot through which the food was passed each day.

"This was the daily treatment of all of the prisoners, including Nelson Mandela. There were special rooms for solitary confinement. The building next to this one was the holding pen, as it was called. If prisoners tried to talk to each other, they were placed there for a week at a time. Mr. Mandela was not a man to remain silent. He spent almost as much time in solitary confinement as on the rock pile."

As we walked around the compound, I noticed there was a golf green not far from the end of one of the buildings.

"Is this a golf course?" I asked.

"Yes. The guards had access to it on their days off."

In contrast to most golf courses, this one was nothing more than sand or hard packed dirt from the tees to the greens. The greens were the only part of the course having grass on them. It was only a nine-hole course which was now no longer being used.

Once again, the island reflected a dark and impressive glimpse into the tyranny with which South Africa was at one time ruled by ruthless whites caring only for themselves with no consideration for the interests, rights, or justice for the blacks.

One of the interesting features of Martin and Lynne's home on Hout Bay which really intrigued me was what they told us about whales coming into the bay. I took out my field glasses each morning and scanned the bay for whales. I often thought I saw them surfacing near some of the larger islands.

"I saw some of the whales surfacing this morning," I said at breakfast.

Martin and Lynne laughed.

"Those aren't whales, Dad. Those are submerged rocks which give the appearance of whales because they're so big!" Lynne laughed.

"Have you ever noticed whether or not they moved from the same position each day, Dad?" Martin asked. "You won't notice any movement from one day to the next. The rocks will still be in the same position every morning!"

Sure enough. When I looked every day thereafter, the "whales" I thought I saw were in exactly the identical spot each day!

Martin and Lynne took the children and us swimming on one of the southern beaches. We seemed to be surrounded by miniature penguins. They had nested in the bushes just behind the beach.

"Aren't these birds a long way from home?" Julie asked Lynne.

"These are miniature penguins, Mom. They wouldn't survive in Antarctica. They're indigenous to this southern coast of Africa," Lynne told us. "Their feather coats are not heavy enough for the really cold temperatures farther south. That's why they nest here. They do go swimming in the ocean for their food like the other penguins, but they have to build their nest along the shore in this warmer climate."

Martin told us to be careful if we swam some distance out into the ocean.

"A friend and I were swimming several hundred yards offshore when the current caught us. We couldn't swim directly back into shore. We had to swim along with the current some half mile down the beach before we could make it back to land. If you swim out too far, don't forget you can't win against the current. We were just lucky we made it back when we did."

It was another lesson which we learned from one who had had the experience of trying to go against the current. Bigger forces will overwhelm you every time if you try to oppose them!

We had some excellent meals at various restaurants along the coast of South Africa. Lynne and Martin had discovered them when Lynne's folks were visiting the year before. If the distance were not so great (more than twenty-two hours by air from the United States), these restaurants would have great appeal for frequent visits.

Our next trip overseas was to Thailand in February 2003. Martin had been reassigned to Bangkok after his two-year stay in South Africa. He was in charge of expending the Chevron facilities in the country. Martin had found a beautiful home not far from the American school in one of Bangkok's expanding suburbs. Lynne enrolled Corinne, Colin, and Christine as soon as they arrived. It was only a one-half-mile trip or a ten-minute bicycle ride from their home to the school. Martin rode his bicycle with Corinne, Colin, and Christine to school each morning before he went to work.

They had a beautiful home with a swimming pool in the backyard, a large open area surrounded by a sidewalk and numerous trees and flowers next to the common area available to all of the residents. Their house was a two-story home with a large staircase ascending from the den and living room to the second floor. Martin and Lynne's bedroom was on the first floor. Corinne and Christine shared Christine's bedroom on the second floor. Colin occupied a second upstairs bedroom, while Julie and I used Corinne's bedroom. The housekeeper and a cook shared another room off the kitchen next to the garage on the first floor.

The neighborhood included many Americans, British and Canadian compatriots so that making friends with neighbors was relatively easy. There were cookouts and picnics twice a month in the common area. Lynne enrolled the children on the various classroom baseball teams so that each of them had an opportunity to play weekly. Julie and I attended a couple of games and saw them play as if they were stateside. There were also adult softball teams upon which Martin and Lynne usually played on a Sunday afternoon. After a few days in Bangkok, Martin and Lynne suggested, "Why don't we spend a week at Hua Hin, Mom and Dad? It's one of the best resort areas in Thailand."

I had been there in 1954 with a group of students and faculty from Chulalongkorn University on our way to the southernmost area of Thailand at Songkhla. I only saw the beach area at the time but was enthralled by its beauty.

"That's a great idea. I haven't been there in over forty-seven years and your Mom has never been there! Do you want us to rent a car and driver?"

"No, that won't be necessary. We've got a large van that seats seven people, has a television screen and eating table. There should be plenty of room for all of us," Lynne said.

It was, indeed, a very comfortable ride to Hua Hin. Their driver knew the way. While Corinne, Colin, and Christine watched a movie, Julie, Martin, Lynne, and I played pitch. It was a very enjoyable time for all of us although Lynne complained of some pain in her groin area for which she was taking medication. We stopped along the way when the driver thought we might like to take in the sights as we travelled through the region. After we arrived, we were taken to our rooms on the third floor of the three-story hotel. Our room looked out over the large swimming pool between the hotel and the beach. We swam not only in the saltwater of the gulf but also in the freshwater of the pool. We did both during our time at the resort. Martin and Lynne had arranged for Julie and me to have the private use of two massage ladies followed by a hot tub "lovemaking" experience as it was called. The theory was if you have a really good massage, then sex should follow as a natural course of events! It proved to be a very satisfactory sequel to our "massage"!

A short time after we arrived, Martin said, "Dad, why don't you and I go golfing? The ladies and kids can go swimming the while. I've found out about a course nearby from the hotel clerk."

"That's okay with me. I'll have to rent some clubs since I didn't bring mine along."

Martin's driver knew where the course was and drove us there. When we went into the pro shop, I almost couldn't believe what I heard.

"That'll cost each of you two hundred dollars."

"What?" I exclaimed. "There's nothing cheaper?"

"All of the courses cost the same, Dad. I'll pay for it if you can't."

"No. That's okay, Martin. I was just a bit overwhelmed. I've heard it costs three hundred dollars to play a round of golf in Japan. This is at least not that expensive!"

I paid the fees and found out we also had "hired" two female caddies who rode on the rear of our carts standing on the bumper behind our clubs and hanging on to the cart struts. They told us to go to the driving range first. Our tee time wasn't for another twenty minutes. After we arrived, Martin's caddy and my caddy gave each of us our drivers and a bucket of balls.

"Use your drivers and hit five balls," the older one told us.

After our fifth ball, the caddies handed us the three wood and five balls.

"Use this three wood to hit five balls."

We dutifully did. The girls then handed us each club in our bags until everyone of them had been used.

"Now go to first tee," the older caddy instructed. (With the four-hundred-dollar fee, we each were given a cart to use.)

After we arrived on the first tee, each of them picked out the driver from our bags and handed them to us. We thought it was some kind of a test to see if we really knew how to play golf. We discovered they had watched us using our clubs to determine how far we hit the ball with each one. Generally, they were on target although when I wanted to use a four iron to reach the distance which she said was 160 yards from the green, I asked for the four iron. She handed me the five iron.

"No. I want the four iron. I can't hit the ball that far with a five iron!"

"No, no. You should use the five iron!" she protested. "I know. I watch players all the time!"

She handed me the five iron, and I proceeded to hit the ball about five yards in front of the green. "See, that's why I wanted to use the four iron!" I told her sharply.

"You weak old man!" she answered. "You should hit green with five iron!"

Following the golf match (which Martin won by several strokes), the girls hung around as we were eating and drinking. It occurred to me they probably wanted their tips.

"We better give them each one hundred baht, Dad," Martin told me. "That's why they're waiting."

I remembered something from years ago in Thailand which one of my roommates told me.

"Don, if the girls hang around after providing some service, it's not unusual for them to be willing to provide sex, for an additional gratuity, if their sponsors wish."

Julie and I were both impressed with the way Martin played tag with their kids in the pool. All of them seemed to enjoy it immensely. What an idyllic existence, I thought, for Martin and his family! Living high on the hog at very little cost to themselves! Few people can enjoy what their family was taking for granted!

Upon our return to Bangkok, Julie and I had the use of Martin's driver, Ong-Arg, and their van to visit some of the sights in and around the city. One of our trips was to the many *klongs* (canals) branching off the Chao Phraya River which flows through the city of Bangkok. We also visited a museum and artists' colony where elephants were available for rides by the tourists. I took some pictures of Julie on an elephant and she took one of me sitting on the outstretched front leg of an elephant who had lain down at the behest of his trainer. It wasn't so bad until the elephant decided to place his head on my left shoulder. I couldn't believe how heavy it was! Fortunately for me, Julie took the picture very quickly! I couldn't have held out much longer!

One of our other trips was to Chulalongkorn University where I had taught from 1954 to 1956. I wanted to show Julie around the campus. The driver took us to a ten-story high-rise just behind what I recognized as the College of Arts and Sciences where I had done most of my teaching.

"Ong-Arg, this isn't the Arts and Sciences building. That's it over there!" I pointed it out to him.

"That's where it used to be, Acharen, but it isn't there anymore. This is the main campus office building now. All of the different departments are in this building now."

"Those buildings are where I used to teach. What are they being used for now?"

"They're still used for classes, Acharen, but also for libraries for the whole campus. The Department of Modern Languages is in this building on the tenth floor."

Ong-Arg let us out at the front door. "Take the elevator to the tenth floor, Acharen," he said.

We took the elevator as directed by Ong-Arg to the tenth floor. We got out and there on the door was the Department of Modern Languages. I opened the door for Julie and introduced ourselves to the secretary.

"Hello, I'm Donald Megnin and this is my wife, Julie. Could I talk with the chairman of the Modern Language Department? I taught in this department from 1954 to 1956. I'd like to introduce my wife to the chairman and look over your facilities."

"Acharen Megnin, the chairman is not in just now. There's no one from the department available just now."

"When I was here, Acharen Nopakhun Tongyai was the vice chairman of the Department of Modern Languages and Prince Prem was the chairman. I don't suppose there's anyone around anymore from that time."

"That's a long time ago! No. There's no one here from that time still teaching. But I do know Acharen Nopakhun's daughter. She's a doctor that lives not far from me. I'll call her and see if she's available."

The secretary called but was unable to reach her. "She's not at home at present."

"Well, she probably wouldn't remember me at any rate. She was just a little girl when I was here then. This is a real high-rise for this campus. Are classes held here in this building, or is this mainly an office building?"

"This is mostly an office building. The classes are still held in the older buildings."

"I see the building is air-conditioned. We didn't have that back in the fifties. We just left out doors open and the wind blew through. This is quite a change from that time!"

The secretary, obviously, didn't care for my comment. "This building has been air-conditioned for more than twenty years! All of our classroom buildings are air-conditioned!"

As two women students came in, I excused us with the comment, "I guess we better be on our way."

Ong-Arg drove us around the campus. The rain tree avenue which once lined the gateway drive from the Phaya Thai Road into the main campus no longer existed. Most of the old buildings were still there but were overshadowed by the new ones.

"It's nothing like I remember, Julie. The shelter under which I kept my motorcycle is gone. The Arts and Sciences building still looks the same, but with these high-rises, the old campus seems much smaller than I remember it."

We should have stopped and walked around a bit, but we didn't. I thought we might come back again, but we never did. Ong-Arg took us to the Oriental Hotel along the Chao Phraya River where Julie, Martin, and I had stayed on our way back from India in 1966. We met Martin and Lynne for lunch in the hotel. When I was in Bangkok in the fifties, I wouldn't have thought of eating there. It was much too expensive! The hotel had been upgraded to become an even more elaborate and expensive one than in those days. The food was excellent and the decor appropriate for foreigners to see something of the old Thai architecture and furnishings. The view of the river scenes were still much the same except there were now mostly power boats and very few still paddled by men. We returned a few more times to the Oriental Hotel for dinner with Martin, Lynne, and the grandchildren.

The country had changed significantly over the past fifty-plus years. While the activities undertaken by families were still much the same with visits to the zoo and the many Buddhist temples. But Thailand had changed. It was different. The people whom I had known and worked with were long gone. The new ones had no idea what life was like in the era in which I had spent there. I thought back on what Nopakhun had told me about the World War II era. The country was occupied by the Japanese.

"The women all had to wear hats during the occupation. I never really knew why. It was a government requirement. There were a lot of things we couldn't do, but wearing hats has always remained with me," she laughed. "It was something all of us women had to do! We also had to dress formally at the university. Men were expected to wear suits and ties. Do you see anyone on the faculty doing that today? Except for the difference in age, you couldn't tell the difference between the students and the faculty! We've become very casual these days. Perhaps too casual. The faculty seems to think so long as they do their job of teaching, the rest of their lives are for their own enjoyment!"

What she was touching on were "moments in time." What do you do with the time that you have? I was certainly not one to wear a sport coat while teaching. Not only was it too hot, but my shirt was sweated through by the end of a lecture without a sport coat! Nopakhun had grown up in an earlier era than I and most of the younger faculty members.

"Just look around you," she said. "The foreign faculty take Thai girls as cooks and housemaids and before long they are expected to do whatever their employer desires. You'll probably fall into the same pattern, if you live in your own house!"

"Yes, Nopakhun. I know what you're referring to. But that's not my lifestyle. I'm not here to exploit Thai girls. I know what happens. Once the men are no longer assigned here, they return to their households and act as if they were as innocent as the day they arrived. No thanks! I'm going to be the same person I was when I leave Thailand as the day I arrived! My 'moments in time' are too precious to waste on the exploitation of women or anyone else! I'm not going to take advantage of some innocent young girls who think their foreign employer is going to take them back home with him when he leaves. Do you know what Mrs. Harris [another Chulalongkorn faculty member from the States] said to me when she first met me?"

"No."

"When she found out I was single, she said, all single men should be shot! They shouldn't be allowed to come to Thailand without a wife!'"

Nopakhun laughed. "That may be a bit extreme, but what she's referring to is what seems to happen every time a single American male comes to Thailand! They think they can get away with whatever they want! And when they leave, the women are left behind!"

The daily life of a person is like a few moments in the space of a lifetime. Whatever he or she does is reflected as a positive contribution to the welfare of others, or as a negative impact upon the life or lives of their fellow human beings. I had seen for myself to what she was referring. Not only had I witnessed what was happening from the actions of the two Americans with whom I lived for a year, but also among the faculty members who retired and returned to their native homelands. One British faculty member had lived and taught at Chulalongkorn

University for more than twenty years. When he finally retired at age sixty-five, he returned to Britain without the woman who had taken care of all of his "needs" for the many years he lived in Bangkok. He did give her some money before he left. He had a family in Britain to whom he returned without her.

Thailand was and is an intriguing country in which to live and work. The temptations are only as flagrant as persons will allow themselves to lose control of their actions. One of my compatriots, with whom I lived for the first year, was a contact for American scholars visiting Bangkok on their way to attend conferences en route to other Asian countries. He told me on one occasion, "The first thing these guys want to do is to be taken to a place where they can have access to Thai girls. These guys aren't just researchers! They're established scholars in their fields. They know what Thailand has to offer!"

"Are they bachelors?" I asked.

"Some of them are, but most of them have families back in the States."

By the time I left Thailand in 1956, I often thought how wise Mrs. Harris's comment about bachelors was! I recalled too how she said her husband didn't hire any development aid specialists unless they were married. He also required that the wife accompany her husband to Thailand for his tour of duty.

"That's the only way they behave," she said emphatically.

If only that were also the case! Not always. I met some very angry wives in Thailand, whose husbands had also strayed while they were busy taking care of the children!

Our last trip overseas was in May 2004. We had made arrangements with the Daytona Beach Mercedes-Benz dealer to buy a new E320 in Germany. We left on the twenty-third of May and flew into Stuttgart to pick up the car at the Mercedes-Benz plant in Sindelfingen on the twenty-fifth. On our previous purchase of a Mercedes, the company paid for Julie's airfare, three nights in a five-star Stuttgart hotel, three dinners, a tour of the plant, car insurance, and shipment of the car back to the States. On this occasion, Mercedes only paid for one night in a five star hotel, a tour and dinner at the plant, two-weeks for car insurance and shipment of the car to the United States. The Company was no longer as generous as previously.

After picking up the car, we drove to Vaihingen/Enz to stay with Hans Grossmann (Liz's husband) at his home in the basement of his son Martin and daughter-in-law's (Regina) house on Znaimer Strasse Nr. 5. Hans sacrificed his bed for our use while he slept on the living room couch. We got together with both of his sons and families. Martin and Regina have four children: Benjamin, Julia, Diana, and Lauren. Mattz and Simi have three children: a daughter, Vivian, twin brothers, Jona and Luka.

Our trip coincided with the annual Mai'en Tag (May Day festivities) in Vaihingen/Enz. There was a parade of children, musicians, elders, visitors from abroad, singers, and horse and buggy carts led this year by Martin and Regina's oldest son, Benjamin, to the city park. He had been chosen because of his outstanding scholastic achievement in the Vaihingen/Enz Gymnasium (high school). Upon arrival at the park, there were speeches, singing, dancing, poems recited by children, and an address made by the mayor as he introduced the assembled dignitaries. The festivities were followed by beer drinking and sausage consumption in the huge tent which had been set up for the occasion. We joined Mattz, Simi, Martin, and Regina and their children in the tent after the program for something to eat and drink.

While we usually stayed in the little attic room in the house that had belonged to Hans and Liz (they had purchased it from her mother, my mother, Tante Lina, and Tante Maria), Mattz and Simi were in the process of remodeling and adding additional rooms to the house. Hence our stay with Hans in his apartment. We had a picnic in the backyard of Martin and Regina's house and ate out with Hans in the local restaurants. He prepared breakfast and supper for us each day. We helped him wash the dishes prior to going out.

One of the sights Julie and I wanted to visit again was Salzburg, Austria, where we had such fond memories and experiences over the years. We had lived in Groedig (a suburb of Salzburg) and in Salzburg while teaching on three different occasions under the Slippery Rock University's Summer Studies Program (1969, '89, and '94). We drove to Salzburg in a few hours and spent the night in the Untersberg Hotel not far from the cable car that took people to the top of the Untersberg Mountain. After visiting the locales where we had stayed, we returned to Germany and stopped in Munich to visit Hermann (my cousin) and his wife, Kunigunde Luipold; their son, Thomas; his wife, Ursel; and their daughter, a student at the University of Munich. We also visited Michael Roth, the son of my deceased cousin; Marianne, Liz's best friend; Renate; and her husband, Dieter Kuckenburg, before returning the car to the Mercedes plant for shipment to the United States. It took us longer to find the correct office at which to leave the car so that we barely got to the airport in time to catch our plane. When we arrived at the flight gate, it had already been closed. The one attendant just closing up took pity on us and led us in, via the back door, in order to board the plane without having had to go through the screening mechanism usually required before entering the aircraft. We made it just as the stewardess was closing the door of the plane!

Other than our yearly flights to either the West Coast, to spend time with Martin's family, or Denver, to spend time with Dan and Katie's family each alternating Christmas season, we have not done any other traveling except for our annual automobile trips to and fro between New Smyrna Beach and Syracuse.

XVII.
Life's Changing Moments

On September 11, 2001, Judy Robinson, the neighbor across the street in Erie Village, called at 8:45 a.m., "Why don't you turn on your television. An airplane has just hit one of the Twin Towers in New York City!"

I did. Julie and I watched in suspense as first the one tower and then the other, which was also hit by another airplane, gradually burned, shook, and collapsed in a thundering shower of dust, dirt, and debris scattered over several blocks of New York City! Almost three thousand of our compatriots were killed in this attack. Men and women could be seen jumping out of the upper-story windows to their death more than a thousand feet below! It was a tragedy which will never be forgotten either by the families of the victims or by us as the bystanders unable to do much to save so many who died not knowing how or why such an attack by a group of terrorists could vent their anger upon innocent persons here in the United States. Fanatical religious extremists have declared war upon those persons who refuse to follow their religious beliefs, practices, and behavior. Religion has, historically, been one of the worst purveyors of hatred, intolerance, and indifference to the needs of people to find their own way amidst the cacophony of conflicting religious views held by those who believe themselves to be the agents of God on earth! We need to be reminded periodically about the counsel and words of Siddhartha Gautama (the Buddha): "Believe nothing just because a so-called wise person said it. Believe nothing just because a belief is generally held. Believe nothing just because it is said in ancient books. Believe nothing just because it is said to be of divine origin. Believe nothing just because someone else believes it. Believe only what you yourself test and judge to be true."

If nothing else, this act of terrorism has set the course for future behavior among peoples and nations around the world. We are now being counseled to become more wary, suspicious, and critical of the actions of others forgetting our need to deal kindly and justly with our families, friends, and neighbors wherever they live and irrespective of their views or beliefs.

It was the first weekend in June 2001. Eva had died in January. Volkmar was at something of a loss as to what his future might hold now that he was all alone. He called and asked if he might stay with us in June. He wanted to attend his sixtieth class reunion from the College of Environmental Sciences and Forestry at Syracuse University.

"That's no problem, Volk. Just come on up and you stay with us over the weekend. We've got plenty of room, as you well know."

That previous year, while attending our annual Fayetteville High School Reunion, an older lady came up to me and asked, "Are you by any chance Volkmar Megnin's brother?"

"Yes, I am. Are you Claire Hossbein, by any chance? I remember you from the nineteen thirties." (I had read her name tag.)

"Yes. I'm Claire Hossbein Wilcox. I was married to Bill Wilcox in 1942. Your brother was a Boy Scout in my dad's troop in Kirkville."

It was the start of an interesting conversation. We renewed our acquaintance and agreed we would get together at some point in the future.

"Give Volkmar my regards, Donald."

"I will, Claire. Good-bye for now."

With Volkmar coming to his college reunion on that first Saturday in June, Julie and I talked over of what we might want to do while he was with us in Erie Village.

"What would you think about getting together with Claire Hossbein while he's here, Julie? It might be a very pleasant surprise for both of them."

"That's an excellent idea. Why don't you call her and find out if she might join us for dinner at the Canteen Restaurant on Sunday afternoon?"

"Okay, I'll give her a call."

I found her number in the phone book and called.

"Hi, Claire. This is Don Megnin. We met last year at the Fayetteville High School Reunion."

"Oh yes. You're Volkmar's brother."

"Claire, how would you like to join Julie and me for dinner this next Sunday around twelve thirty at the Canteen Restaurant in Chittenango?"

"Thanks. I'd like that."

"Okay, see you on Sunday, Claire."

When Volkmar arrived on Friday, we had one of Julie's special dinners (roast pork) followed by a good time playing cards. We discussed all kinds of subjects with him: how he was getting along all by himself, how things were going at the mill, whether he was getting enough to eat cooking by himself, and what he was doing to overcome his loneliness. He gave quite a litany of his work schedule, the hours alone (which he found the hardest to take with Eva's death).

"How would you like to join us for dinner at the Canteen Restaurant in Chittenango this Sunday afternoon and meet someone whom you've not seen since 1942?"

"Not since 1942? Is it a man or a woman?"

"It's a woman, Volkmar. Don says you were really sweet on her years ago," Julie laughed.

"I've arranged for Claire Hossbein Wilcox to join us for dinner, Volk. You remember her, don't you?"

"Heck yes. I haven't seen her since I went into the army in 1942!"

"She doesn't know you're going to be with us, Volk. You can take her by surprise on Sunday when you see her."

He had a good time at his class reunion in Syracuse. But we noticed he was really more interested in meeting Claire the next day. He went off to the Catholic Church in Chittenango Sunday morning to attend mass. He was all dressed up in a sport coat, tie, pressed slacks, and new shoes. At a little after twelve o'clock, we drove down to Chittenango and walked into the Canteen Restaurant. The woman greeter asked where we preferred to sit.

"Actually, we're meeting someone for dinner."

"Follow me. I think I know where she's sitting."

We followed the maitre de' into the dining room looking out on Route 5. There was Claire waiting for us to arrive. Imagine the shock when she saw Volkmar. She didn't have time to say hello because he came up to her and kissed her full on the mouth! After the kiss, he said, "Hello, Claire. It's been a long time since we've seen each other!"

"Yes, it has, Volkmar. It's nice to see you again!"

"It's wonderful to see you, Claire. Julie and Donald told me you were going to join us for dinner."

"Donald called me to invite me for dinner. He didn't say you were going to be here too!"

"We wanted it to be a surprise, Claire," Julie said.

And that's how the romance began again after more than a fifty-nine-year interim. Clare was really shocked to see him. She did seem to like seeing him again, and a kiss like that was something she hadn't had in years! It was a very pleasant start to a romance which blossomed over the summer. Shortly after Volkmar returned to Pennsylvania, he called Claire and asked if he might come to visit her. She said yes. From there, she reintroduced him to her mother, Mrs. Hossbein. She was in the Nottingham Nursing Home and at age 104; she was no longer able to care for herself. Mrs. Hossbein remembered the Boy Scout who lived down on the county line farm. A few days after being told by Claire and Volkmar they were going to be married, Mrs. Hossbein told Claire, "Well, you're in good hands, Claire. I can go now." A few days later she died.

The date for the marriage was set for Saturday, October 6, 2001, in the Kirkville Methodist Church. I conducted the service, and at its conclusion, a reception was hosted by Claire's niece and her husband, Daryl and Deanna Johnston, at the Johnston Golf Course at Rogue's Roost. The two old friends had once again found each other and are now living in Seneca, Pennsylvania, where Volkmar has lived since 1951. It's been a real pleasure to have Claire in the family. She takes far better care of Volkmar than he ever did himself!

On December 10, 2003, Heath Wood Megnin was born to Dan and Katie in Denver, Colorado. He is the oldest of their two boys and was born on my seventy-fifth birthday. What a pleasure it is to have another link between the past, present, and future! He is of a similar blue-eyed, blond, and stocky build reflective of his father. We visited them that next summer and spent a week in the mountains driving back and forth to see them as much as possible. Heath's birth also set the precedent for alternating Christmas spent first one year in California and the next in Denver (which I mentioned earlier), bringing together Martin's family and Dan and Katie's. It's an event we all look forward to each year.

On February 25, 2005, Seth Bartholomew Megnin was born to Dan and Katie. He is their second son and has the same attractive features favoring his mother: dark hair, tall, and slender build and a very pretty smile. Corinne, Colin, and Christine very much enjoy getting together with their younger cousins during our annual Christmas reunions. I'm looking at the five of them as I'm typing this page. Their bright smiles and faces reflect the love and joy of their parents and grandparents for the children. Corinne is a high school junior, Colin is a high school freshman, Christine is an eighth grader, Heath is in kindergarten, and Seth is in preschool. The path to educational success is going well, and the beginnings of bright futures are not only what their parents wish, but also their grandparents. We wish them all a bright and successful future in the coming years!

On November 4, 2008, another of those brilliant examples of a political transformation took place here in the United States. Our first African-American president (Barack Hussein Obama) was elected to confront a litany of problems left over from the previous administration. Confrontation of international terrorists, an unnecessary and tragic war in Iraq, the mistreatment and torture of Iraqi prisoners of war, an economic debacle and near depression, the bankruptcy of the American automotive industry, the example of too many people trying to live beyond their means (the housing fiasco), unbridled and unconscionable investment frauds by banks and investment firms, the expansion of illegal settlements in the Palestinian territory by expansionist Israelis, and a continuing war in Afghanistan which should have been completed in 2001-02. These are what might be called carryovers for which this new administration is already being blamed for the actions of the Bush administration over the past eight years! These are, indeed, part of the tragic and now hopeful aspects of life's ever-changing moments. May these moments, instead, become productive of the kinds of changes which enhance and support improving the quality of life for human beings wherever they may be found!

Get Published, Inc!
Thorofare, NJ 08086
22 January, 2010
BA2010022